HISTORY OF THE
WORLD CUP

HISTORY OF THE
WORLD CUP

KEIR RADNEDGE

igloobooks

igloobooks

Published in 2014
by Igloo Books Ltd
Cottage Farm
Sywell
NN6 0BJ
www.igloobooks.com

Project managed by HL Studios

SHE001 0314
2 4 6 8 10 9 7 5 3 1
ISBN: 978-1-78197-952-5

Printed and manufactured in China

The publisher would like to thank the following for permission to reproduce
the following copyright material:

Cover images: Thinkstock (main background); Getty Images (bl); Mirrorpix (tl); ©
Oliver Berg/dpa/Corbis (tr); © Matthew Ashton/AMA/Corbis (br).

Endpapers: Thinkstock

Wallchart: Getty Images (player images)

Mirrorpix: 17, 18 (tl, tr, and br), 19 (tl, tc, c, bl, tr, br), 36 (tl, c, bl, tr, and br), 112 (tl, bl, c, tr, br),
113 (tl, bl, c, tr, br), 130, 133, 135, 138, 139 (b), 141, 144 (tr, br), 145 (tr), 149, 162
(tr, cr, br), 163 (tl), 172 (tl, tr, c, bl, br), 173 (tl, tr, tc, bl, bc, br).

Getty Images: 2, 3, 6, 7, 8, 10, 11, 12, 13, 14, 15, 16, 18 (c and bl), 20, 21, 22, 23, 25, 26, 27, 28,
29, 30, 31 (t and b), 33 (t and b), 34, 35 (t and b), 37 (tl, cl, b, tr, and br), 38, 39, 40, 41 (t and
b), 42, 43 (t and b), 44, 45 (t and b), 46, 47 (t and b), 48, 49 (t and b), 50, 51 (t and b), 52,
53 (t and b), 54, 55 (t and b), 56, 57 (t and b), 58, 59 (t and b), 60, 61, 62, 63, 64, 65, 66,
67, 68, 69, 70, 71, 72, 73, 74, 75, 76, 77, 78, 79, 80, 81, 82 (tl, tc, tr, bl, br, bc), 83 (tl, tr, bl, br),
84, 85, 86, 87, 88, 89, 90, 91, 92, 93, 94, 95, 96, 97, 98, 99, 100, 101, 102, 103, 104, 105,
106, 107, 108, 109, 110, 111, 114, 115, 116, 117, 118, 119, 120, 121, 122, 123, 124, 125,
126, 127, 128, 129, 131, 132, 134, 136, 137, 139, 140, 142, 143, 144 (tl, bl, c), 145 (tl, bl,
tc, cr, br), 146, 147, 148, 150, 151, 152, 153, 154, 155, 156 (t and b), 157, 158
(t and b), 159, 160, 161 (t and b), 162 (tl, bl), 163 (cl, tc, tr, cr, b), 164 (t and b),
165, 166 (t and b), 167, 168 (t and b), 169 (t and b), 170, 171
(t and b), 174, 175 (t and b).

Istock: 4, 5.

Every effort has been made to obtain permission to
reproduce copyright material, but there may be cases
where we have been unable to trace a copyright
holder. The publisher will be happy to correct any
omissions in future printings.

CONTENTS

THE ORIGINS

OF THE GAME

Modern football is only a century-and-a-half old, but competitive ball-kicking games can be traced back much earlier. FIFA recognizes the ancient Chinese game *tsu-chu* (or *cu-ju*) as modern football's oldest ancestor.

Tsu-chu was popularized around 200–300BC as an exercise in the army. In one variation, players kicked a feather-filled ball into a 12–16 inch (30–40cm) net hung between two 30 foot (9m) high bamboo poles. In AD600, the Japanese game *kemari* was invented. Players passed a small, grain-filled ball between themselves without letting it touch the ground.

Early versions of football in Europe came from the Greek and Roman Empires. These games were more similar to rugby than modern football, with players able to use their hands as well as their feet. The Roman version, known as *harpustum*, grew into *calcio*, a notoriously violent Renaissance game, which gives its name to modern Italian football.

MEDIEVAL FOOTBALL

Records of medieval football (called fute-ball) in France and Britain tell of violent mobs charging through towns, using anything from a pig's bladder

RIGHT Gabriele Bella's painting of a game of football in Venice in the eighteenth century

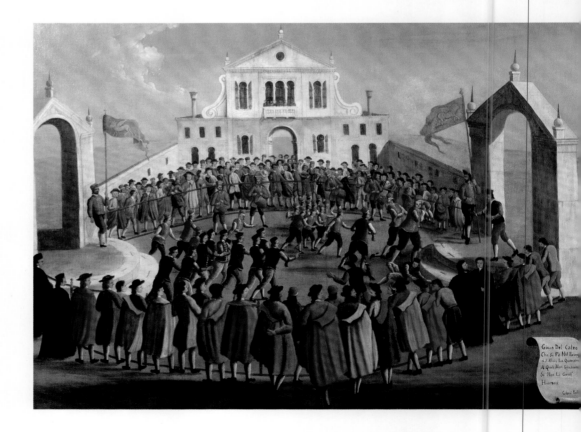

to the head of a defeated Danish prince as a ball. Football was so competitive, popular, and disruptive that it caused riots. Both the Lord Mayor of London in 1314 and Henry VIII in 1540 attempted to ban the sport, despite Henry having his own pair of football boots.

RULES AND REGULATIONS

By the 19th century, football—or soccer, as it was also known from its earliest years—had started to take a more recognizable shape as part of British public school curriculums. Two unofficial sets of rules, one from Cambridge University and another developed by clubs in the north east of England, were established to govern the game.

The English Football Association (FA) was formed in 1863 and published the first consolidated set of formal laws. Rebel schools, which wanted to permit running while holding the ball, abandoned association football and launched rugby football.

AN INTERNATIONAL GAME

Football quickly spread around the world as sailors, engineers, bankers, soldiers, and miners introduced it wherever they went.

Clubs were formed in Copenhagen, Vienna, and Genoa, with British colonial outposts further aiding the spread of the game. In 1891, Argentina became the first nation outside the UK to establish a football league and British sailors helped to popularize the game in Brazil. Even the United States had its own "soccer" teams as far back as the 1860s. By the end of the century, leagues—albeit not necessarily national ones at this early stage—were running in England, Scotland, Italy, Holland, and pre-communist Russia.

The first international match took place the year after the inaugural FA Cup, when England played Scotland in 1872, at Hamilton Crescent, Partick, Glasgow. The British Home Internationals quickly became a fixture.

ABOVE Members of Harrow School's Soccer Eleven, 1867

THE ORIGINS
OF THE GAME

THE CREATION OF FIFA

By the start of the 20th century, national football associations had been formed in countries across Europe and South America, including Uruguay, Chile, Paraguay, Denmark, Sweden, Italy, Germany, Holland, Belgium, and France.

Carl Anton Wilhelm Hirschman of Holland suggested convening an international meeting of football associations to the English FA's secretary, F. J. Wall. The English FA was initially positive, but left the call unanswered. Robert Guerin from the French Sports Association didn't want to wait indefinitely and, at a match between France and Belgium in 1904, he invited the European associations to join together.

This time the English FA made it clear it was not interested. However, the others agreed and FIFA (Fédération Internationale de Football Associations) came into being on 21 May 1904, in Paris, when representatives agreed a list of

FOOTBALL FACTS

300–200BC *tsu-chu* popularized in China
AD600 *kemari* developed by the Japanese aristocracy
12th century both women and men took part in huge games in England
1314 "football" banned by the Lord Mayor of London
1530 a famous *Calcio* game takes place during the siege of Florence
1848 "Cambridge Rules" published by Cambridge University
1863 English Football Association founded with a set of codified laws for modern football

RIGHT Crowds build at the 1923 FA Cup "White Horse Final" between West Ham United and Bolton Wanderers

regulations, including playing matches according to the English Football Association's law book. Represented at the meeting were France, Belgium, Denmark, Holland, Spain, Sweden, and Switzerland. The seeds were sown for the World Cup, with Article Nine stipulating that FIFA would be the only body with the authority to organize such an international tournament.

Although none of the British nations attended the founding meeting of FIFA, they joined two years later and England's D. B. Woodfall became president.

ENGLAND'S INFLUENCE

The English game remained revered around the world in those days, proof of which is to be found in the English clubs names which survive far and wide. Clubs named after Arsenal are to be found in countries as far apart as Ukraine and Argentina and the famous amateur team, the Corinthians, saw their title adopted by what is now one of Brazil's greatest clubs.

In Italy, the English legacy is still evident in the names of clubs such as Milan and Genoa—not the Italian "Milano" and "Genova"—while the fervent Basque supporters of Athletic Bilbao in northern Spain maintained a private insistence on "Atleti" despite the Franco dictatorship imposing the Spanish-language "Atletico" label.

Students who came to England for an education also took home with them more than the latest developments in engineering, finance, and commerce. One such was Charles Miller, whose Scottish father, a railway engineer in Sao Paulo, had sent his son "home" for an English boarding school education. Young Miller returned to Brazil in 1894 with two footballs in his baggage—and sparked a passion which resulted in a record five World Cup triumphs.

Jimmy Hogan, William Garbutt, and Arthur Pentland were outstanding among English football coaches who taught the finer points of the game on the continent in the first half of the 20th century. Hogan worked in Hungary and then in Austria whose national team he coached in their famously narrow 4-3 defeat by England at Stamford Bridge in 1932.

THE ORIGINAL LAWS OF THE GAME

(as adopted by the Football Association on December 8, 1863)

1. The maximum length of the ground shall be 200 yards, the maximum breadth shall be 100 yards, the length and breadth shall be marked off with flags; and the goal shall be defined by two upright posts, eight yards apart, without any tape or bar across them.

2. A toss for goals shall take place, and the game shall be commenced by a place kick from the center of the ground by the side losing the toss for goals; the other side shall not approach within 10 yards of the ball until it is kicked off.

3. After a goal is won, the losing side shall be entitled to kick off, and the two sides shall change goals after each goal is won.

4. A goal shall be won when the ball passes between the goal-posts or over the space between the goal-posts (at whatever height), not being thrown, knocked on, or carried.

5. When the ball is in touch, the first player who touches it shall throw it from the point on the boundary line where it left the ground in a direction at right angles with the boundary line, and the ball shall not be in play until it has touched the ground.

6. When a player has kicked the ball, any one of the same side who is nearer to the opponent's goal line is out of play, and may not touch the ball himself, nor in any way whatever prevent any other player from doing so, until he is in play; but no player is out of play when the ball is kicked off from behind the goal line.

7. In case the ball goes behind the goal line, if a player on the side to whom the goal belongs first touches the ball, one of his side shall be entitled to a free kick from the goal line at the point opposite the place where the ball shall be touched. If a player of the opposite side first touches the ball, one of his side shall be entitled to a free kick at the goal only from a point 15 yards outside the goal line, opposite the place where the ball is touched, the opposing side standing within their goal line until he has had his kick.

8. If a player makes a fair catch, he shall be entitled to a free kick, providing he claims it by making a mark with his heel at once; and in order to take such kick he may go back as far as he pleases, and no player on the opposite side shall advance beyond his mark until he has kicked.

9. No player shall run with the ball.

10. Neither tripping nor hacking shall be allowed, and no player shall use his hands to hold or push his adversary.

11. A player shall not be allowed to throw the ball or pass it to another with his hands.

12. No player shall be allowed to take the ball from the ground with his hands under any pretence whatever while it is in play.

13. No player shall be allowed to wear projecting nails, iron plates, or gutta-percha on the soles or heels of his boots.

THE WORLD CUP

The World Cup is the planet's greatest sports event. In terms of competing nations, television viewers and finance, it dwarfs every other tournament. Uruguay were the first hosts—and first winners—in 1930, but the worldwide game is quite evenly balanced: South American nations have won nine cups and Europe's finest have won ten. Brazil has carried off the golden trophies a record five times, followed by Italy (four) and Germany (three).

THE WORLD CUP

FOUNDATION & 1930s

After a string of false starts, the World Cup was launched in 1930. The inaugural international tournament was the British Home Championship, but FIFA's first attempt to launch a truly international championship in 1906 had fallen flat. Switzerland agreed to host the tournament and even made a trophy, but no-one turned up.

PAGE 10 Italy score the first goal in the 1982 World Cup final

PAGE 11 Italy's Fabio Cannavaro lifts the 2006 trophy

THE RESULT 1930

Location: Montevideo
Final: Uruguay 4 Argentina 2
Shirts: Uruguay white, Argentina light blue-and-white stripes
Scorers: Dorado, Cea, Iriarte, Castro; Peucelle, Stabile

England, now a member of FIFA, organized the first large-scale international football tournament as part of the 1908 London Olympic Games.

FIFA became a genuinely international body as countries from North and South America started to join. The Olympic football tournament continued, and from 1914 FIFA took a lead role, officially designating it the "world championship of amateur football."

Yet FIFA still harbored ambitions of launching its own tournament. Not only was the status of football in the Olympics insecure—it was almost dropped entirely from the 1932 Games at Los Angeles—but interest was hampered by the sudden spread of professionalism.

URUGUAY WIN ON HOME TERRITORY

In the 1920s, two Frenchmen, FIFA President Jules Rimet and French Federation Secretary Henri Delaunay, set up a steering committee. In 1928, the FIFA Congress in Amsterdam voted to support a first world championship and Uruguay's bid to host the event easily beat off European competition. As part of the country's centenary celebrations, the event was guaranteed financially by the government. The Uruguayans boasted an impressive pedigree as double Olympic champions—in 1924 they won in France and four years later they triumphed in Amsterdam— and built the massive Centenario Stadium in Montevideo.

Lucien Laurent of France scored the first-ever World Cup goal in the 4-1 victory over Mexico, but Uruguay's generosity in hosting the tournament was rewarded with ultimate victory, when 80,000 fans packed the Centenario Stadium to witness their 4-2 win over Argentina in the final.

RIGHT Czech goalkeeper Planicka punches clear in the 1934 final

WORLD CUP 1934

Italy were both hosts and winners of the first finals to be staged in Europe. Dictator Benito Mussolini wanted to put on a show to impress his international visitors. But World Cup title holders Uruguay stayed away because they feared their top players would remain in Europe.

Vittorio Pozzo, Italy's manager, included three Argentinian-born players in his squad, while his best home-grown players were forwards Giuseppe Meazza and veteran Angelo Schiavio.

Spain became Italy's most awkward opponents. The heroics of the legendary Spanish goalkeeper Ricardo Zamora held the hosts to a 1-1 draw in the quarter-finals. However, Zamora took such a battering from Italy's over-physical forwards that he was not fit enough to play in the replay.

Italy won 1-0 and then defeated Austria, Europe's other top nation, by the same score. In the final they beat Czechoslovakia 2-1, but only after extra time, with Schiavio scoring the winner.

ABOVE Leonidas (left) leads Brazil to their victory over Sweden in 1938

WORLD CUP 1938

Four years later, Italy won a second time, this time in France. The atmosphere was very different compared to 1934, when Pozzo's team had benefited from home advantage, generous referees, and home support. In France they were jeered by fans angered by Italy's fascist politics.

England, despite being outside FIFA, were invited to compete at the last minute in place of Austria—which had been swallowed up by Adolf Hitler's Germany. However, England's Football Association declined the invitation, even though they had thrashed Germany 6-3 in Berlin shortly before the finals.

The favorites included Brazil, following their astonishing first round match against Poland. Brazil won 6-5 in extra time: Brazil's Leonidas and Poland's Ernst Wilimowski both scored hat-tricks.

Brazil were so confident of beating Italy in the semi-finals that they rested Leonidas to keep him fresh for the final, but their gamble misfired because they lost 2-1. Italy went on to defeat Hungary 4-2 in the final to become the first-ever back-to-back World Cup winners.

1950s

"All I remember was everyone in tears."

PELÉ RECALLS THE 1950 FINAL

A nation was traumatized when the host, and one of the favorites, Brazil lost to Uruguay in the climax of the first postwar World Cup. The competition ended not with a one-off final but a four-team group, a format not used since.

1950

The closing match, in front of a record crowd of nearly 200,000 in Rio's Maracana Stadium, proved decisive as Uruguay claimed their second title.

Free-scoring Brazil needed only a draw to win their first World Cup, and looked to be on their way when Friaça fired them into the lead. But underdogs Uruguay, captained and marshaled by center half Obdulio Varela, stunned the hosts with late goals by Juan Schiaffino and Alcides Ghiggia. Brazilian fans were furious with their team's failure, with much of the blame heaped on unfortunate goalkeeper Barbosa.

The defeat marked the very last time that Brazil wore an all-white uniform, which was believed to be so unlucky that it was replaced by the now famous yellow shirts. Because of the result, the Uruguay players remained in their dressing room for hours after the final whistle until it was safe to emerge.

The final was not the only shock of the tournament—England had been humbled in the first round by the United States. England lost 1-0 at Belo Horizonte, courtesy of a goal from Haiti-born Joe Gaetjens.

1954

When runaway favorites Hungary thrashed under-strength West Germany 8-3 in their opening round group game, no one expected these sides to meet again in the final—let alone for the West Germans to triumph.

West Germany's coach Sepp Herberger rested several key players for their first game, while Hungary's captain Ferenc Puskás suffered an ankle injury that was meant to rule him out of the rest of the tournament. Yet Puskás, as the star player, was controversially brought back for the final and even gave his Magical Magyars a sixth-minute lead. Left winger Zoltan Czibor scored again almost immediately, with another rout looking likely.

RIGHT 1954 souvenir postcard featuring the Maracana Stadium and views over Rio de Janerio

THE RESULT 1950

Location: Rio
Final: Uruguay 2 Brazil 1
Shirts: Uruguay light blue, Brazil white
Scorers: Schiaffino, Ghiggia; Friaça

URUGUAY

Máspoli

Gambetta   Gonzáles

Andrade   Varela   Tejera

Ghiggia Julio Pérez Miguez Schiaffino Morán

Chico   Jair   Ademir   Zizinho   Friaça

Danilo   Bauer   Bigode

Juvenal   Augusto

Barbosa

BRAZIL

WEST GERMANY

Turek

Posipal   Liebrich   Kohlmeyer

Eckel   Mai

Rahn   Morlock   O Walter   F Walter   Schäefer

Tóth   Puskás   Hidegkuti   Kocsis   Czibor

Zakarias   Bozsik

Lantos   Lantos   Buzánszki

Grosics

HUNGARY

LEFT Brazil's 17-year-old Pelé shoots for goal in the 1958 final

BRAZIL

Gilmar

D Santos   Bellini   Orlando   N Santos

Zito   Didi

Garrincha   Vavá   Pelé   Zagallo

Skoglund   Liedholm   Simonsson   Gren   Hamrin

Parling   Börjesson

Bergmark   Gustavsson   Axbom

Svensson

SWEDEN

But the Germans made a spirited comeback. Led by captain Fritz Walter and two-goal hero Helmut Rahn, the Germans battled back for what is known in footballing history as "Das Wunder von Bern"— the miracle of Berne.

Hungary entered the tournament as Olympic champions and overwhelming favorites, but remarkably the final would be their only defeat between 1950 and early 1956.

They thought they had done enough to take the match into extra time, only for an 88th-minute Puskás strike to be controversially disallowed for offside by Welsh linesman Mervyn Griffiths.

The competition produced an amazing 140 goals over 26 matches, including the World Cup's highest-scoring match during Austria's thrilling 7-5 triumph over Switzerland.

1958

Brazil finally ended their wait for their first World Cup crown, with a little help from their latest superstar, Pelé, in Sweden. The 17-year-old Santos prodigy had to wait until Brazil's final group game to make Vicente Feola's starting line-up, with mesmerizing winger Garrincha also given his first opportunity at the finals.

The pair proved irresistible by setting up Vavá for both goals to beat the Soviet Union, before Pelé grabbed a hat-trick in the 5-2 semi-final success over France. Brazil defeated hosts Sweden by the same score in the final, including two goals by Pelé, who broke down in tears at the end.

Yet Brazil were not the only ones to impress. French striker Just Fontaine scored 13 goals, a record for a single World Cup tournament that no one has since come close to emulating. The 1958 finals were also the only time that all four of the UK's Home Nations qualified, although England had lost Duncan Edwards and several other international players in the Munich air disaster.

West Germany lost a bitter and violent semi-final to Sweden. Captain Fritz Walter was fouled out of the game and could not be replaced because substitutes were not allowed at the time.

1960s

Even without Pelé at the helm, Brazil were unstoppable as they comfortably retained their title in South America. Pelé scored in Brazil's first game but was injured in the next match, so he played no further part in the tournament.

RIGHT Garrincha (left) and Amarildo celebrate Brazil's equalizer against Czechoslovakia in the 1962 final

THE RESULT 1962

Location: Santiago
Final: Brazil 3 Czechoslovakia 1
Shirts: Brazil yellow, Czechoslovakia red
Scorers: Amarildo, Zito, Vavá; Masopust

BRAZIL

Gilmar

D Santos   Mauro   Zozimo   N Santos

Zito   Didi   Zagallo

Garrincha   Vavá   Amarildo

Jelínek   Kvasnak   Scherer   Pospichal

Masopust   Kadraba

Novák   Popluhár   Pluskal   Tichý

Schrojf

CZECHOSLOVAKIA

1962

Pelé's deputy was Amarildo from Botafogo of Rio de Janeiro. Known as "the white Pelé," he made an immediate impact by scoring two goals in the 2-1 win over Spain in their decisive concluding group match. Amarildo also notched an equalizer in the final, but the undisputed star of the tournament was Garrincha, nicknamed "the Little Bird."

Garrincha, the world's greatest-ever dribbler, was the two-goal man of the match as Brazil saw off England 3-1. He even overcame the embarrassment of being sent off in the 4-2 semi-final win over hosts Chile.

Brazil managed to persuade the disciplinary panel not to ban their star player, so he played in the final. The defending champions suffered an early shock when midfielder Josef Masopust shot the Czechoslovakians into an early lead. However, mistakes by goalkeeper Vilem Schroif helped

Brazil hit back to register a 3-1 victory. Masopust's consolation, months later, was to be voted as the European Footballer of the Year.

Chile's preparations had been marred by an earthquake two years earlier, yet they surpassed expectations not only off the pitch but on it as they clinched a deserved third place.

The Chileans caused a quarter-final upset by knocking out the highly rated Soviet Union, despite the outstanding efforts of legendary goalkeeper Lev Yashin.

1966

A historic hat-trick hero, a Soviet linesman, and a dog named Pickles were all made famous by the World Cup hosted in England.

West Ham's Geoff Hurst, who started the finals as a reserve striker, became the only man ever to score three goals in a World Cup final as the hosts beat West Germany 4-2 at Wembley Stadium.

But his second strike was one of the most controversial in football history. West Germany leveled through Wolfgang Weber's 89th-minute goal to take the final into extra time. In the first-half of extra time, Hurst produced an angled shot that struck the underside of the crossbar and went down behind the goal line before bouncing back out again for the Germans to clear it to safety.

England claimed they had scored and, despite West Germany's protests, linesman Tofik Bakhramov told Swiss referee Gottfried Dienst that the ball had indeed crossed the line. Hurst, who fell while shooting at goal, was unsighted. However, fellow striker Roger Hunt was so certain that the ball had crossed the line that he did not bother even following up to put it back into the net. The controversial goal left the Germans deflated and Hurst capped his performance by claiming his hat-trick—and England's greatest footballing triumph—with virtually the last kick of the contest.

Alf Ramsey's hard-working side, nicknamed the "Wingless Wonders," had edged past Uruguay, Mexico, France, Argentina, and Portugal en route to the final. However, there were some complaints that England had been able to play all their matches in their stronghold of Wembley Stadium.

Their quarter-final against Argentina proved to be the most bitter. Visiting captain Antonio Rattin was sent off for dissent by German referee Rudolf Kreitlein but initially refused to leave the pitch and eventually had to be escorted by police.

The tournament had been boycotted by African nations, who were unhappy at their "winner" having to qualify via a play-off with the champions of Asia or Oceania.

BRAZIL MISS PRESENCE OF PELE

For the second successive World Cup finals, Pelé limped out of the tournament early on after being the victim of relentlessly tough tackling. His aging team-mates were unable to raise their game without their star player, and Brazil surprisingly crashed out in the first round.

It was also a story of woe for former champions Italy, whose squad were pelted with rotten vegetables on their return home. They suffered a 1-0 defeat to the minnows of North Korea, whose winner was drilled home by dentist Pak Doo Ik. The Koreans raced into a 3-0 quarter-final lead over Portugal, before Mozambique-born Eusébio inspired the Portuguese to a 5-3 comeback and slotted home four goals.

Eusébio, dubbed the "Black Panther" for his goal scoring prowess, ended the tournament as top scorer with nine goals but was denied a place in the final by Bobby Charlton's two goals, which guided England to a 2-1 semi-final success.

Less than four months before England captain Bobby Moore accepted the Jules Rimet trophy from Queen Elizabeth II, it had been stolen from a London exhibition. Fortunately, a mongrel dog called Pickles dug up the trophy from a South London garden and was promptly rewarded with a lifetime's supply of pet food.

THE RESULT 1966

Location: London
Final: England 4 West Germany 2
Shirts: England red, West Germany white
Scorers: Hurst 3, Peters; Haller, Weber

ENGLAND

Banks

Cohen   J Charlton   Moore   Wilson

Ball   Stiles   B Charlton   Peters

Hurst   Hunt

Emmerich   Held   Seeler

Overath   Beckenbauer   Haller

Schnellinger   Weber   Schulz   Höttges

Tilkowski

WEST GERMANY

ABOVE Pickles, the dog who found the stolen World Cup

LEFT England captain Bobby Moore holds aloft the Jules Rimet trophy

WORLD CUP MOMENTS

ABOVE Just Fontaine parades his top-scoring golden boot

RIGHT France striker Fontaine on the way to his record 13 goals

ABOVE Portugal's Eusébio is floored for a penalty against North Korea

BELOW Geoff Hurst rises above the West German defense at Wembley

ABOVE Czech forward Jan Riha ouwits Brazil's Domingos da Guia

LEFT Romania and England line up in the first round in Mexico

BELOW Brazil's Jairzinho is sent flying by a Uruguayan defender

ABOVE Top-scoring Gerd Müller eludes Yugoslav keeper Enver Maric

BELOW Franz Beckenbauer (white) breaks up a Dutch attack

ABOVE England left back Terry Cooper outwits West German captain Uwe Seeler

LEFT Weary England await extra time in their quarter-final in Leon

THE WORLD CUP

1970s

This was the first World Cup to be broadcast in sun-soaked color around the world. Nothing could match Brazil's famous yellow shirts as Mario Zagallo showcased arguably the most dazzling attacking side in footballing history.

THE RESULT 1970

Location: Mexico
Final: Brazil 4 Italy 1
Shirts: Brazil yellow, Italy blue
Scorers: Pelé, Gerson, Jairzinho, Carlos Alberto; Boninsegna

BRAZIL

Felix

Alberto   Brito   Piazza   Everaldo

Clodoaldo   Gerson   Rivelino

Jairzinho   Tostao   Pelé

Riva   Boninsegna
(Rivera)

De Sisti   Mazzola   Bertini   Domenghini
(Juliano)

Facchetti   Rosato   Cera   Burgnich

Albertosi

ITALY

1970

Spearheaded by Pelé, Jairzinho, Rivelino, and Tostão, Brazil were allowed to keep the Jules Rimet trophy after becoming the first country to win three World Cups. Pelé became the only player with a hat-trick of victories, although in 1962 he had been injured very early in the tournament.

Brazil featured in a classic first round contest, when they defeated England 1-0. However, both sides qualified for the quarter-finals. England's title defense came to a dramatic end when West Germany avenged their 1966 final defeat to bounce back from a two-goal deficit to register an extra time 3-2 win over Sir Alf Ramsey's men. The effort of overcoming England undermined the Germans in their semi-final against Italy, and West Germany ran out of steam and lost another epic, to be edged out 4-3.

Brazil wrapped up the tournament with a 4-1 triumph over Italy in Mexico City. Brazil's fourth goal was the finest of the tournament, and one of the most memorable ever scored in a final. A smooth passing move, the length of the pitch, was finished off by captain Carlos Alberto. Manager Mario Zagallo became the first man to win the World Cup both as a player and a manager.

1974

Franz Beckenbauer achieved the first half of his own leadership double when he captained hosts West Germany to victory over Holland. The final was played in Munich's Olympic Stadium, the footballing home to Beckenbauer and his FC Bayern team-mates—goalkeeper Sepp Maier,

defenders Hans-Georg Schwarzenbeck and Paul Breitner, and strikers Uli Hoeness and Gerd Müller.

Yet the dominant personality of the finals was Holland's center forward Johan Cruyff who, as captain, epitomized their revolutionary style of total football, characterized by a high-speed interchange of playing positions.

Hosts West Germany surprisingly stuttered in the first round but managed to qualify despite suffering a shock defeat to East Germany, who had emerged through the Berlin Wall for the first and last time in World Cup history. Jürgen Sparwasser made a name for himself with an historic strike in the 77th-minute to secure a slender 1-0 success.

West Germany topped their second round group ahead of Poland—qualifying victors over

RIGHT Holland's Johan Cruyff holds off a West German defender

England—while Holland topped the other group ahead of an over-physical Brazil.

English referee Jack Taylor awarded the first World Cup final penalty—Cruyff had been fouled in the opening minute at Munich. Johan Neeskens stepped up to put the Dutch ahead before the hosts had even touched the ball.

West Germany soon leveled matters through a penalty kick and went ahead decisively, courtesy of Müller, just before the half-time interval.

1978

Holland had to settle for second best again, this time without the inspirational Cruyff, who refused to travel to Argentina, amid kidnap fears.

Cruyff's absence was particularly missed in the final as the hosts clinched their inaugural World Cup 3-1 after extra time. Argentina's only European-based player, Mario Kempes, finished as top scorer, with six goals, including two goals in the final.

A ticker-tape assisted storm of home support carried manager César Menotti's Argentina through the first round and to the second group with a tricky meeting against Peru. Needing to win by at least four clear goals, Menotti's men ran out contentious 6-0 winners to deny Brazil a final berth. Instead, Brazil settled for a 2-1 win over Italy in the third place play-off.

In the final, Holland went behind to a Kempes strike before half-time and equalized through substitute striker Dick Nanninga. On the verge of the full-time whistle, Rob Rensenbrink's effort was denied by the post and proved a costly miss as Argentina pulled away in extra time with further goals from Kempes and Daniel Bertoni.

Scotland failed to progress beyond the first round and were shamed by Willie Johnston being kicked out of the tournament after failing a dope test. The dazzling left winger protested his innocence, insisting he was taking Reactivan tablets to treat a cold, but he was banned from internationals and his playing career fizzled out.

ABOVE Jairzinho scores Brazil's third goal against Italy

1980s

The competition swelled to 24 sides in 1982, as Spain played hosts for the first time. Italy ended a 44-year wait for their third title, with captain Dino Zoff becoming the oldest player to win a World Cup at the grand age of 40.

THE RESULT 1982

Location: Madrid
Final: Italy 3 West Germany 1
Shirts: Italy blue, West Germany white
Scorers: Rossi, Tardelli, Altobelli; Breitner

ITALY

Zoff

Scirea Gentile Bergomi Collovati Cabrini

Conti Oriali Tardelli

Rossi   Graziani
(Altobelli) (Causio)

Rummenigge Fischer Littbarski
(H Müller)
Dremmler Breitner B Förster
(Hrubesch)
Briegel K Förster Stielike Kaltz

Schumacher

WEST GERMANY

1982

Toni Schumacher, West Germany's goalkeeper, was fortunate to have been playing in the final. Despite having knocked unconscious France's Patrick Battiston with a brutal foul during a thrilling semi-final in Seville, he somehow escaped punishment.

In the final, Schumacher faced a spot kick from Antonio Cabrini and the Italian left back made history by becoming the first player to miss a penalty in the title decider. In the same match, German Paul Breitner wrote himself into the annals of history when he became the first player to score a penalty in two separate finals.

But second half goals from Paolo Rossi, Marco Tardelli, and Alessandro Altobelli handed Enzo Bearzot's attacking side the trophy. Rossi's hat-trick in a 3-2 win had earlier knocked out a Brazil team that included Falcao, Socrates, and Zico.

Rossi finished up as the tournament's six-goal leading marksman to claim the Golden Boot. This was an astonishing achievement because the Juventus striker had returned to top-class football only six weeks earlier, following a two-year suspension for his role in a match-fixing scandal.

Holders Argentina struggled from the outset and they introduced their new hero, 21-year-old Diego Maradona, who had narrowly missed out on a place in their previous World Cup squad. Yet Maradona was stifled in the opening match, beaten 1-0 by Belgium, and then sent off for retaliation during a second round defeat by Brazil.

Spain were one of the more disappointing World Cup hosts out on the pitch, sensationally beaten by Northern Ireland in their opening match and later eliminated after finishing bottom of a three-nation second round group behind West Germany and England.

A further change of format saw the knockout semi-finals restored. Italy defeated Poland 2-0 in Barcelona to make the final, then West Germany saw off France in Seville, courtesy of the first penalty shoot-out in World Cup history. A magical match swung one way, then the other: Germany opened the scoring but trailed 3-1 before battling back with two goals to force extra time. Schumacher went from villain to hero by stopping the crucial last French penalty from Maxime Bossis.

RIGHT Claudio Gentile and skipper Dino Zoff celebrate in Madrid

1986

After his previous World Cup disgrace, Maradona jumped into the spotlight when, virtually single-handedly, he won Argentina their second World Cup by combining audacious skills with equally audacious law-breaking.

The world saw the best and worst of Maradona in a five-minute spell of Argentina's quarter-final contest against England. Although the Argentinian captain punched the ball into the back of the net, Tunisian referee Ali bin Nasser allowed the goal to stand (this was his first and last World Cup game as a referee).

Maradona claimed the goal was "a little bit of Maradona, a little bit the hand of God," a boast that accompanied him for years to the delight of a nation that considered the trick a belated answer to Argentina's military and naval defeat by Britain in the 1982 Falkland Islands conflict.

However, no one could dispute the majesty of Maradona's second strike. A solo slalom took him the full length of the England half, before he swept the ball past embattled goalkeeper Peter Shilton with his left foot, for one of the best-ever goals. Just to prove this had been no accident, maverick Maradona scored a similar solo goal in the 2-0 semi-final victory over Belgium.

Despite being closely marked by West Germany's Lothar Matthäus in the final, Maradona escaped long enough to provide the defense-splitting pass that set up Jorge Burruchaga's late goal to once more clinch World Cup success. The Germans had clawed their way back from a two-goal deficit and looked to be heading toward extra time, before the glittering run and pass from match-winner Maradona.

Franz Beckenbauer, a World Cup winner with West Germany in 1974, was in charge of the national team. Yet even his magic touch off the pitch was simply no match for the genius of Maradona on it.

England's consolation was that striker Gary Lineker went on to win the Golden Boot as the tournament's leading scorer with six goals. His tally included a hat-trick in England's first round defeat of Poland, which sent them to the quarter-finals against Paraguay. England had struggled initially, losing their opening game 1-0 to Portugal, and in the scoreless draw against Morocco they lost key players—Ray Wilkins was sent off and captain Bryan Robson was helped off with an injury.

European champions France sneaked past Brazil on penalties in their quarter-final, but for the second successive World Cup fell in the semi-final to West Germany. The Germans simply cruised into the final against Argentina, courtesy of goals from Andreas Brehme and Rudi Völler.

ABOVE Diego Maradona sends Peter Shilton the wrong way

THE RESULT 1986

Location: Mexico City
Final: Argentina 3 West Germany 2
Shirts: Argentina blue and white, West Germany green
Scorers: Brown, Valdano, Burruchaga; Rummenigge, Völler

ARGENTINA

Pumpido

Cuciuffo   Brown   Ruggeri

Giusti Burruchaga Batista Olarticoechea Enrique
(Trobbiani)

Valdano   Maradona

Rummenigge   Allofs
(Völler)

Brehme   Eder   Magath   Matthäus
(Hoeness)

Briegel K Förster Jakobs Berthold

Schumacher

WEST GERMANY

THE WORLD CUP

1990

West Germany overcame Diego Maradona and Argentina, gaining revenge for their 1986 final defeat, which meant Franz Beckenbauer joined Brazil's Mario Zagallo as the only other man to win a World Cup as player and coach.

Victory in the Stadio Olimpico saw history made as Franz Beckenbauer became the first man to have won separate World Cups as coach and captain (Zagallo had not captained Brazil), while Argentina saw red and paid the penalty for their negative tactics in the final. Beckenbauer stepped down after the triumphant return home and was promptly succeeded by his former assistant Berti Vogts. However, the Germans have not won a World Cup since.

Unlike four years earlier, the final showdown of Italia '90 was a dull defensive game. Settled by Andreas Brehme's controversial late penalty, it was marred by red cards for Argentina's Pedro Monzon and Gustavo Dezotti. This was the first time that a player had been sent off in a World Cup final.

The 1990 finals were later considered as one of the poorest tournaments in the event's history, partly because of the inferior quality of refereeing. Sepp Blatter, then the general secretary of world governing body FIFA and later its president, decided then and there to launch a campaign to improve refereeing standards.

CAMEROON BRING AN AFRICAN BEAT

Argentina were not a patch on the team who had won the World Cup for the second time in their history just four years earlier. Inspirational captain Diego Maradona was carrying a knee injury and in their showpiece opening match they were pulled apart by nine-man Cameroon, the African surprise package. The Africans, making their debut in the World Cup finals, beat the holders 1-0, thanks to a historic strike from François Omam Biyik.

Cameroon's secret weapon was veteran striker Roger Milla. He provided some of the tournament's highlights but Cameroon were let down by their indiscipline. The Africans led England, managed by Bobby Robson, 2-1 in their quarter-final contest in Naples, but slack defending opened up gaps, which prompted them into conceding two penalties. Both were converted by Gary Lineker, who helped drive England through to their first semi-final appearance for 24 years.

But England's fortune with penalties ran out when they faced West Germany. England finished 1-1 after extra time, but lost the penalty shoot-out 4-3 after Stuart Pearce and Chris Waddle missed their spot-kicks.

England, managed for the last time by Robson, who was moving to PSV Eindhoven, lost to hosts Italy in the third place play-off. By then, the Tottenham midfielder Paul Gascoigne had become a national icon, both for his performances as well as for the tears he shed after being shown a yellow card in the semi-final defeat by the Germans. The card was Gascoigne's second of the tournament, which meant he would have missed the final had England reached that grand stage. Later, Gascoigne returned to Italy to play for Lazio.

England were not the only nation to suffer the pain of penalty punishment. In the second round, Romania fell in the shoot-out to the Irish Republic, who were making an impressive debut under manager Jack Charlton, and Argentina edged past both Yugoslavia in the quarter-finals and hosts Italy in the last four through penalty kicks.

The finest match in the tournament was arguably the second round duel between old rivals

THE RESULT 1990

Location: Rome
Final: West Germany 1 Argentina 0
Shirts: West Germany white, Argentina blue
Scorers: Brehme (pen)
Sent Off: Monzón, Dezotti

Holland and West Germany. Tension surrounding the game was exacerbated in the first half by the expulsions of Holland midfielder Frank Rijkaard and German striker Rudi Völler. Ultimately, West Germany won 2-1, thanks to a sensational performance by striker Jürgen Klinsmann—possibly the best of his career—who scored and made the other goal.

Argentina's new hero, especially in the shoot-outs, was goalkeeper Sergio Goycochea. The first choice, Nery Pumpido, was injured in Argentina's opening group game against the former Soviet Union, so Goycochea played instead.

MARADONA AT HOME IN NAPLES

The duel between Italy and Argentina was staged in Naples, where Maradona was plying his trade at club level. His appeal for Napoli fans to cheer for Argentina backfired, yet they still won.

The downside for Argentina was that their outstanding winger, Claudio Caniggia, received a yellow card for a second time in the tournament and so was suspended from playing in the final.

Maradona had played remarkably throughout Italia '90, considering his injury. But in the final his luck ran out, and he pointed the blame at everyone except himself, including FIFA's Brazilian president João Havelange.

The final straw for Maradona was the controversial award of a late penalty to West Germany for a foul on striker Völler. Lothar Matthäus was the designated German penalty taker. But, citing a muscle strain, the captain handed over the responsibility to Brehme, who made no mistake in shooting past Goycochea.

RIGHT Andy Brehme celebrates his World Cup-winning penalty against Argentina

THE WORLD CUP
1994

After missing out to Mexico in 1986, the United States finally hosted a World Cup and proved better than expected on the pitch by reaching the second round before bowing out to the eventual champions—Brazil.

RIGHT Diana Ross launches the World Cup party in Chicago

The Americans had set themselves a goal of staging the event back in the late 1960s. They had failed with a bid to host the finals in 1986, but won FIFA approval through both their commercial potential and a promise to build a solid professional league.

Bora Milutinovic, a freelance Yugoslav coach, was hired to build a national team on the strength of his work in guiding Mexico, as hosts, to the quarter-finals in 1986. His "Team America" reached the second round before narrowly losing to Brazil, the eventual winners.

The finals proved surprisingly successful, with the average attendance for the tournament reaching its highest-ever figure of 69,000. The total attendance of 3.6 million became the then highest attendance in World Cup history.

The tournament was also the most attended single sport sporting event in US history, and featured the first-ever indoor match in the World Cup finals, when the US hosted Switzerland in the Pontiac Silverdome in Michigan, Detroit.

The competition kicked off at Soldier Field Stadium in Chicago with another penalty miss, when veteran pop star Diana Ross rolled a pretend spot-kick wide during a glitzy opening ceremony in front of US President Bill Clinton.

The opening match saw holders Germany edge past Bolivia 1-0, courtesy of Jürgen Klinsmann's

strike on the hour mark. Ultimately, the Germans, playing for the first time as a unified team since the collapse of the Berlin Wall, were dethroned 2-1 by Bulgaria in the quarter-finals.

One of the favorites to win overall had been Colombia, led by their maverick frizzy-haired playmaker Carlos Valderrama, who was dubbed "El Pibe"—the kid. The Colombians had been tipped

THE RESULT 1994

Location: Los Angeles
Final: Brazil 0 Italy 0 (after extra time; Brazil 3-2 on penalties)
Shirts: Brazil yellow, Italy blue

BRAZIL

Taffarel

Jorginho (Cafu) Aldair Márcio Santos Branco

Mazinho II Dunga Mauro Silva Zinho (Paulo Viola)

Romário Bebeto

R Baggio Massaro

D Baggio (Evani) Albertini Berti Donadoni

Maldini Baresi Mussi (Apolloni) Benarrivo

Pagliuca

ITALY

for great things by no less a judge than Pelé, after an incredible 5-0 win away to Argentina during the qualifying competition, in which winger Faustino Asprilla exploded onto the international scene. Unfortunately, their campaign proved both short-lived and tragic. They failed to progress beyond the first group stage, when central defender Andrés Escobar scored an own goal in their 2-1 defeat by the United States.

Colombia's squad returned home to a furious reception from fans and media. The furore was cut short within days, after Escobar was shot dead after an argument near his home. His killer was later jailed for 43 years, but served only 11 years of the sentence before being paroled.

MARADONA MAKES HASTY EXIT

Diego Maradona's final World Cup also proved controversial and short-lived. In 1991 he had fled Italy in disgrace after failing a dope test for cocaine and was banned for 15 months while playing for Napoli. He made a comeback in Spain and then Argentina, playing his way back into the national squad in time for the World Cup finals.

However, after scoring and starring in an opening win against World Cup newcomers Greece, Maradona then failed a further dope test for the stimulant ephedrine, following Argentina's 2-1 win over Nigeria, and was immediately expelled from the tournament. Maradona later blamed the dope test failure on the weight-loss drugs he had been taking prior to the World Cup finals.

His shocked team-mates were not long in following him home to Buenos Aires after their unexpected 3-2 exit at the hands of Romania in the last 16 knockout stage. The Romanian side was built around the creative midfield talents of Gheorghe Hagi, known as the "Maradona of the Carpathians."

For the first time since the four British Home Nations returned to the FIFA fold after World War II, none of them qualified for the finals. However, the Republic of Ireland—largely built around English league players—emerged impressively from a first round group that featured Italy, Mexico, and Norway. They fell at the next hurdle, soundly beaten 2-0 in the last 16 by Holland at the Citrus Bowl Stadium in the midday humidity of Orlando, Florida.

BRAZILIAN BLEND FAITH AND FLAIR

Brazil, despite lacking the flair of some of their previous sides, boasted the most effective strike partnership of the tournament in the European-based pair of Bebeto and Romario. But a disappointing final against Italy ended scoreless, making it the first in the history of the World Cup to be settled by a penalty shoot-out.

The decisive kick was missed by Italian forward Roberto Baggio, whose goals had been crucial in taking his country all the way to the final at the Rose Bowl Stadium in Los Angeles, California.

Mario Zagallo, the assistant manager of Brazil to Carlos Alberto Parreira, became the first man to be involved in four World Cup winning teams, 20 years after his first attempt at gaining this distinction. Zagallo had been an invaluable outside left in Brazil's victorious teams at Sweden in 1958 and four years later in Chile. He successfully managed Brazil in 1970, but four years later his side crashed out to finish fourth.

ABOVE Consolation for Italy's Roberto Baggio after his decisive penalty miss

THE WORLD CUP

1998

Zinedine Zidane's distinctive balding head won France their first World Cup. The midfielder's headed goals, either side of half-time, was overshadowed by a Brazilian side subdued by striker Ronaldo's pre-match collapse.

THE RESULT 1998

Location: Paris
Final: France 3 Brazil 0
Shirts: France blue, Brazil yellow
Scorers: Zidane 2, Petit
Sent Off: Desailly

FRANCE

Barthez

Thuram Leboeuf Desailly Lizarazu

Petit Deschamps Karembeu Zidane
(Boghossian)

Djorkaeff
(Vieira)

Guivarc'h
(Dugarry)

Ronaldo Bebeto

Leonardo Rivaldo Dunga César Sampaio
(Denílson) (Edmundo)

Carlos Baiano Aldair Cafu

Taffarel

BRAZIL

Internazionale striker Ronaldo had been a member of the 1994 Brazil squad, but did not play a game. Yet, by 1998 he was the team's key player and goal scorer. But crucially, on the morning of the World Cup final, he collapsed in the hotel room that he shared with Roberto Carlos, and was taken to hospital for an emergency check-up.

Manager Mario Zagallo, not expecting Ronaldo to be available to play, named an official line-up that featured Edmundo in Ronaldo's place. Surprisingly, Ronaldo appeared in the line-up after being given the medical all clear. Zagallo swiftly obtained FIFA clearance to alter the team line-up and later denied that he had been pressured into including Ronaldo by FIFA officials and/or sponsors. Although Ronaldo did play the entire match, he was never a force in the game and rarely threatened to add to his personal tally of four goals scored during the previous rounds.

Zidane's double and a last-minute third goal from midfielder Emmanuel Petit provided France with a comfortable victory in Saint-Denis, north of Paris. The 3-0 triumph was astonishing because the French side were reduced to ten men after defender Marcel Desailly was sent off.

Desailly's red card cost Thierry Henry an opportunity to make an appearance in the final. The striker had played in all the previous games and as a substitute was expected to play a part. But manager Aimé Jacquet opted to bring on a replacement defender for Desailly instead.

An earlier red card, in England's second round loss to Argentina, had already made David Beckham notorious. England had reached the finals by qualifying from a tough group that included Italy. Under the management of former international midfielder Glenn Hoddle, England had beaten Tunisia and Colombia in their first round group but finished in

RIGHT Referee Kim Milton Nielsen sends off England's David Beckham

second spot because of a 2-1 reversal to Romania. It proved a costly slip up because it meant England had to tackle old rivals Argentina in the second round instead of Croatia.

England's Michael Owen, the outstanding new Liverpool striker, scored a superb solo goal, but early in the second half Manchester United midfielder Beckham was sent off by Danish referee Kim Morten Nielsen for flicking a retaliatory foot at the Argentinian midfielder Diego Simeone. England, without the influential Beckham, fought bravely and even had a potential winning "goal" by defender Sol Campbell contentiously disallowed before they eventually succumbed in the lottery of a penalty shoot-out.

Argentina's midfielder Ariel Ortega was given his marching orders during their next game against Holland. Being reduced to ten men meant the same ultimate outcome of defeat. Holland progressed to the finals with a 2-1 win, courtesy of a superb winning goal from Arsenal striker Dennis Bergkamp—later voted the best goal of the finals.

FRANCE FIND WINNING FORMULA

Dutch luck finally ran out. In their semi-final they lost on a penalty shoot-out to Brazil while hosts France, gathering speed and confidence, sneaked past Croatia thanks to the first and second goals of defender Lilian Thuram's international career. France won despite finishing with ten men after Laurent Blanc was sent off after a tussle with Slaven Bilic.

Croatia went on to finish third on their debut at the finals, less than a decade after the country had gained independence out of the wreckage of the former Yugoslavia. Star striker Davor Suker ended up as the tournament's six-goal leading marksman to crown a remarkable season and win the coveted Golden Boot. Less than two months earlier, Suker had became a European club champion with Real Madrid following their slender 1-0 victory over Juventus in the Champions League final.

France went on to defeat Brazil and duly celebrate the triumph for which they had been waiting since fellow countryman Jules Rimet had launched the inaugural World Cup 68 years earlier. Thousands of delirious fans poured into central Paris to celebrate, and the victorious team

undertook an open-top bus parade the following day down the Champs-Elysées. Manager Aimé Jacquet, a former international midfielder, was delighted with the manner of victory because he had been subjected to a barrage of relentless criticism for his tactics and team selection by the daily sports newspaper *L'Equipe*.

Jacquet stepped down after the finals and handed over to assistant Roger Lemerre. The new manager proved that the World Cup triumph had been no fluke by leading France to a further international victory at the subsequent European Championships two years later with a 2-1 success over Italy.

BELOW Team-mates join Zinedine Zidane in celebrating his second goal against Brazil

THE WORLD CUP

2002

"We proved the World Cup belongs to everyone."

JAPAN'S HIDETOSHI NAKATA

Although the trophy went to hot favorites Brazil, the tournament was full of upsets. Holders France made a swift exit, while co-hosts South Korea stunned Portugal, Italy, and Spain to reach the semi-finals.

RIGHT Park Ji-sung of South Korea enjoys that winning feeling against Portugal

THE RESULT 2002

Location: Yokohama
Final: Brazil 2 Germany 0
Scorers: Ronaldo 2
Shirts: Brazil yellow, Germany white

BRAZIL

Marcos

Cafu   Lúcio   Roque Júnior   R Carlos

Ronaldinho   Edmilson   Silva   Kléberson
(Paulista)

Ronaldo   Rivaldo
(Denílson)

Klose   Neuville
(Bierhoff)

Bode   Hamann   Jeremies   Schneider
(Ziege)   (Asamoah)

Metzelder   Ramelow   Linke   Frings

Kahn

GERMANY

South Korea were beaten to third place by Turkey, who had previously never progressed beyond the first round.

This was the first World Cup to be played in Asia. Japan had long been campaigning for the right to stage the finals, and one major step in their bid to impress the world authority FIFA had been the launch of the professional J.League in 1993.

Less than two years before the hosting decision, in 1996, the Japanese were challenged in the bidding race by neighbors South Korea. A major political battle within FIFA ended with a compromise that resulted in both countries being awarded the finals jointly. This decision meant that not only was the 2002 event the inaugural Asian finals but the first, and so far the only, World Cup finals to be co-hosted.

The co-hosting proved highly expensive for FIFA and highly complex in logistical terms. The match schedule for the finals had to be especially organized to ensure that each co-host played all matches in their country. In the end, the tournament organization ran remarkably smoothly.

FRANCE FAIL TO SCORE A GOAL

Out on the pitch, the first of many shocks kicked off with the tournament's grand opening match. Defending champions France were narrowly beaten 1-0 by Senegal, who were making their debut in the finals. Midfielder Papa Bouba Diop scored the goal for the impressive and organized Senegal side.

France may have been reigning world and European champions but, in a disastrous defense of their World Cup, they were knocked out in the first round without even scoring a goal in their three group games. It was the worst record of any defending nation in the tournament's history, although they were handicapped by the initial absence of Zinedine Zidane. The key midfielder had been injured in a warm-up friendly against South Korea on the eve of the finals. Manager Roger Lemerre, who had guided France, or "Les Bleus," to victory in the European Championship two years earlier, was fired on France's return home, despite having been awarded a contract extension before the finals.

The once-mighty Argentina also failed to make the second round, after finishing third in their

group behind England and table-topping Sweden. With memories of the 1998 World Cup penalty shoot-out still fresh in their memories, Argentina tackled England indoors at Tokyo's Sapporo Dome. England emerged as 1-0 winners courtesy of a penalty converted by David Beckham, who avenged his 1998 World Cup expulsion against the South Americans.

England were guided by Swede Sven-Göran Eriksson, their first foreign manager, and beat Denmark surprisingly easily 3-0 in the second round but then lost 2-1 to Brazil in the quarter-finals. The decisive goal was a long-range fluke shot from Ronaldinho that drifted over the head of helpless England keeper David Seaman. Ronaldinho was sent off in the 57th minute, but Brazil held onto their lead without the influential midfielder for both the rest of this contest and for their semi-final 1-0 victory over Turkey.

SEMI-FINAL SLOTS FILLED BY UNDERDOGS

Japan reached the second round before being eliminated 1-0 by Turkey, while South Korea made the most of their fervent home support to race into the semi-finals and finish fourth overall. South Korea were astutely organized by the Dutch coach Guus Hiddink and inspired by attacking players such as Ahn Jung Hwan, whose extra time goal beat Italy in a dramatic second round tie. Turkey had rarely appeared before in the finals of any major tournament, let alone the World Cup. But they made the most of this opportunity by reaching the semi-final stage. Veteran striker Hakan Sükür scored the fastest-ever goal in the World Cup by taking just 10.8 seconds to give Turkey the lead in a 3-2 win over South Korea in the third place play-off.

The final, played at the International Stadium Yokohama in Japan, belonged to Brazil's prolific striker Ronaldo. He scored twice against a competitive but uninspired German team that clearly missed their key midfielder Michael Ballack, who was suspended after collecting a second yellow card of the tournament in the semi-final.

Ronaldo finished the tournament as its eight-goal leading marksman to not only pick up the Golden Boot but to equal Pelé's Brazilian record of 12 goals overall in World Cup finals.

Oliver Kahn, Germany's captain, became the first goalkeeper to be voted as the best player of the tournament despite making a crucial error to concede the first goal in the final.

Cafu, Brazil's captain, also made history by becoming the first footballer to play in the final of three consecutive World Cups.

ABOVE Ronaldo scores Brazil's first goal after a mistake by goalkeeper Oliver Kahn

BELOW David Seaman is fooled by Ronaldinho's long shot

THE WORLD CUP

2006

Italy collected their fourth World Cup, although the final will always be associated with Zinedine Zidane's violent act. The French master was aiming for a fairytale ending to his illustrious career, but instead bowed out disgracefully.

THE RESULT 2006

Location: Berlin
Final: Italy 1 France 1 (after extra time, Italy 5-3 penalties)
Shirts: Italy blue, France white
Scorers: Materazzi; Zidane (pen)
Sent Off: Zidane

The final pitched France against Italy in Berlin's Olympic Stadium and saw Real Madrid midfielder Zinedine Zidane give France the lead with a cheeky penalty, in what was to be his final game before retiring from the sport.

Italy equalized through a header from rugged central defender Marco Materazzi, which sent the game into extra time. With ten minutes of extra time and the contest still at stalemate, Zidane suddenly launched his head into Materazzi's chest and was sent off for violent conduct by the Argentinian referee Horacio Elizondo.

Subdued France had no Zidane to help them in the penalty shoot-out. Italy, coached by Marcello Lippi, became the second side to win the World Cup on penalties after the French striker David Trezeguet hit the bar with his attempt.

Despite such a disgraceful end to his career, Zidane was voted player of the tournament because of his efforts in masterminding victories over Spain, Brazil, and Portugal to reach the final.

Italy proved to be the tournament's most consistent team, largely thanks to the contributions of the outstanding goalkeeper Gianluigi Buffon, center back and captain Fabio Cannavaro, and influential midfielder Andrea Pirlo.

Their success was all the more dramatic since it occurred at the same time as a trial in Italy, in which senior figures in club football were being accused and found guilty of systemic match-fixing. Juventus official, Luciano Moggi, was the controversial central figure in the corruption scandal. Five of Italy's successful squad and seven other World Cup players returned to Italy after

the tournament to find that their club had been relegated to Serie B as punishment. The once mighty trio of Juventus, Lazio, and Fiorentina were demoted.

Italy had beaten Germany 2-0 during extra time at the semi-final stage. The hosts had been one of the most exciting teams to watch under the guidance of former striker Jürgen Klinsmann.

KLINSMANN LEADS GERMAN REVIVAL

The German federation had appointed Klinsmann, a World Cup winner in 1990, as coach in the summer of 2004, following their nation's disappointing showing at the UEFA European Championship. Klinsmann demanded a free hand, which included the right to continue to live in California and bring in his choice of new staff—coaches, assistants, and fitness experts. His approach drew initial skepticism among other coaches and fans. By the time the World Cup finals started, it became clear that Klinsmann was winning fans with his tactics and approach to matches.

Germany made an adventurous—and, crucially, winning—start, by defeating Costa Rica 4-2 in the opening game. New heroes included young striker Lukas Podolski and defender Philipp Lahm. Ultimately, the German effort was halted in a semi-final in Dortmund by Italy in what was arguably the finest game of the tournament. Italy snatched victory through last-gasp goals in extra time from Fabio Grosso and Alessandro Del Piero.

The Germans scored a 3-1 third place play-off win over Portugal, resulting in a far better finish to their campaign than many home fans had feared.

DULL ENGLAND SUFFER ON SPOT-KICKS

In contrast to the Germans, England's World Cup performances were dreary, in Sven-Göran Eriksson's third and last tournament as national coach. The quarter-finals were once again the end of the road as England lost on penalties for the second time in three World Cups, beaten by Portugal in a shoot-out for the second time in a row—after a similar finish in the 2004 UEFA European Championship held in Portugal.

England's hopes had been hindered by a pre-tournament foot injury to star striker Wayne Rooney, which delayed his arrival. Then fellow striker Michael Owen was seriously injured during a freak accident in a group game against Sweden.

Rooney was sent off for stamping on defender Ricardo Carvalho during the quarter-final contest. Cristiano Ronaldo, Rooney's Manchester United team-mate, endured a hate campaign on his return to English football after having been caught smiling and winking at the Portuguese bench following Rooney's expulsion.

Portugal's progress was ended by France, who inflicted a 1-0 semi-final defeat in a lackluster match through Zidane's 33rd-minute penalty.

South America's challenge ended in the quarter-finals. In the group stage, a surprisingly adventurous Argentina had contributed the goal of the tournament against Serbia & Montenegro, a 24-pass move finished by Esteban Cambiasso. But they lost to Germany on penalties in the quarter-finals while Brazil lost their hold on the trophy at the same stage by a 1-0 reversal to France.

German striker Miroslav Klose finished top scorer with five goals, the lowest tally since 1962, for the winner of the Golden Boot.

BELOW Italy's Marco Materazzi acclaims his equalizer in the final

BOTTOM Zinedine Zidane beats Gigi Buffon to open the score for France

THE WORLD CUP

2010

Spain lifted their first World Cup at a tournament where attractive, attacking football emerged triumphant for the major European sides.

The final itself should have been a marvellous spectacle as the Spanish, already the European champions, came up against Holland, who had won all their matches en route to the final in Johannesburg, eliminating Brazil and surprise package Uruguay along the way. However, rather than trying to outplay the Spanish, which with stars like Wesley Sneijder and Arjen Robben in their team was not impossible, Dutch coach Bert van Marwijk sent his side out to nullify their opposition. This made for an underwhelming and at times brutal contest, with referee Howard Webb dishing out 14 yellow cards and dismissing Holland's Jonny Heitinga for a second booking.

Eventually settled by Andres Iniesta's winner four minutes from the end of extra time, the 2010 final will not be remembered as a classic.

It confirmed Spain as worthy champions, despite a 1-0 loss in their opening game to Switzerland. They recovered well with wins over Honduras and Chile, then three consecutive 1-0 wins over Portugal, Paraguay and Germany booked them a place in their first World Cup final and allowed Iniesta to consign the Dutch to a third final defeat without ever having lifted the trophy.

Hosts South Africa had started the party with a 1-1 draw against Mexico, but would go on to become the first home team in a World Cup not to progress from the group stage. They were dumped out despite beating the troubled French, whose players had gone on strike against manager Raymond Domenech's coaching methods.

Argentina had looked like early contenders under Diego Maradona's leadership, picking up maximum points from their group, while Brazil and Portugal emerged ahead of Ivory Coast in what was regarded as the 'group of death'. The

Portuguese hit whipping boys North Korea for seven, the tournament's greatest margin of victory, but their journey would end at the last 16.

Germany were given an early scare when they lost to Serbia, but recovered to book their place in the knockout stages. They would go on to thrash an underperforming England in the first knockout round, although it could all have been different had the assistant referee seen Frank Lampard's long-range drive bounce well over the German goal-line before bouncing back into play. Germany progressed to meet Argentina in the quarter-final, where their performance in a 4-0 win led many to tip Joachim Low's enterprising young side as potential winners.

Indeed, the South American giants were not faring so well and Brazil were eliminated by the Netherlands, who came from behind to win 2-1, though they were helped on their way by an own goal and a red card to Felipe Melo. Both Maradona and Dunga, playing greats in their respective countries, would leave their jobs after the tournament.

RIGHT Frank Lampard's shot clearly bounces over the German line, but the goal was not given

It was left to Uruguay to carry the South American flag, though their campaign will be remembered for Luis Suarez's controversial handball against Ghana in the quarter-finals. With the score tied at 1-1 in the dying moments of extra time, the forward handled a goalbound header on the line and was subsequently sent off. Asamoah Gyan then missed the penalty for the Ghanaians, who passed up the chance to become the first African side ever to make the last four. Uruguay won the shootout, and not for the first time in his career, Suarez had won few friends.

Minus Suarez's talents, the Uruguayans were undone by two goals in three minutes from Sneijder and Robben, after Gio van Bronckhorst and the excellent Diego Forlan had set the game up for an exciting finale. Maxi Pereira pulled one back late on, but it was the Dutch who would march on to their first final since 1978.

It would be an all-European encounter, with their opponents to come from either Spain or Germany, who had also contested the Euro 2008 final two years earlier.

Once again, the Spaniards would win 1-0 and deservedly so. They controlled the encounter for long periods, with Low's bold side unable to get a grip on the game or create the chances they had in their earlier fixtures. As they did in 2006, the Germans would finish third thanks to a 3-2 win over Uruguay in Port Elizabeth.

That game featured the men voted the tournament's best player, Diego Forlan, and best young player, Thomas Muller; they also shared the golden boot along with David Villa and Wesley Sneijder. All four scored five goals during the course of the tournament.

ABOVE Luis Suarez handles the ball on the line, denying Ghana a goal. Ghana would then miss the crucial penalty

BELOW Spain celebrate their first World Cup triumph in Johannesburg

WORLD CUP MOMENTS

ABOVE Keeper Jan Jongbloed comes to Holland's rescue

RIGHT Diego Maradona celebrates victory over England

BELOW Argentina's fans hail Daniel Passarella

ABOVE Andy Brehme converts Germany's penalty winner in the final

BELOW Gary Lineker wins the golden boot with six goals

ABOVE Romario celebrates a quarter-final goal against Holland

RIGHT Dennis Bergkamp fires the final's best goal past Carlos Roa

ABOVE Sent-off Zinedine Zidane makes an exit

BELOW Siphiwe Tshabalala (number 8) of South Africa celebrates the opening goal of the tournament, which brought a continent together

LEFT David Beckham scores England's winner against Argentina

THE WORLD CUP 2014

Brazil is the place to be in 2014 for the greatest show on earth. Opportunities like this do not come around for players every day. It is 64 years since the World Cup was last played here and nobody wants to miss it. All the major nations qualified, just, which promises a footballing party like never before. Included here are profiles of every team, their qualifying record and the men to watch when the action starts on June 12.

ARGENTINA

Aside from the hosts, there is no side better placed for success in Brazil than the ludicrously talented Argentina.

ROAD TO WORLD CUP 2014

Argentina	4-1	Chile
Venezuela	1-0	Argentina
Argentina	1-1	Bolivia
Colombia	1-2	Argentina
Argentina	4-0	Ecuador
Argentina	3-1	Paraguay
Peru	1-1	Argentina
Argentina	3-0	Uruguay
Chile	1-2	Argentina
Argentina	3-0	Venezuela
Bolivia	1-1	Argentina
Argentina	0-0	Colombia
Ecuador	1-1	Argentina
Paraguay	2-5	Argentina
Argentina	3-1	Peru
Uruguay	3-2	Argentina

KEY PLAYERS

Lionel Messi
Sergio Aguero
Javier Mascherano

Not only do the *Albiceleste* possess some of the planet's best attacking players, their squad will be more familiar with the climate and surrounds of a South American tournament than many of their European counterparts. It is no surprise to see them installed among the frontrunners to lift the World Cup trophy for the third time this summer.

However, it is a surprise the two-time champions have not progressed beyond the quarter final stage since being in the 1990 final.

In 2014, expectations are understandably high. Led by Lionel Messi, coach Alejandro Sabella has almost too many star players to choose from. Alongside the Barcelona forward, there is Sergio Aguero, Gonzalo Higuain, Angel Di Maria, Ezequiel Lavezzi and Javier Pastore all jostling for places and positions while representing Champions League clubs. Such is their strength that Carlos Tevez, now of Juventus, has not been selected by Sabella since 2011.

Messi's team-mate in Catalonia, Javier Mascherano, provides a defensive partnership with Ezequiel Garay of Benfica, a classy centre-back, comfortable in possession with a useful turn of pace. That pair will be as important to any Argentine success as those grabbing glory at the other end of the field and will be expected to help improve a questionable defensive shield in midfield.

Argentina's campaign began in late 2011 with a Higuain hat-trick and Messi strike seeing off Chile, before a shock 1-0 defeat in Venezuela and a home draw with Bolivia.

Six wins in seven followed as qualification became a question of 'when' rather than 'if'. Goals flowed from the golden group of Higuain,

Messi, Aguero and Di Maria, while old-timer Maxi Rodriguez also chipped in as Argentina surged to the top of the South American table, beating Colombia, Ecuador, Paraguay, Uruguay, Chile again and then taking revenge against Venezuela to cap an impressive run.

Three straight draws allowed Colombia to climb a little closer but Argentina would not be beaten and a 5-2 win in Paraguay sealed qualification last September, allowing Sabella to experiment by using some fringe players in the final two games.

Inter Milan forward Rodrigo Palacio made the scoresheet in a 3-1 victory over Peru in Buenos Aires, while Rodriguez struck twice in the 3-2 defeat to rivals Uruguay in the final game, a result that saw Uruguay clinch a place in the play-offs.

Sabella thus has plenty of options, perhaps as many as any Argentine coach since Cesar Menotti in 1978, when they lifted the trophy at home after beating Holland in the final.

Diego Maradona, in so many ways comparable

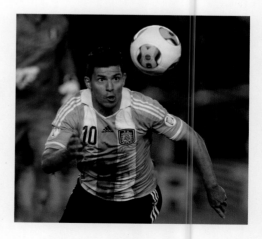

to Messi, led Argentina almost singlehandedly to glory in 1986 and almost repeated the trick in 1990, only for West Germany to triumph against a brutally physical Argentine side.

Since then, there has been huge underachievement. Four years later in 1994, Maradona was sent home for a failed drug test, while in 1998 they fell victim to one of the all-time great goals, scored by Holland's Dennis Bergkamp in the quarter-final.

The ignominy of a group stage exit followed in 2002, despite a strong squad and at both 2006 and 2010 they lost out at the last eight.

Four years ago, Maradona was coach in South Africa after overseeing a bumpy qualification campaign. Things started well with three straight wins, before Mexico were seen off in the first knockout round. Germany awaited in the quarters where, despite Argentine pressure and possession, they were stunned 4-0 by a brilliant display of counter-attacking football.

It left Argentina in need of a boost and hosting the 2011 Copa America should have been the ideal opportunity, but again they slipped up, finishing behind Colombia in their group to set up a quarter-final with Uruguay, who were victorious on penalties. It was a painful defeat, which signalled the end of Maradona's replacement Sergio Batista's short reign, ushering in a new era under Sabella.

This time around, a straightforward qualifying campaign (in the absence of Brazil) has instilled confidence to a gifted squad. Argentina possess all the ingredients for a third success, if Sabella can find the right blend.

ABOVE Argentina players react to defeat against Venezuela

LEFT Sergio Aguero is just one of coach Alejandro Sabella's attacking options

RIGHT Javier Mascherano can provide steel behind the more creative Argentines.

WORLD CUP 2014, TEAMS

BRAZIL

Never has the weight of expectation on a country been as eagerly felt as it is in Brazil in the lead-up to the 20th World Cup.

KEY PLAYERS

Neymar
Oscar
Thiago Silva

RIGHT Coach Luiz Felipe Scolari delivers his message.

No other nation has qualified for all 20 World Cups and no other nation has been crowned world champions as many times. It is probably fair to say that no other nation identifies itself through its football team quite as much as five-times champions Brazil.

In 2014, it will be 12 years since Ronaldo scored twice to secure their last success and that is too long to wait for a country that expects to win. The pressure is on.

Yet last summer, Brazil hosted the Confederations Cup as a warm-up to this global occasion and the *Selecao* responded in the best way possible – they won every game en route to lifting the trophy, seeing off Japan, Mexico, Italy, Uruguay and Spain.

An underwhelming showing at the 2011 Copa America, where Brazil were eliminated on penalties by Paraguay, was followed by the disappointment of losing to Mexico in the final of the 2012 Olympics. This saw coach Mano Menezes dismissed as the Brazil Football Federation sought 'new methods' to boost their chances in 2014.

The choice was perhaps a surprise, but in Luiz Felipe Scolari they have a man who led the team to glory in 2002 and is seen as a passionate father figure to Brazilian football and a huge patriot, though not a tactical genius.

Defeat to England at Wembley in his first friendly game (as hosts, Brazil did not need to qualify), followed by draws with Italy and Russia, suggested all was not well for 'Felipao', but a 3-0 win over France on the eve of their first competitive fixtures under the new man brought confidence and once the Confederations Cup kicked off in Brasilia, they did not look back.

Star man Neymar struck an irresistible half-volley in the opening minutes against Japan in the first game, setting the tone for a tournament that would unite a population that had been taking to the streets to protest against its government.

Scolari found a settled side, with attacking full-backs Marcelo and Dani Alves complementing the creative force of Hulk, Oscar and Neymar in attack, while midfielders Luiz Gustavo and Paulinho provided energy and steel ahead of ball-playing centre-backs David Luiz and captain Thiago Silva.

In short, there is talent wherever you look, though the two question marks hanging over Brazil will be at either end of the field. First-choice goalkeeper Julio Cesar was relegated from the English Premier League with Queens Park Rangers in 2013 and has been lacking regular football since, while centre-forward Fred can appear off the pace and clumsy in possession. However, the Fluminense striker did end last summer's tournament with five goals and looks likely to lead the line in the absence of major competition. Jô has found form in Brazil after struggling in the Premier League, while Alexandre Pato and Robinho are back in contention after rediscovering their form at club level.

With most of their players based abroad in Europe, there have been huge burdens placed upon them by travelling either to South America or around the world for a series of meaningless friendlies, but recent results for the Brazilians have been good.

Despite defeat to Switzerland in Basel, they have beaten Australia at home, Portugal in Massachusetts, South Korea in Seoul and Zambia in Beijing. When Scolari finally gets his men all together on home soil, they will be expected to gel even more.

The message the 65-year-old Scolari will try to deliver is that there awaits an opportunity to write history. When Brazil previously hosted the World Cup in 1950, they were beaten in the final by Uruguay. They have won it five times since, but neither Pele, Romario nor Ronaldo ever experienced it in front of their own supporters.

There will be strong opposition from around the world. Neighbours Argentina will be well-fancied, while Spain will be expected to give a better showing than they did in the Confederations Cup. Italy, Germany and Holland will all be capable of an upset, yet the Brazilians will fancy their chances against all of them on their day.

It is 36 years since a host nation won the World Cup. Brazil will be expecting to put an end to that run on July 13.

ABOVE There are doubts over Fred's quality, but his goals helped Brazil win last summer's Confederations Cup

BELOW Defensive pair Thiago Silva and David Luiz talk tactics

ENGLAND

After repeated disappointment in Germany and South Africa, failure to qualify for the European Championships in 2008 and a mediocre showing in Ukraine and Poland at the 2012 Euros, expectations on England seem to have finally lowered.

ROAD TO WORLD CUP 2014

Moldova	0-5	England
England	1-1	Ukraine
England	5-0	San Marino
Poland	1-1	England
San Marino	0-8	England
Montenegro	1-1	England
England	4-0	Moldova
Ukraine	0-0	England
England	4-1	Montenegro
England	2-0	Poland

KEY PLAYERS

Wayne Rooney
Steven Gerrard
Joe Hart

RIGHT Roy Hodgson's bold selection of Andros Townsend paid dividends

The 'Golden Generation' of earlier campaigns has largely now dispersed, leaving a younger nucleus of talent for coach Roy Hodgson to lead, mixed with the remaining experienced talents of captain Steven Gerrard, Wayne Rooney and Frank Lampard.

After taking the job following Fabio Capello's resignation shortly before Euro 2012, Hodgson was charged with bringing pride and hope back to a country that had only once made the semi-finals since lifting the World Cup on home soil back in 1966.

The qualification process began well as Lampard struck twice in the opening half-hour in Moldova, with squad players Jermain Defoe, James Milner and Leighton Baines adding gloss, but four days later it took a Lampard penalty three minutes from time at Wembley to prevent defeat to an impressive Ukraine side.

San Marino were swept aside as England notched five again, but once more England struggled against more established opposition, labouring to a draw in Poland thanks to Wayne Rooney's second goal of the campaign.

Creativity was proving a problem, the 4-2-3-1 shape favoured by Hodgson struggled to break down better organised opposition.

San Marino proved less troublesome, conceding eight as England ran riot, substitute Daniel Sturridge getting on the scoresheet after impressing since joining Liverpool.

At the halfway point in the campaign, England had won three and drawn two. They travelled to Montenegro, a familiar opposition having been paired together in European qualifying two years earlier, with a point to prove.

Rooney gave England the perfect start six minutes in as he headed home from close range but Hodgson's side failed to capitalise on early superiority, eventually losing control and allowing a late Montenegrin equaliser to keep the Three Lions off the top spot in Group H.

Four games remained, including a daunting trip to Kiev for the return game against Ukraine. Before this, however, the autumn period began with a straightforward dismantling of Moldova, memorable for Rickie Lambert's header and a Danny Welbeck double, which elevated England above Montenegro for the first time.

Welbeck, a favourite of Hodgson, received a yellow card, however, and would be suspended in Kiev. With Rooney also missing due to a gashed head, perhaps predictably, England's attack was blunted in eastern Europe, but the defence of Kyle Walker, Gary Cahill, Phil Jagielka and Ashley Cole performed well and emerged with a 0-0 draw that had been low on excitement but high on importance.

Two home wins against Montenegro and Poland would be enough. Yet England were still to beat recognised footballing opposition.

Hodgson was under pressure, but rather than play it safe, for which he was renowned, he gambled, offering a debut to young Tottenham winger Andros Townsend against Montenegro. From the outset, the 22-year-old showed no fear and attacked the visitors at will.

Rooney and a Branko Boskovic own goal had England in control, but Dejan Damjanovic pulled one back to set the nerves jangling, only for Townsend to fire home from 25 yards to seal the

win, Sturridge adding an injury-time penalty.

Poland were the final visitors to Wembley and brought with them 18,000 supporters. They could no longer qualify themselves, but were determined to make it difficult for England.

Once again Townsend was heavily involved but it fell to Rooney, scoring his seventh of the campaign, to head home an opening goal, while captain fantastic Gerrard delivered a late trademark run and finish to confirm qualification for Brazil.

The mood now is brighter than it was when Hodgson took over but there remain huge question marks. Goalkeeper Joe Hart's club form has been erratic, Cahill and Jagielka remain inexperienced at the very top; in midfield Lampard and Gerrard battle the effects of ageing while in attack, bar Rooney, there is a scarcity of world-class talent.

Yet there is still hope. Unbeaten in qualifying, Hodgson will hope to call on exciting young talent. Not only Townsend, but Arsenal's spring-heeled pair of Alex Oxlade-Chamberlain and Theo Walcott show promise, while Jack Wilshere, if he stays fit, could impress from the centre of midfield.

With pre-tournament expectations uncharacteristically low, England may yet surprise, but improvement will be needed if they are to be in South America after the quarter-final stages.

ABOVE Question marks surround Joe Hart and Gary Cahill at world level

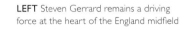

LEFT Steven Gerrard remains a driving force at the heart of the England midfield

FRANCE

It took a stunning comeback in the European play-offs to seal a fifth consecutive World Cup appearance for the 1998 champions.

ROAD TO WORLD CUP 2014

Finland	0-1	France
France	3-1	Belarus
Spain	1-1	France
France	3-1	Georgia
France	0-1	Spain
Georgia	0-0	France
Belarus	2-4	France
France	3-0	Finland
Ukraine	2-0	France
France	3-0	Ukraine

KEY PLAYERS

Franck Ribery
Karim Benzema
Hugo Lloris

At 2-0 down to Ukraine after the first leg in Kiev, where they had been well beaten, it looked as though France would miss out on their place in Brazil, but a Mamadou Sakho brace and one from Karim Benzema turned the tie on its head in favour of Didier Deschamps' side.

The French were unfortunate in qualifying, having missed out on a group seeding and then being paired with reigning world and European champions Spain, who would inflict their only defeat, in Paris, during the eight league games. It was the only group around the world, bar South America, to feature two former winners of football's greatest prize.

Until that point, the campaign had started well, with a 1-0 win in Helsinki, a difficult place to visit, followed by a 3-1 win over Belarus on home soil and an impressive 1-1 draw with the Spanish in Madrid, where Olivier Giroud's injury-time equaliser ended Spain's run of 24 consecutive qualifying wins.

Another Giroud strike in overtime, this time at the end of the first half, followed by strikes from Mathieu Valbuena and Franck Ribery, set up a comfortable home win over Georgia as France went to the top of the group, but their fate would be sealed when Spain's Pedro bundled a winner over the line at the Stade de France

A goalless draw in Tbilisi in September followed, and then France had to come from behind twice to beat Belarus, with goals from Ribery (two), Samir Nasri and midfielder Paul Pogba, who had been sent off against Spain. Finland were brushed aside 3-0 in the final group game thanks to goals from Benzema, who had endured a 1,200-minute goal drought at international level, and Ribery.

The play-off draw pitted France against Ukraine, who had met at Euro 2012. The French were favourites, so it was a shock to leave Kiev with a two-goal deficit, a late Andriy Yarmolenko

RIGHT Karim Benzema is back in goalscoring form for the French

penalty and a Laurent Koscielny red card looking to have sealed their fate.

No side had ever completed a comeback from such a position, and Ukraine had now kept eight consecutive clean sheets, but France showed their class on a memorable night in Paris. Their 24 attempted shots was a high for their qualification campaign, though they had defender Sakho to thank for his two goals, the second, and decisive, effort taking a heavy deflection off Oleg Gusev.

Sakho had only been called into the side to replace the out-of-form Eric Abidal, whose own involvement in any football, let alone the elite international game, is remarkable given his own inspirational fight against liver cancer. Philippe Mexes and the exceptional young Raphael Varane are the other central defensive options, though a good second half to the campaign may see Adil Rami or Eliaquim Mangla creep into the 23-man squad for Brazil.

Goalkeeper Hugo Lloris, who is quick off his line and boasts excellent reflexes, is the captain and a safe bet between the sticks, while veteran Patrice Evra, a key figure in the farce of the 2010

tournament, and Mathieu Debuchy are first-choice full-backs.

In midfield, Deschamps is blessed with both style and steel. Rio Mavuba and Etienne Capoue can provide box-to-box stamina and tough tackling, while Pogba and Yohan Cabaye have guile to complement the dangerous Ribery and Nasri. Benzema is the main man up front while the more physical Giroud and the pacy Loic Remy supply backup options to trouble most defences.

There is no doubt that if they can gel, France are capable of seeing the later stages in Brazil. That the 2006 finalists and 1998 winners are not seeded means they could face tough opposition in the group stages, but if they can avoid the internal problems that spoiled their campaign in South Africa, they should have plenty in the tank to make the quarter-finals.

After that it could be down to luck, but recent experience of meeting the Spanish will have helped, while a friendly against the Dutch in March will offer tough European opposition, though they will need to improve on defeats to Uruguay and Brazil in the summer of 2013 if they are to match the South Americans.

Having very nearly not made it, the French will not want to waste their chance in 2014.

ABOVE Olivier Giroud celebrates his equaliser in Spain

LEFT France captain and first-choice goalkeeper Hugo Lloris

GERMANY

It was no surprise to see Germany top their World Cup qualifying group for Brazil 2014.

ROAD TO WORLD CUP 2014

Germany	3-0	Faroe Islands
Austria	1-2	Germany
Republic of Ireland	1-6	Germany
Germany	4-4	Sweden
Kazakhstan	0-3	Germany
Germany	4-1	Kazakhstan
Germany	3-0	Austria
Faroe Islands	0-3	Germany
Germany	3-0	Republic of Ireland
Sweden	3-5	Germany

KEY PLAYERS

Mesut Ozil
Bastian Schweinsteiger
Manuel Neuer

RIGHT Joachim Low (left) has a squad full of quality to choose from

Not only have the Germans never failed to qualify for a finals (they were banned in 1950), their current crop is among the best the country has ever produced. That is some claim for the three-time winners (two as West Germany) and four-time runners-up. Put simply, Germany is synonymous with the World Cup.

Joachim Low's young side excelled four years ago in South Africa, taking the best of their Under-21 side that had lifted the European title a year earlier, Mesut Ozil, Sami Khedira, Thomas Muller and goalkeeper Manuel Neuer, mixing them with the more experienced Phillip Lahm, Bastian Schweinsteiger and Miroslav Klose to create an exceptional unit, strong in defence, creative yet sturdy in midfield and dynamic in attack.

Not considered among the frontrunners, they took the competition in South Africa 2010 by storm, topping their group before putting four past both England and the well-fancied Argentina, but were unlucky to meet Spain in the semi-final, losing 1-0 and missing out on a record eighth final. They did, however, beat Uruguay 3-2 in the third-place play-off to earn the bronze medal.

The semi-finals also spelled the end of the road at Euro 2012, but Low had been able to bring even more fresh blood into the setup, with Mario Gotze, Marco Reus, Toni Kroos and Andre Schurrle all in the final squad. They were four names that all figured regularly in qualifying, slotting comfortably into a squad that will be among the strongest in South America in 2014.

The qualification process began with Gotze and an Ozil brace seeing away the minnows of the Faroe Islands, before Reus joined Ozil on the scoresheet in a narrow away win in Austria. Ireland, finalists at Euro 2012, were dismantled

6-1 as Germany's youngsters ran riot in Dublin. By the time they were 4-0 up at home to Sweden four days later, they had scored 10 in just over a game-and-a-half, but inspired by the great Zlatan Ibrahimovic, the Swedes fought back to earn a draw. It was the first time Germany had ever let a four-goal lead slip and Low spoke afterwards of his amazement at the collapse.

It was to be the only blot on the Germany's qualifying copybook, otherwise winning every game and scoring 36 goals in their 10 matches. After the Sweden embarrassment in Berlin, they put seven past Kazakhstan over two matches, three past each of Austria, the Faroes and Ireland, their qualification secured with that final

game in Cologne, and another five past the Swedes during a second eight-goal thriller.

In that final game, Schurrle hit the first hat-trick of his career and Ozil struck his eighth goal of the campaign. Bearing in mind that Miroslav Klose, who has 14 World Cup finals goals to his name and even at 35 featured in qualifying, should also be available, goals will not be a problem in Brazil.

It is hard to see where, in fact, the Germans will struggle. Their domestic game is in its best shape for many years and in Bayern Munich and Borussia Dortmund they have the two teams who competed in the 2013 Champions League final, arguably the two most exciting teams in Europe, each packed with home-grown talent.

In goalkeeper Neuer they have one of the best in the world, a commanding presence behind a no-frills defence typified by the excellent captain Lahm and steadying presence of Per Mertesacker and Mats Hummels.

Schweinsteiger, Ozil and Thomas Muller would all be vying for places in a World Cup XI and will start if fit, while up front Low can choose from Klose, the maligned but prolific Mario Gomez and Lukas Podolski, while Max Kruse and Stefan Kiessling could force their way into his plans with good seasons in the Bundesliga.

In the modern game, they have never been eliminated before the quarter-final stage and will be expecting a place in at least the semis, as they have achieved in six of the last eight tournaments. Indeed, were Germany not to make the final in Rio, it would be the first time since the 1950 World Cup that they had been missing from three finals in a row.

History tells us they can go all the way. By studying the form book and their ludicrously talented squad, there is little to argue against the Germans.

ABOVE Manuel Neuer is among the world's best goalkeepers

BELOW Germany's next generation of talent is already shining through

HOLLAND

Finalists in 2010, Holland had few problems in reaching Brazil 2014, racking up 28 points out of a possible 30 in qualifying.

ROAD TO WORLD CUP 2014

Holland	2-0	Turkey
Hungary	1-4	Holland
Holland	3-0	Andorra
Romania	1-4	Holland
Holland	3-0	Estonia
Holland	4-0	Romania
Estonia	2-2	Holland
Andorra	0-2	Holland
Holland	8-1	Hungary
Turkey	0-2	Holland

KEY PLAYERS

Arjen Robben
Robin van Persie
Kevin Strootman

RIGHT Louis van Gaal is in his second spell as Dutch coach

The only blip came playing away in Estonia, when Robin van Persie spared their blushes with an injury-time equaliser. Only Germany matched their points tally, or indeed bettered their 34 goals scored, during an eye-catching campaign.

Returning coach Louis van Gaal, who failed to reach the 2002 World Cup when previously in charge, began with a straightforward 2-0 win over Turkey, recording an impressive 4-1 win in Hungary four days later.

Minnows Andorra conceded three in Rotterdam before a 3-1 win away to Romania, Holland's closest rivals, confirmed what most expected, that the Dutch would dominate Group D in Europe.

Estonia and Romania then went for a combined seven goals in Amsterdam without reply, leaving the Dutch firmly in command. The draw in Estonia would have caused embarrassment, but van Persie's 94th minute leveller preserved the unbeaten run dating back to August 2012, when they were beaten 4-2 in a friendly by neighbours Belgium.

A low-key win away to Andorra secured qualification—no European side achieved it earlier—and was followed by one of the biggest wins of the whole qualifying campaign, an 8-1 thrashing against Hungary in which van Persie grabbed a hat-trick and was joined on the scoresheet by high-profile team-mates Rafael van der Vaart and Arjen Robben, who remain central to Dutch plans. A 2-0 win in Istanbul rounded things off nicely.

So where do the Dutch stand as they prepare to embark for Brazil?

Four years on from their first World Cup final in 32 years, Holland have retained key individuals. Van Persie is touted by many as the best striker on the planet and his form since joining Manchester United from Arsenal has been excellent. His fitness will be vital, particularly with Klaas-Jan Huntelaar having his own injury problems.

Out wide, Bayern Munich winger Robben, another who is susceptible to knocks, can trouble any defence, while van der Vaart and Wesley Sneijder are among Europe's best playmakers when on top of their game. Nigel de Jong remains a well-respected stopper in midfield.

There is also a younger generation of talent emerging, as there always seems to be in Holland. Kevin Strootman will be important in central midfield and has matured well since switching to Roma, while at the back 22-year-old Bruno Martins is expected to partner Ron Vlaar in central defence.

Daryl Janmaat should be first choice at right-back, though Gregory van der Wiel could challenge if he has a good end to the season in France with Paris St-Germain and at left-back Daley Blind has edged ahead of Jetro Willems, the teenager who played at Euro 2012.

In goal, van Gaal has options. Maarten Stekelenburg was the custodian in 2010 and remains on the scene, though he played only three times in qualifying. Tim Krul at Newcastle began the campaign but has since been back on the bench, while Swansea's Michel Vorm, PSV youngster Jeroen Zoet and Ajax pair Kenneth Vermeer and Jasper Cillessen have all been considered. Van Gaal will need to identify one in the pre-tournament friendlies and stick with him. He will regret no longer having the great Edwin van der Sar to call on.

A country of less than 17 million people, Holland have regularly overachieved, but with their appearances in two finals in the 1970s and the great Ajax team they were built around, expectations rose and the pressure will be on again in 2014. Infighting has also damaged a few Dutch campaigns in the past, but with a young squad, van Gaal will hope to foster a family atmosphere with the influential senior players helping the less experienced members.

If they can gel, and van Gaal can find a preferred goalkeeper, the *Oranje* could go all the way. Three-time beaten finalists and never a champion, there are few countries who could argue that they deserve a title quite so much. Of course, football does not always provide what is deserved and there are a number of rivals who are equally well equipped.

The re-emergence of neighbours Belgium as a major rival will serve as a motivation to the Dutch, while Germany are long-term footballing adversaries and Spain had the upper hand four years ago. Brazil and Argentina are both closer to home and will expect to be in the later stages, so it is likely the Dutch will need to beat at least two of these sides. On the right day, they are capable of doing so.

ABOVE If fit, Arjen Robben remains a danger man for Holland

BELOW Strong team spirit will be vital in Brazil

ITALY

The 2006 winners return to the World Cup for their 14th consecutive finals and will once again be hoping to go the distance.

ROAD TO WORLD CUP 2014

Bulgaria	2-2	Italy
Italy	2-0	Malta
Armenia	1-3	Italy
Italy	3-1	Denmark
Malta	0-2	Italy
Czech Republic	0-0	Italy
Italy	1-0	Bulgaria
Itay	2-1	Czech Republic
Denmark	2-2	Italy
Italy	2-2	Armenia

KEY PLAYERS

Andrea Pirlo
Mario Balotelli
Daniele De Rossi

RIGHT Forward Pablo Osvaldo will be a problem for opposing defences

As four-time World Cup winners, only Brazil have a better record than the Italians, who last lifted the trophy eight years ago after a penalty shootout victory over France, ending a 24-year wait to hold the trophy again.

Coach Cesare Prandelli, who took over following a disappointing campaign in 2010, has committed to an attacking style of football that contrasts with the traditional *catenaccio* approach. It paid dividends in qualifying as Italy quickly took control of their competitive group, remaining unbeaten throughout their 10 games.

Two goals from Pablo Osvaldo earned a draw in their opening game away to Bulgaria, before comfortable victories against Malta and Armenia.

In their fourth game, Italy were 2-0 up at home to Denmark thanks to goals from Riccardo Montolivo and Daniele De Rossi, but the Danes pulled one back just before half-time. Then 18 seconds after half-time, Osvaldo was dismissed. A home defeat could have been damaging, but the Italians rallied and Pirlo laid on a third goal for Mario Balotelli, moving them four points clear at the top of the group.

From that point, there was no doubt that Italy would be at the finals and four more points were picked up before the 2013 summer break, which saw Prandelli's team sample the Brazilian atmosphere at the Confederations Cup.

This presented an opportunity to test themselves against a variety of opposition and, after narrowly beating Mexico and Japan, they were beaten 4-2 by the hosts, but gave an encouraging display and progressed to the quarter-finals. There, an entertaining exchange

with reigning world champions Spain finished goalless, though defeat on penalties spelled the end of the road.

Back in World Cup qualifying, it took just two more games to confirm Italy's place at the finals, as first Bulgaria were beaten 1-0 in Palermo before they came from behind in Turin to beat Czech Republic, Balotelli converting the all-important penalty just three minutes after Giorgio Chiellini had drawn the *Azzurri* level.

Two 2-2 draws, with Denmark and Armenia, were perhaps not the best way to end the campaign, but in coming from behind to earn a

point in both, the Italians proved they have steel and spirit, both of which will be required in Brazil.

The unpredictable Balotelli and the immaculate Pirlo aside, there are fewer stars in the Italy setup than they have previously known, though they are not lacking quality.

At 36, goalkeeper and captain Gianluigi Buffon will be appearing in his fourth World Cup, but remains indispensable to the cause and ahead of him Chiellini and Leonardo Bonucci, the Juventus pair, will provide a solidity in defence.

Pirlo will dictate the play from his deep-lying midfield role and although Daniele De Rossi, Claudio Marchisio and Alberto Aquilani could all partner him, there may yet be a space for 21-year-old Marco Verratti, who has been in excellent form for Paris St-Germain.

Balotelli's goals helped Italy to the final of Euro 2012 and will be vital once more in Brazil. The bustling Osvaldo should also expect to feature, while AC Milan's Stephan El Shaarawy and the experienced Alberto Gilardino will expect to be on the plane.

Eliminated at the group stage in South Africa, Italy will be hoping 2014 can be more like 2006, when Fabio Cannavaro lifted the trophy in Berlin.

Bizarrely, they are not seeded for the forthcoming tournament, which will mean facing one of the top-ranked sides in the group stage. Provided they can produce the goods against so-called lesser sides, unlike four years ago when they were beaten by Slovakia and failed to beat Paraguay or New Zealand, the Italians will be in the later stages, where their experience and team spirit could come into their own.

ABOVE Giorgio Chiellini heads home against Czech Republic in qualifying

RIGHT Veteran Andrea Pirlo is a driving force in the Italian midfield

PORTUGAL

For the second World Cup in a row, a talented Portugal side needed the play-off stage to qualify, but now they are there they will have their sights on the later stages.

ROAD TO WORLD CUP 2014

Luxembourg	1-2	Portugal
Portugal	3-0	Azerbaijan
Russia	1-0	Portugal
Portugal	1-1	Northern Ireland
Israel	3-3	Portugal
Azerbaijan	0-2	Portugal
Portugal	1-0	Russia
Northern Ireland	2-4	Portugal
Portugal	1-1	Israel
Portugal	3-0	Luxembourg
Portugal	1-0	Sweden
Sweden	2-3	Portugal

KEY PLAYERS

Cristiano Ronaldo
Joao Moutinho
Miguel Veloso

RIGHT Helder Postiga scored six times during qualifying

This time it was Sweden they saw off, in a tie billed around the world as Cristiano Ronaldo versus Zlatan Ibrahimovic. The encounter was true to form too, with two of the planet's most in-form forwards offering up a goalscoring masterclass.

Ronaldo struck first blood with his winner in Lisbon, a low diving header to give his side the narrowest of advantages heading to the second leg in Solna, where he opened the scoring again with a fine finish after a swift Portuguese counter-attack. Ibrahimovic levelled things up with two in five minutes, however, only for Ronaldo to take centre-stage once again, and grab two more inside two minutes to claim a hat-trick and confirm a 4-2 victory for his side.

Portugal are far from a one-man team and can field genuine quality throughout their side, but at times it can seem as though Ronaldo is playing on his own, such is the attention on the Real Madrid man.

He scored his country's first goal of the qualifying campaign, an equaliser against lowly Luxembourg, before Helder Postiga struck in the second half to spare their blushes, but after a 3-0 win over Azerbaijan in which goals came from Silvestre Varela, Postiga once more and defender Bruno Alves, Portugal's campaign became extremely disjointed.

A defeat to eventual group winners Russia was followed four days later by a home draw against Northern Ireland, in which Portugal again had to come from behind against lesser opposition. It took another late comeback in Israel, with an injury-time equaliser from Fabio Coentrao to earn a point, by which time the Russians were four points ahead with a game in hand.

Portugal closed the gap thanks to a 1-0 win when the two sides met in Lisbon, but after a Ronaldo hat-trick inspired a 4-2 comeback against Northern Ireland in Belfast, a late Israeli equaliser

following Ricardo Costa's opener meant Russia only needed a draw against Azerbaijan to qualify top, which they duly achieved.

So Paulo Bento's side did it the hard way, just like they did against Bosnia-Herzegovina in 2010, when two 1-0 wins were enough to see them to South Africa, eventually losing 1-0 to Spain in the round of 16. No shame in that, of course, but they will want to advance further in Brazil.

Ronaldo, in particular, will want to display his outrageous talents to the world, but behind the captain there are others who deserve some time in the spotlight.

Postiga's six goals in qualifying were a decent return for the forward, while on the opposite flank to Ronaldo is Manchester United winger Nani, himself capable of brilliance when he feels like it.

In midfield, Joao Moutinho was one of Europe's most sought after talents before opting to join Monaco, his vision and range of passing reminiscent of Deco in the great Portugal side of a decade ago, while behind him Raul Meireles and Miguel Veloso offer bite in the tackle but also ability on the ball.

In defence, Pepe and Bruno Alves will be among the most respected central partnerships at the World Cup, while full-backs Joao Pereira and Fabio Coentrao like to attack as much as defend, though the latter may need to increase his match fitness after struggling to hold down a place at Real Madrid.

Goalkeeper Rui Patricio, of Sporting Lisbon, was an ever-present in qualifying and looks to have made the spot his own ahead of number two Eduardo, and is seen as a capable pair of hands.

Outside of the starting 11, Portugal are arguably weaker, but certainly less experienced than at any time in the last 15 years. The "Golden Generation" has now long passed, without silverware, and there is less pressure on this side than at any recent tournament. This may play in their favour.

Argentina, Brazil, Germany and Spain all possess more strength in depth than the Portuguese, but if they can steer clear of injuries, there is an outside chance Portugal could go all the way. If Ronaldo is in the mood and his team-mates can provide the type of service they did against Sweden in November, there is no doubting they have the talent to stick around in South America.

ABOVE Miguel Veloso during the 1-0 defeat to Russia in qualifying

BELOW Portugal celebrate play-off success against Sweden

SPAIN

The reigning champions return to Brazil with a point to prove after their humbling in last summer's Confederations Cup final.

ROAD TO WORLD CUP 2014

Georgia	0-1	Spain
Belarus	0-4	Spain
Spain	1-1	France
Spain	1-1	Finland
France	0-1	Spain
Finland	0-2	Spain
Spain	2-1	Belarus
Spain	2-0	Georgia

KEY PLAYERS

Andres Iniesta
Cesc Fabregas
Sergio Ramos

RIGHT Gerard Pique (left) and Sergio Ramos will both be key members of the Spanish defence

As holders of both the World and European titles, Spain arrived in South America with a strong desire to take the intercontinental crown too. They made good progress in reaching the final after group victories over Uruguay, Tahiti and Nigeria and a penalty shootout win against Italy, only for the hosts to sweep them away with a brilliant display. The score of 3-0 did not flatter Brazil, who remain unbeaten in competitive games on home soil since 1975.

It brought to an end an unbeaten run of 29 competitive games for the Spanish, a sequence stretching back to the group stages of the 2010 World Cup, and created doubts around a side that had previously seemed invincible.

Vicente Del Bosque's squad strongly resembled that which had been victorious three years earlier and it is unlikely to drastically change before 2014.

Goalkeeper and captain Iker Casillas, a legend for both club and country, has only been on the fringes of the Real Madrid team for the last year and could yet see his place threatened by the rejuvenated Pepe Reina, youngster David De Gea or Barcelona's Victor Valdes, who replaced him for the penultimate qualifying game last Autumn, when Spain secured their place at the forthcoming finals with a 2-1 win over Belarus.

A year earlier, the campaign began with a narrow win away to Georgia, striker Roberto Soldado sweeping home from close range four minutes from time following a dominant if stuttering display.

A Pedro hat-trick against Belarus helped Spain to a 4-0 win in their second game, the other goalscorer young left-back Jordi Alba, a newcomer to the squad since their South African success.

Olivier Giroud's injury-time equaliser earned France a point in Madrid, before Finland claimed the same result in March 2013. Goals were proving a problem for the Spanish, whose scorer in each game had been defender Sergio Ramos.

Pedro struck a decisive winner in Paris to leapfrog the French back to the top of the group with three games remaining and there would be no further slip-ups.

Alba and forward Alvaro Negredo, struck the decisive goals in Finland before second-half strikes against Belarus, from midfield maestro Xavi and Negredo again, ensured a place at their tenth successive finals.

Negredo and Juan Mata were the goalscorers in the final group game, a 2-0 home win against Georgia, in which Del Bosque rotated his side to give starts to fringe players Juanfran, Jesus Navas and Alberto Moreno.

It all amounted to a solid qualification campaign for the Spanish, who are renowned for their possession game and interchangeable formation, a surplus of midfield talent sometimes seeing them play without a recognised forward.

What people tend to miss, however, is Spain's solid defensive record. Their eight goals scored and two conceded were both the lowest ever figures for a World Cup-winning side. Attack is often regarded as the best form of defence, and so it seems. If Spain's opponents do not have the ball, they cannot score.

So Del Bosque takes his squad to Brazil in pursuit of their fourth consecutive major title. Much of their squad picks itself, barring injuries. The defence will most likely feature Ramos, the youngest European ever to win 100 international caps, playing centrally alongside Gerard Pique, with Alba and Alvaro Arbeloa either side.

The coach will probably stick with Xavi, Fabregas and Iniesta pulling the strings in midfield ahead of protector Sergio Busquets, with Pedro a shoo-in on the flank, having played in all eight qualifiers.

Major question marks remain in attack, where Negredo's three goals in the final three qualifiers probably did enough to book his flight to Brazil, but Fernando Torres and Soldado must improve their club form before the end of the season to figure. David Villa, Spain's all-time leading scorer, should also be in the final 23, having rediscovered some of his old magic since transferring to Atletico Madrid.

Four years ago, Spain became the first European country to win the tournament outside of their own continent. To repeat that feat in 2014 would confirm this generation as among the game's greatest ever teams and whoever

Del Bosque selects, he will have enough talent available to see that his side are well-backed to lift the World Cup trophy on July 13.

Crucially, there will also be experience of lifting major silverware, not just internationally but at club level too. That could prove priceless when the pressure is on.

ABOVE Sergio Busquets (left) and Fernando Torres reflect on Confederations Cup defeat to Brazil

LEFT Pedro scores in Paris to put Spain in control of their qualifying group

URUGUAY

The surprise package in South Africa four years ago, Uruguay will have high hopes this time around having booked their place through the play-offs.

ROAD TO WORLD CUP 2014

Uruguay	4-2	Bolivia
Paraguay	1-1	Uruguay
Uruguay	4-0	Chile
Uruguay	1-1	Venezuela
Uruguay	4-2	Peru
Colombia	4-0	Uruguay
Uruguay	1-1	Ecuador
Argentina	3-0	Uruguay
Bolivia	4-1	Uruguay
Uruguay	1-1	Paraguay
Chile	2-0	Uruguay
Venezuela	0-1	Uruguay
Peru	1-2	Uruguay
Uruguay	2-0	Colombia
Ecuador	1-0	Uruguay
Uruguay	3-2	Argentina
Jordan	0-5	Uruguay
Uruguay	0-0	Jordan

KEY PLAYERS

Luis Suarez
Edinson Cavani
Diego Godin

RIGHT Powerful striker Edinson Cavani will lead the line in Brazil

Having finished a disappointing fifth in South American qualifying, and that was without the Brazilians, Oscar Tabarez' side were fortunate to have the two-legged intercontinental play-off against Jordan to fall back on, the fourth successive time they have been involved in such a tie.

The qualification process for 2014 began well enough with 11 points from their opening five games, scoring 12 times in their three home games and picking up draws in Paraguay and Venezuela, but three consecutive away defeats threw the campaign into doubt.

First they were humbled 4-0 in Colombia, then 3-0 in Argentina and four days later 4-1 in Bolivia, meaning that they had taken just two points from five away games and shipped 13 goals in the process, with their campaign firmly in freefall.

Uruguay would eventually go six games without a win after a late Paraguay equaliser in Montevideo and a 2-0 defeat in Chile, before eking out a crucial 1-0 win in Venezuela, their first win there in 17 years, courtesy of a fine Edinson Cavani goal.

Those three points took them back into fifth spot ahead of the Venezuelans and a Luis Suarez brace in Peru earned another three points before Cavani and Cristian Stuani did the business late on against the Colombians.

The penultimate group game took La Celeste to Ecuador, where a win would have seen them into the automatic qualifying spots. Unfortunately, they lost 1-0 to Jefferson Montero's first-half goal, ensuring it would be the play-offs once again, despite a 3-2 win over weakened group winners Argentina in the final group game.

Luis Suarez ended the group with 11 goals, making him the top scorer in South American qualifying, though he was absent from the scoresheet in Jordan despite Uruguay hitting five to all but confirm their place in Brazil, following it up with a goalless draw at home to reach their 12th finals.

Winners of the inaugural tournament at home in 1930 and again in Brazil in 1950, Tabarez will hope his talented Uruguayans can emulate the team of 64 years earlier. By reaching the semi-finals in 2010, they made the world sit up and notice and they also lifted the 2011 Copa America in Argentina.

Suarez and Cavani, though very different in their styles, will stretch any opposition defence.

The scheming Liverpool forward has subtlety, pace and devilment, while Paris St-Germain striker Cavani is the embodiment of the traditional number nine, big and brutish, his game based on power and athletic ability.

There is also veteran Diego Forlan, who was voted the best player of the tournament in South Africa. Forlan will be 35 when the World Cup in Brazil begins, but his experience will be hugely important to younger members of the squad, such as forwards Stuani and Abel Hernandez, who may be competing for selection, and playmaker Nicolas Lodeiro, who ended an unhappy stay in Europe to play for Botafogo in Rio de Janeiro.

There is creativity elsewhere in winger Cristian Rodriguez, now with Atletico Madrid, and Gaston Ramirez, who has struggled for game time with Premier League club Southampton.

Defensively too, there is strength. Walter Gargano and Egidio Arevalo are an experienced holding midfield pair and behind them, captain Diego Lugano and Diego Godin are a fairly accomplished pair. Fernando Muslera is a solid goalkeeper who will not let anybody down, while wide defenders Maxi Pereira and Alvaro Pereira,

who can also play further forward, enjoy joining in with attacks and will help create chances.

There is no doubting that Uruguay has what it takes to repeat their performance from four years ago. There is a reason why they are ranked inside the world's top 10. Tabarez is one of the most experienced and longest-serving coaches at the tournament and will know how to get the best from a settled squad. He used 28 players in qualifying, less than any other side in South America.

Yet in qualifying, they struggled, particularly on the road, and will need to solve their travel sickness by the time they get to Brazil. They seemed resigned to the play-offs before it was a certainty, knowing they could easily come past Jordan. At the World Cup proper, there is no such safety net. They will need to perform from the outset if they are to progress.

ABOVE Uruguay celebrate booking their place in Brazil after a goalless draw at home to Jordan

LEFT Veteran Diego Forlan remains a goalscoring threat

ALGERIA

Not many sides cut it quite as fine as Algeria in qualifying, who only made it to Brazil on away goals after an entertaining play-off against Burkina Faso.

ROAD TO WORLD CUP 2014

Algeria	4-0	Rwanda
Mali	2-1	Algeria
Algeria	3-1	Benin
Benin	1-3	Algeria
Rwanda	0-1	Algeria
Algeria	1-0	Mali
Burkina Faso	3-2	Algeria
Algeria	1-0	Burkina Faso

KEY PLAYERS

Madjid Bougherra
Sofiane Feghouli
Islam Slimani

The hero who scored the all-important goal was defender Madjid Bougherra, scrambling home a decisive winner shortly into the second half of the second leg after a 3-2 defeat away from home.

Algeria's recent form has been impressive, turning around their failure to qualify for the 2012 African Nations followed by their last-place finish in 2013, by reaching their fourth World Cup and ensuring that the five African sides in Brazil will be the same five that made it to South Africa four years earlier.

Despite being beaten by Mali in qualifying, the Algerians picked up 15 from a possible 18 points to meet the in-form *Burkinabe*, who themselves had been finalists at the continental championship in January. A 3-2 defeat left qualification in the balance, but Magherra provided the all-important touch to seal a spot in Brazil.

Algeria's top scorer during qualifying was Sporting Lisbon striker Islam Slimani, who netted five in seven games, and he and El Arabi Soudani will be the main goal threats in Brazil, while playmaker Sofiane Feghouli, of Valencia, will be expected to create chances for his team-mates.

At the back, Bougherra is the captain and defensive mainstay, while Carl Medjani was the only man to play in all eight qualifying games.

Coach Vahid Halilhodzic, who was sacked from Ivory Coast just months before the 2010 World Cup, has plenty of decisions to make. Regardless of personnel, he will need to make his side hard to beat, as they were four years ago, when they failed to score but conceded just twice in three group games.

If they are to go further this time, Algeria must find a way of keeping and using the ball better than they did in South Africa. Feghouli is capable, but will need those around him to be at their very best if progression is to become a realistic aim.

RIGHT Madjid Bougherra celebrates the goal that booked his country's place in Brazil.

AUSTRALIA

Despite being among the first teams to book their tickets to Brazil, Australia dispensed with coach Holger Osieck following consecutive 6-0 friendly defeats to Brazil and France last autumn.

Osieck had overseen a slightly troublesome qualification, in which the *Socceroos* finished second in their Asian qualifying section behind Japan thanks to late victories over Jordan and Iraq.

In their opening fixture in the preliminary group, they needed a second-half revival to overcome Thailand in Brisbane, Alex Brosque's 86th minute winner sparing their blushes, but wins over Saudi Arabia (3-1) and Oman (3-0) put them in control of the group.

Oman then beat them by a single goal in Muscat but there would be no more slip-ups and they progressed comfortably to the next stage. Once again Oman were there, with Iraq, Jordan and Japan to contend with.

A goalless draw with the Omanis, followed by a draw with the Japanese which needed a penalty to draw them level and then a defeat in Jordan left an uphill task.

Further late comebacks provided some hope, with an away win in Iraq, with goals in the final

10 minutes from veterans Tim Cahill and Archie Thompson and then at home to earn a draw against Oman.

The penultimate game against Jordan would see the victors into second place and here Australia finally showed their potential with a 4-0 win. Another experienced midfielder, Mark Bresciano, opened the scoring before Cahill, Robbie Kruse and captain Lucas Neill sealed a comfortable win.

With Jordan beating Oman in their final game, Australia still had to win against Iraq and, eventually, they did as Kennedy struck an 83rd minute winner to avoid a play-off and book automatic qualification behind Japan.

So what to expect in Brazil? Australia's squad is experienced, with several members approaching their third consecutive World Cup, but there is a lack of top-level talent beyond that 30-something crowd. New coach Ange Postecoglou faces a huge challenge to get the team beyond the group stages.

ROAD TO WORLD CUP 2014

Australia	2-1	Thailand
Saudi Arabia	1-3	Australia
Australia	3-0	Oman
Oman	1-0	Australia
Thailand	0-1	Australia
Australia	4-2	Saudi Arabia
Oman	0-0	Australia
Australia	1-1	Japan
Jordan	2-1	Australia
Iraq	1-2	Australia
Australia	2-2	Oman
Japan	1-1	Australia
Australia	4-0	Jordan
Australia	1-0	Iraq

KEY PLAYERS

Tim Cahill
Josh Kennedy
Brett Holman

LEFT Approaching their third consecutive World Cup, Australia's squad possesses a wealth of experience

WORLD CUP 2014, TEAMS

BELGIUM

Unbeaten in qualifying, Belgium's exciting young side are the dark horses of Brazil 2014.

ROAD TO WORLD CUP 2014

Wales	0-2	Belgium
Belgium	1-1	Croatia
Serbia	0-3	Belgium
Belgium	2-0	Scotland
Macedonia	0-2	Belgium
Belgium	1-0	Macedonia
Belgium	2-1	Serbia
Scotland	0-2	Belgium
Croatia	1-2	Belgium
Belgium	1-1	Wales

KEY PLAYERS

Eden Hazard
Vincent Kompany
Marouane Fellaini

RIGHT The Belgians are delighted to have qualified, but Axel Witsel (left) and Steven Defour will want to go far in Brazil

Long cast in the shadows of neighbours France, Holland and Germany, the Red Devils had failed to qualify for the previous two tournaments, with the golden days of 1986, when they finished fourth, feeling like a long time ago. But suddenly Belgium has an embarrassment of riches, with strength in depth which is the envy of their rivals.

From the outset of the qualifying campaign, there was little doubt that this side would be in Brazil and having amassed eight wins from their 10 games, there are plenty who believe they could yet go all the way, particularly after being seeded for the group stage.

A 2-0 victory in Wales thanks to goals from defenders Vincent Kompany and Jan Vertonghen was followed by a 1-1 draw at home to Croatia. A solid start, but the Belgians then went on a seven-game winning streak that saw them leave their opposition trailing far behind.

Serbia were brushed aside 3-0 in Belgrade with goals from Christian Benteke, Kevin De Bruyne and Kevin Mirallas, Scotland beaten easily in Brussels and Macedonia twice fell victim to the mercurial Eden Hazard.

Once De Bruyne and midfielder Marouane Fellaini had seen off Serbia once more, it was only a matter of time before qualification was sealed and it finally came with another noteworthy win over Croatia, as young striker Romelu Lukaku notched twice in Zagreb.

Coach Marc Wilmots must now pick his first-choice 11. Everywhere there are options. Young goalkeeper Thibaut Courtois has impressed at Atletico Madrid, but Wilmots can also choose Liverpool's Simon Mignolet.

Captain Kompany is the lynchpin of a solid defence that also calls upon the dynamic Vertonghen and highly-rated Toby Alderweireld, while in midfield Fellaini and Axel Witsel are challenged for places by Mousa Dembele and Stephen Defour.

In attack, there is creativity wherever you look, be it through the tricky Hazard, pacy Mirallas or powerful De Bruyne and up front there is the choice between Lukaku and Benteke, each offering raw muscle and a keen eye for goal.

Few sides will fancy facing the Belgians who, unlike other top teams, do not have to live up to the weight of history. If key players stay fit, they should be aiming for at least the semi-finals.

BOSNIA-HERZEGOVINA

Bosnia-Herzegovina will be at their first ever World Cup in 2014, thanks to a superb qualifying campaign that saw them excel at both ends of the field.

With 30 goals, they were the fourth-highest scorers in Europe and began well by thrashing minnows Liechtenstein, where forward pairing Edein Džeko and Vedad Ibišević grabbed a hat-trick each, setting the tone for an impressive run of results.

Four days later Latvia were hammered in Zenica, as Zvjezdan Mišimović took his own tally to four in two games. Next, a 0-0 draw away to main qualification rivals Greece was seen as a good result that left the Bosnians in command of the group.

BELOW Edin Džeko will be Bosnia-Herzegovina's danger man

By beating the Greeks at home, with Džeko and Ibišević both scoring again, Bosnia-Herzegovina put clear daylight between themselves and their challengers, following it up with a 5-0 win in Latvia.

Defeat at home to Slovakia raised questions but Safet Sušić's squad held its nerve to end the campaign with three straight wins, a narrow win in Lithuania tying up their place in Brazil.

With a population of less than four million, the Bosnians, who have emerged from the horrors of civil war in the last 20 years, have overachieved in reaching the World Cup, but with a number of top-class players in their ranks they will not just be making up the numbers.

Džeko and Ibišević scored 18 between them in qualifying and are prolific in England and Germany respectively, while Miralem Pjanić has been a revelation for Roma and has developed into their main playmaker since making his debut as an 18-year-old. Goalkeeper Asmir Begović has long been admired by some of Europe's top clubs, and he will be reliable when called upon, something the Bosnians may consider an advantage when comparing themselves to some of the other unseeded sides in South America.

Although not among Europe's traditional frontrunners, Bosnia-Herzegovina will hope to announce themselves to the world in 2014 and they could succeed at the expense of one of the big names. The lack of previous World Cup appearances to compare their achievements against means the Bosnians have everything to gain in Brazil.

ROAD TO WORLD CUP 2014

Liechtenstein	1-8	Bosnia-Herzegovina
Bosnia-Herzegovina	4-1	Latvia
Greece	0-0	Bosnia-Herzegovina
Bosnia-Herzegovina	3-0	Lithuania
Bosnia-Herzegovina	3-1	Greece
Latvia	0-5	Bosnia-Herzegovina
Bosnia-Herzegovina	0-1	Slovakia
Slovakia	1-2	Bosnia-Herzegovina
Bosnia-Herzegovina	4-1	Liechtenstein
Lithuania	0-1	Bosnia--Herzegovina

KEY PLAYERS

Miralem Pjanić
Edin Džeko
Vedad Ibišević

CAMEROON

Think of Cameroon at the World Cup and it is nigh on impossible not to think of Roger Milla dancing in front of a corner flag, but since that memorable summer in 1990, the "Indomitable Lions" have qualified for all but one tournament.

ROAD TO WORLD CUP 2014

Cameroon	1-0	Congo DR
Libya	2-1	Cameroon
Cameroon	2-1	Togo
Togo	0-3	Cameroon (match awarded to Cameroon)
Congo DR	0-0	Cameroon
Cameroon	1-0	Libya
Tunisia	0-0	Cameroon
Cameroon	4-1	Tunisia

KEY PLAYERS

Samuel Eto'o
Alex Song
Stephane Mbia

They are there again in 2014 having successfully negotiated their way through their qualifying campaign, and will be hoping to go past the group stages for the first time since Milla and co became the first African side to reach the quarter-finals 24 years ago.

A tricky regional group was well navigated, with Congo DR beaten in the opening game thanks to an Eric Choupo-Moting penalty, though pacesetters Libya inflicted Cameroon's only standing defeat with an injury-time winner in the second game.

A Samuel Eto'o brace brought a 2-1 win over Togo, which was followed by a 2-0 loss against the same side in Lome, only for the result to be overturned and Cameroon awarded a 3-0 win, after it emerged that the Togolese had fielded an ineligible player, Alaixys Romao. Those extra three points would prove very handy indeed, and after a 0-0 draw in Kinshasa, they booked a place in the play-off with a narrow win over Libya.

Tunisia were a potential banana skin, but Cameroon, coached by Volker Finke, were favourites and held out for a 0-0 draw in the first leg before a comfortable 4-1 win on home soil in Yaounde with goals from Pierre Webo, Benjamin Moukandjo and two from Jean Makoun.

Rennes midfielder Makoun is part of a strong Cameroon midfield, which also houses Barcelona enforcer Alex Song and Stephane Mbia, who has had valuable match practice on loan with Sevilla in Spain after a move to England with Queens Park Rangers went sour.

Choupo-Moting, who played in 2010, can be a threat but the main danger will again be Eto'o, who at 33 will be playing in his fourth World Cup. He remains a world-class striker and has sharpened since swapping Russia for England in his club career.

Cameroon probably won't better their 1990 appearance, but they will want to at least make the knockout rounds, which may mean getting the better of one of the big European sides.

RIGHT Captain Samuel Eto'o remains Cameroon's main threat, even at his fourth World Cup

WORLD CUP 2014, TEAMS

CHILE

Chile's qualifying campaign for Brazil was an incredible journey of ups and downs which ended with success on the final day.

Heavy defeats to highly-rated Argentina and Uruguay teams were put aside with four wins in the opening six fixtures, including a 2-0 win in Venezuela that saw *La Roja* score both goals in the final five minutes. At this stage things were looking good, but three straight defeats followed and coach Claudio Borghi was dismissed.

His replacement Jorge Sampaoli was beaten in his first game, but then oversaw an excellent run that saw Chile go unbeaten in their final six games, picking up 16 points from a possible 18.

The sequence began with a 2-0 win over the Uruguayans in Santiago and continued with wins over Paraguay, Bolivia and Venezuela. The campaign was almost derailed when they surrendered a three-goal first-half lead in Colombia in the penultimate game, but they recovered their nerve in the final game by beating Ecuador thanks to another five-minute double salvo, this time in the first half, a result that saw them qualify for their ninth World Cup.

As they did in South Africa, Chile will hope to reach the knockout rounds in Brazil and will believe they have the individuals to do it.

Alexis Sanchez is a regular at Barcelona and will be their main goalscoring threat, though Eduardo Vargas will be expected to contribute too. Arturo Vidal is capable of dominating games from central midfield and Matias Fernandez can carve out opportunities for those ahead of him.

Defensively, Gary Medel, nicknamed 'Pitbull', snaps away at opposition attackers, while Mauricio Isla can impress from right-back. Experienced goalkeeper Claudio Bravo is the captain and will have benefited from Champions League experience with Real Socieded this season.

Chile finished third as hosts in 1962, but otherwise have never gone beyond the last 16. It is a huge challenge, but if luck is with them, this could be the year they make the leap.

ABOVE Gary Medel (left) and Alexis Sanchez epitomise Chile's contrasting qualities

ROAD TO WORLD CUP 2014

Argentina	4-1	Chile
Chile	4-2	Peru
Uruguay	4-0	Chile
Chile	2-0	Paraguay
Bolivia	0-2	Chile
Venezuela	0-2	Chile
Chile	1-3	Colombia
Ecuador	3-1	Chile
Chile	1-2	Argentina
Peru	1-0	Chile
Chile	2-0	Uruguay
Paraguay	1-2	Chile
Chile	3-1	Bolivia
Chile	3-0	Venezuela
Colombia	3-3	Chile
Chile	2-1	Ecuador

KEY PLAYERS

Alexis Sanchez
Arturo Vidal
Matias Fernandez

COLOMBIA

The story of Colombia at the World Cup is as depressing as it is disappointing.

ROAD TO WORLD CUP 2014

Bolivia	1-2	Colombia
Colombia	1-1	Venezuela
Colombia	1-2	Argentina
Peru	0-1	Colombia
Ecuador	1-0	Colombia
Colombia	4-0	Uruguay
Chile	1-3	Colombia
Colombia	2-0	Paraguay
Colombia	5-0	Bolivia
Venezuela	1-0	Colombia
Argentina	0-0	Colombia
Colombia	2-0	Peru
Colombia	1-0	Ecuador
Uruguay	2-0	Colombia
Colombia	3-3	Chile
Paraguay	1-2	Colombia

KEY PLAYERS

Radamel Falcao
James Rodriguez
Cristian Zapata

RIGHT There are matchwinners throughout the Colombia squad, which will want to improve its poor World Cup record

A fine footballing pedigree has produced some incredible talent, notably Carlos Valderrama and Faustino Asprilla, yet a study of their World Cup record lurches from disqualification and embarrassment in 1954 to tragedy and murder in 1994.

Only once have Colombia ever gone beyond the groups, in 1990, when they lost in the first knockout round. Simply by qualifying for Brazil, they have gone beyond their achievements in any of the previous three tournaments.

Surprisingly, Colombia have also secured a seeding for the World Cup draw, which promises a potentially easier group and avoidance of major opposition such as Germany and Spain. It has raised eyebrows that a country that has won fewer finals matches than Italy has won trophies will be seeded above the *Azzurri*.

Yet on the field, Colombia are in good health, with potential matchwinners throughout the side. Pekerman, who replaced Leonel Alvarez as coach in early 2012, inherited a team that had already won in Bolivia and was beaten narrowly by Argentina only after losing important figures Radamel Falcao and Fredy Guarin to injury.

A shock defeat to Ecuador was rectified with a massive 4-0 win over 2010 semi-finalists and Copa America holders Uruguay, thanks to Falcao, Juan Zuniga and a double from highly-rated Teofilo Gutierrez. This was followed by an impressive 3-1 win in Chile.

A hard-fought goalless draw in Argentina and defeat to Uruguay sandwiched important wins against Peru and Ecuador. Then a second-half three-goal comeback to earn a draw at home to Chile was enough to guarantee a first qualification in 16 years, with gloss added to the campaign thanks to a brace from captain Mario Yepes in the final game against Paraguay.

History suggests the odds are against them, but if Colombia can find some consistency in Brazil, they could yet find a way into the later stages. Such progress would be long overdue.

WORLD CUP 2014, TEAMS

COSTA RICA

Costa Rica finished second behind USA in an impressive qualifying campaign that saw them reach their fourth World Cup finals.

Having missed out in 2010, *Los Ticos* are back and will be looking to emulate their debut appearance in 1990, when two group stage victories propelled them into the knockout rounds.

Early on in their preliminary qualifiers, it looked as though the Costa Ricans were not going to make it, with back-to-back defeats to Mexico threatening their participation in the final group section. A 1-0 win over El Salvador followed by a 7-0 thrashing of Guyana did the job, however, and they took their place in the six-team group, with three to qualify automatically for Brazil 2014.

A 2-2 draw in Panama, thanks to captain Bryan Ruiz's late equaliser, provided a solid start. Despite defeat to America in a snowy Colorado, four wins from their next six put them in a commanding position as Jamaica, Honduras, Panama and the USA, who were 12 games unbeaten, were all defeated in San Jose, the Costa Rican capital.

On the road, Jorge Luis Pinto's side were less impressive, failing to win any of their five games, though draws in Mexico and Jamaica accrued valuable points, with the game in Kingston ensuring qualification with two games to spare.

So what are their chances in Brazil? Realistically, being there is an achievement and the last 16 would be a bonus for a country of fewer than five million people.

Captain Ruiz, of Fulham, is the star creative talent, while youngster Joel Campbell and veteran Alvaro Saborio could also catch the eye up front. Celso Borges, based in Norway, will look to pull the strings in midfield, though as one of the lesser-fancied sides, gaining prolonged periods of possession in which to inflict damage could be a problem.

Costa Rica are sure to enjoy the World Cup party in Brazil, but it is unlikely they will still be there beyond the group stages.

KEY PLAYERS

Bryan Ruiz
Joel Campbell
Celso Borges

ABOVE Costa Rica are one of the less-fancied sides in Brazil

CROATIA

Croatia eventually succeeded in the play-offs having come second behind the impressive Belgium in their qualifying group.

ROAD TO WORLD CUP 2014

Croatia	1-0	Macedonia
Belgium	1-1	Croatia
Macedonia	1-2	Croatia
Croatia	2-0	Wales
Croatia	2-0	Serbia
Wales	1-2	Croatia
Croatia	0-1	Scotland
Serbia	1-1	Croatia
Croatia	1-2	Belgium
Scotland	2-0	Croatia
Iceland	0-0	Croatia
Croatia	2-0	Iceland

KEY PLAYERS

Luka Modrić
Mario Mandžukić
Darijo Srna

The disappointment of not qualifying for South Africa in 2010 looked as though it would return, but the Croatians recovered from an underwhelming group stage to defeat Iceland over two legs and book their place in Brazil.

A 0-0 draw in Rejkjavik gave Niko Kovač's side the upper hand going into the second leg in Zagreb, and a goal in either half from Mario Mandžukić, who was also sent off, and captain Darijo Srna were enough.

Bayern Munich striker Mandžukić top-scored in qualifying with four; fellow striker Eduardo was the only other player to score more than once. It seems goals may be a problem, with the Croatians only scoring 14 in 12 games, though with the combined creativity of Luka Modrić, Ivan Rakitić, Niko Kranjčar and youngster Mateo Kovačić, creating chances should be the least of their problems.

Goalkeeper Stipe Pletikosa, Srna and defender Josip Šimunić all boast over 100 caps in an experienced backline that also includes the experienced Vedran Ćorluka and Danijel Pranjić,

while the younger Dejan Lovren has excelled in the English Premier League with Southampton and forced his way into the line-up during the later stages of qualifying.

The campaign had begun well with five wins and a draw in Belgium, Lovren scoring a late leveller in Wales before Eduardo scored an even later winner. They were shocked by Scotland at home, however, before being pegged back in Serbia and well beaten by the Belgians. This left them trailing the leaders but grateful of Serbia's poor form, ensuring a play-off spot before the 2-0 reverse at home to Scotland on the final day of the group stage, which cost former coach Igor Štimac his job.

Kovac, then, has a clean slate after negotiating his way past Iceland in his first two games, but time is short to ensure a better performance in Brazil than Croatia achieved during the 2002 or 2006 World Cups, when they exited at the group stage. Having missed the run to the semi-finals at their first World Cup in France in 1998 through injury, Kovač will be desperate to impress in 2014.

RIGHT Croatia can be a match for anyone on their day

ECUADOR

Ecuador's qualifying campaign was overshadowed by the tragic death at 27 of forward Christian 'Chucho' Benitez in July 2013.

Benitez, who suffered heart failure weeks after moving to Qatar, had played in nine qualifying games having also featured at the finals in 2006. To overcome the loss of a much-loved but also talented player and qualify for the World Cup is testament to a strong team spirit in the Ecuadorian squad, which also possesses a number of exciting attacking talents, despite struggling for goals in their South American group.

Felipe Caicedo, a bullish brute of a striker, scored seven times in nine games during qualifying, while Jefferson Montero and Antonio Valencia can trouble top defences if they hit their peak in Brazil. Winger Christian Noboa has impressed at Dinamo Moscow in Russia.

Most of the Ecuadorian defenders are based at domestic clubs, suggesting a lack of elite quality, but veterans Walter Ayovi and Jorge Guagua possess plenty of experience.

Coach Reinaldo Rueda has been in charge since 2010, having led Honduras to the last World Cup finals in South Africa, and oversaw a qualifying campaign that was typified by excellent home results but struggles on the road.

Seven wins from eight home games, Argentina the only side to depart Quito unbeaten with a 1-1 draw, proved the key factor in reaching the finals, but Ecuador failed to win any of their away games, drawing only in Uruguay, Venezuela and Bolivia, and this in a campaign without the mighty Brazilians.

In qualifying, Ecuador have reached only their third World Cup. After progressing to the last 16 in 2006, hopes will be high, but after the loss of Benitez, simply being there is a credit to the country. They will want to honour their former forward in Brazil.

ROAD TO WORLD CUP 2014

Ecuador	2-0	Venezuela
Paraguay	2-1	Ecuador
Ecuador	2-0	Peru
Argentina	4-0	Ecuador
Ecuador	1-0	Colombia
Ecuador	1-0	Bolivia
Uruguay	1-1	Ecuador
Ecuador	3-1	Chile
Venezuela	1-1	Ecuador
Ecuador	4-1	Paraguay
Peru	1-0	Ecuador
Ecuador	1-1	Argentina
Colombia	1-0	Ecuador
Bolivia	1-1	Ecuador
Ecuador	1-0	Uruguay
Chile	2-1	Ecuador

KEY PLAYERS

Antonio Valencia
Jefferson Montero
Christian Noboa

LEFT Antonio Valencia, Jefferson Montero and Felipe Caicedo are key to Ecuador's plans

WORLD CUP 2014, TEAMS

GHANA

Ghana were top scorers in Africa's qualifying section and will be looking for a repeat of their 2010 run, when they reached the quarter-finals.

ROAD TO WORLD CUP 2014

Ghana	7-0	Lesotho
Zambia	1-0	Ghana
Ghana	4-0	Sudan
Sudan	1-3	Ghana
Lesotho	0-2	Ghana
Ghana	2-1	Zambia
Ghana	6-1	Egypt
Egypt	2-1	Ghana

KEY PLAYERS

Asamoah Gyan
Kevin-Prince Boateng
Kwadwo Asamoah

Important members of that squad remain involved, this time under the guidance of Ghanaian coach Kwesi Appiah, who will hope he has gained the experience in the qualifying campaign and the 2013 African Cup of Nations to lead his side at least into the knockout rounds, matching the performance of their first appearance at the finals in 2006.

Sulley Muntari, one of the veterans of those earlier campaigns, got a demanding qualifying process off to the perfect start with an early goal in the 7-0 win over Lesotho, with strikers Dominic Adiyiah and Jordan Ayew, son of the great Abedi Pele, each scoring twice.

Defeat to the much improved Zambia was a blow, but a 4-0 win over Sudan, with a brace from Asamoah Gyan, their most prolific forward, put the "Black Stars" back on track, and they tied the group up with a 2-1 win over the Zambians on the final day, as goals from Majeed Waris and Kwadwo Asamoah put them out of reach.

The play-offs pitted the Ghanaians against seven-time African champions Egypt, but they

removed any doubts with a 6-1 home thrashing of Bob Bradley's side. Gyan added another pair while Muntari and Christian Atsu, the exciting young winger, scored his second of the campaign. A meaningless 2-1 defeat in Cairo followed, but it was significant as it marked the return to the national team of Kevin-Prince Boateng, who had not appeared in over two years.

Schalke midfielder Boateng will be crucial to Ghana's hopes in Brazil. Combative yet classy, his eye for goal and European experience adds another dimension to a midfield also boasting the impressive Asamoah, Muntari and Chelsea's Michael Essien, himself back in the fold after an extended international break.

Goalkeeper Fatawu Dauda has finally wrestled the number one spot from the error-prone Richard Kingson, while up front the unpredictable Gyan will hope to bury the ghost of his missed penalty against Uruguay in 2010. As captain, he may yet produce the inspiration to see Ghana past the last eight. It is a big ask, but they could be Africa's best hope in Brazil.

RIGHT Asamoah Gyan's goals will be crucial to Ghana's hopes

GREECE

Greece reached only their third World Cup by coming past Romania in the European play-offs and will be hoping to go past the group stages for the first time.

Previous appearances in 1994 and 2010 were underwhelming, though by beating Nigeria they did record their first finals victory in South Africa. Key players from that campaign still remain, with veteran captain Giorgos Karagounis, Kostas Katsouranis and forwards Theofanis Gekas and Dimitris Salpingidis all featuring regularly in qualifying this time around.

Goalkeeper Orestis Karnezis appears to have nailed down the number one spot, while Vasilis Torosidis can be a class act at full-back, provided he plays regularly for Italian high-flyers Roma. Sokratis Papastathopoulos is a strong, pacy and accomplished defender, who will benefit from his Champions League and Bundesliga experience with Borussia Dortmund.

Greece's strength is their tight defence, as it was when they became unlikely European champions in 2004, and this time around they conceded just six times in 12 qualifiers, with three of those in a defeat to group winners Bosnia-Herzegovina.

Goals have not always flowed, Gekas and Salpingidis contributed but top scorer was Kostas Mitroglou, who plays his football in the Greek league with Olympiakos. He scored five times and will probably provide the main threat in Brazil, with Celtic striker Giorgos Samaras toiling on the international stage.

Gekas netted the winner in the group opener away in Latvia, before a home win over Lithuania and a goalless draw with the Bosnians. Slovakia, who qualified in 2010, were importantly beaten in Bratislava.

Defeat in Zenica looked to have effectively confirmed Bosnia-Herzegovina as group winners at the halfway point, but four consecutive 1-0 wins (with four different goalscorers) and a 2-0 win in Liechtenstein meant the Greeks ended level on points with their Balkan neighbours, each having dropped just five points and won eight of their 10 games, though the Greeks would have to compete in a play-off.

Mitroglou scored twice to give the Greeks a 3-1 advantage in Athens, before netting again in Bucharest to seal their place in Brazil.

It will be hard going for Fernando Santos' team, but with their firm defence they will be hard to beat. A decade on from their greatest success, they may yet surprise a few people once more, but do not bet on a repeat of that glory.

ROAD TO WORLD CUP 2014

Latvia	1-2	Greece
Greece	2-0	Lithuania
Greece	0-0	Bosnia-Herzegovina
Slovakia	0-1	Greece
Bosnia-Herzegovina	3-1	Greece
Lithuania	0-1	Greece
Liechtenstein	0-1	Greece
Greece	1-0	Latvia
Greece	1-0	Slovakia
Greece	2-0	Liechtenstein
Greece	3-1	Romania
Romania	1-1	Greece

KEY PLAYERS

Giorgios Karagounis
Sokratis Papastathopoulos
Vasilis Torosidis

LEFT Greece celebrate their play-off win over Romania in November

HONDURAS

Honduras qualified for their second successive World Cup by finishing third in the American section, sealing their place in Brazil with a final-day draw in Jamaica.

ROAD TO WORLD CUP 2014

Honduras	0-2	Panama
Canada	0-0	Honduras
Cuba	0-3	Honduras
Honduras	1-0	Cuba
Panama	0-0	Honduras
Honduras	8-1	Canada
Honduras	2-1	USA
Honduras	2-2	Mexico
Panama	2-0	Honduras
Costa Rica	1-0	Honduras
Honduras	2-0	Jamaica
USA	1-0	Honduras
Mexico	1-2	Honduras
Honduras	2-2	Panama
Honduras	1-0	Costa Rica
Jamaica	2-2	Honduras

KEY PLAYERS

Wilson Palacios
Roger Espinoza
Jerry Bengtson

RIGHT *Wilson Palacios will be the driving force from the Honduran midfield*

It was a campaign that began badly with defeat to Panama and a draw with Canada before three wins from four matches saw them through their preliminary group and into the six-team final group.

Victory over USA in their opening game was the perfect start, coming from behind to win 2-1 and then they came from two down to earn a point against Mexico. They then lost three of their next four games as defeats to Panama, who would only miss out on the play-off position on the final day, Costa Rica and USA brought them back down to earth, though three points in the middle of that run against Jamaica would prove important.

Mexico were memorably beaten at home when two goals in four minutes from forwards Jerry Bengtson and Carlo Costly completed an unlikely turnaround to put Honduras back in the driving seat. Then, even though they were pegged back by a last-minute Panama equaliser in Tegucigalpa, Bengtson's goal gave them a 1-0 win over the Costa Ricans in the penultimate game, meaning a 2-2 draw in Kingston would be enough.

Qualification for Brazil has delighted the eight million Hondurans back home, but the squad is not without its problems. Bengtson, who top-scored in qualifying with nine goals, walked out of the squad midway through the campaign, only to be welcomed back by coach Luis Fernando Suarez, who also led the Under-23 side to the quarter-finals of the Olympics in 2012.

Suarez has utilised some of those youngsters alongside his more experienced stalwarts. Wilson Palacios remains the main man, his aggression in midfield allowing the likes of Roger Espinoza and Oscar Garcia to create chances for the forwards, while goalkeeper and captain Noel Valladares is a calming presence at the back.

Progression beyond the group stages will be difficult, but Honduras will be determined to make history and reach the last 16 for the first time. They will probably require a little luck if they are to do it.

IRAN

Iran return to the world stage for a fourth World Cup finals after topping their Asian qualifying section.

It was a confidence-boosting campaign for the Iranians who, in finishing above South Korea, toppled a side that has been at the last eight finals tournaments.

Coach Carlos Queiroz has seen it all in football. He has previously coached his native Portugal twice, United Arab Emirates, and South Africa, while a spell at Real Madrid sandwiched two positions as Sir Alex Ferguson's assistant at Manchester United.

Queiroz' experience will prove invaluable to an Iranian group which has been lauded back home simply for qualifying. The coach himself readily admits his side cannot win the tournament, the aim instead to demonstrate progress for an emerging football nation.

In qualifying, their main strength was defensive solidity, conceding just seven goals and Queiroz will surely look to build from the back.

In midfield, veteran captain Javad Nekounam is Iran's most famous current player, his form

in the 2006 World Cup earning a move to Europe with Spanish side Osasuna, where he was joined by compatriot Masoud Shojaei two years later. Now back in his homeland, Nekounam will want to sign off from World Cup duty with a strong performance and will look to Shojaei, who remains in Spain, for support alongside him.

There may be problems in goal scoring when up against better opposition, but 30 goals from 16 qualifiers suggests competence in attack and Belgium-based striker Reza Ghoochannejhad could provide the answer after hitting three in five qualifying games. The 26-year-old has a decent goals to games ratio at club level, and may catch the eye in Brazil if Iran can create enough chances.

After group stage exits in 1998 and 2006, Iran will hope to show they are a better side in 2014, but face a tough task in reaching the knockout rounds.

ROAD TO WORLD CUP 2014

Iran	4-0	Maldives
Maldives	0-1	Iran
Iran	3-0	Indonesia
Qatar	1-1	Iran
Iran	6-0	Bahrain
Bahrain	1-1	Iran
Indonesia	1-4	Iran
Iran	2-2	Qatar
Uzbekistan	0-1	Iran
Iran	0-0	Qatar
Lebanon	1-0	Iran
Iran	1-0	South Korea
Iran	0-1	Uzbekistan
Qatar	0-1	Iraq
Iran	4-0	Lebanon
South Korea	0-1	Iran

KEY PLAYERS

Javad Nekounam
Masoud Shojaei
Reza Ghoochannejhad

LEFT After a strong showing in qualifying, Iran have plenty to gain in Brazil

IVORY COAST

There will be few more experienced sides at the World Cup than Ivory Coast. Billed as potential winners four years ago, they may still make waves in Brazil.

ROAD TO WORLD CUP 2014

Ivory Coast	2-0	Tanzania
Morocco	2-2	Ivory Coast
Ivory Coast	3-0	Gambia
Gambia	0-3	Ivory Coast
Tanzania	2-4	Ivory Coast
Ivory Coast	1-1	Morocco
Ivory Coast	3-1	Senegal
Senegal	1-1	Ivory Coast

KEY PLAYERS

Kolo Toure
Didier Drogba
Salomon Kalou

Back in 2010, *Les Elephants* were cursed by bad luck—they were drawn alongside the well-fancied Brazil and Portugal in what was billed as the group of death, before star striker Didier Drogba suffered a broken arm in the run-up to the tournament. He returned, but was ineffectual and the Ivory Coast were eliminated.

This time around, the same key players remain, back for their third finals and running out of time to make the jump from dark horses to genuine contenders.

Leading light Didier Drogba will be 36 when the tournament kicks off, but the powerful forward retains plenty of the qualities that saw him crowned African player of the year in both 2006 and 2009. His protégé, former Chelsea team-mate Salomon Kalou, has finally stepped up to deliver consistency, scoring five times in seven qualifying appearances.

Wilfried Bony and Gervinho each offer an alternative option in attack, Bony a short but strong poacher in front of goal, Gervinho the pacy wide man finding his best form in Serie A with Roma.

Midfielder Yaya Toure, driving force behind Manchester City's 2012 Premier League triumph, has such speed, stamina and strength that no midfielder in the world will want to face him, while Cheik Tiote is a tough-tackling, all-action central midfielder that can operate alongside him.

At the back, Toure's brother Kolo, now with Liverpool, and Didier Zokora, both veterans of more than 100 caps, offer old heads and Champions League experience, though lack pace, not that it showed in qualifying.

Ivory Coast remained unbeaten throughout, scoring 19 times and conceding just seven. Having navigated their way past Morocco, Gambia and Tanzania at the group stage, they then beat Senegal 3-1 at home, courtesy of Drogba and Kalou, before securing a draw away from home to book their third straight appearance.

The squad's prime may now have passed, but Ivory Coast could still impress in Brazil. They are certainly due the fortune to take them into the knockout rounds.

RIGHT Ivory Coast have a strong squad, and despite previous failures could still go far in Brazil

JAPAN

Japan qualified for their fifth successive World Cup with little fuss and, like four years ago, will be hoping to make their way into the knockout stages in Brazil.

As one of the bigger boys of the Asian Confederation, coach Alberto Zaccheroni's side were expected to reach Brazil and they became the first side to do so in the summer of 2013.

It was not all plain sailing though. In their preliminary qualifying group, which began in September 2011, they were beaten away in Pyongyang by Korea DPR and lost at home to Uzbekistan, albeit having sewn up progression to the next round already.

At the final group stage, a strong start saw the *Blue Samurai* take 13 points from the opening 15, with a 3-0 win over Oman followed by a 6-0 trouncing of Jordan. Keisuke Honda struck a hat-trick in that game, with Ryoichi Maeda also scoring in both.

By avoiding defeat in Australia in June 2012, they put themselves firmly in the driving seat and victories over Iraq and Oman all but confirmed their place in Brazil as the Australians toiled.

A defeat in Jordan meant qualification would have to wait, but only for one more game when a 1-1 draw at home to Australia, which came thanks to an injury-time Honda penalty saw them book their place in Brazil.

They could not celebrate for long, taking part in the Confederations Cup the same month and while they were beaten in each of their three games, the Japanese impressed in the 4-3 defeat to Italy and will have benefited from improved competition.

With more players based in Europe than ever before, including Manchester United's Shinji Kagawa, a vital performer alongside Honda, and defenders Yuto Nagatomo of Inter and Mayo Yoshida of Southampton, there should be enough experience to make Japan difficult to beat. Zaccheroni's challenge will be in inspiring the rest of the squad to raise their game in Brazil. If the Italian can do it, Japan could progress into the later stages.

ROAD TO WORLD CUP 2014

Japan	1-0	Korea DPR
Uzbekistan	1-1	Japan
Japan	8-0	Tajikistan
Tajikistan	0-4	Japan
Korea DPR	1-0	Japan
Japan	0-1	Uzbekistan
Japan	3-0	Oman
Japan	6-0	Jordan
Australia	1-1	Japan
Japan	1-0	Iraq
Oman	1-2	Japan
Jordan	2-1	Japan
Japan	1-1	Australia
Iraq	0-1	Japan

KEY PLAYERS

Shinji Kagawa
Keisuke Honda
Yuto Nagatomo

LEFT Japan will be hoping their European-based stars will lead them to the later stages

MEXICO

Mexico reached their sixth successive World Cup despite a poor qualifying campaign that had old rivals USA to thank for their narrow escape.

ROAD TO WORLD CUP 2014

Mexico	3-1	Guyana
El Salvador	1-2	Mexico
Costa Rica	0-2	Mexico
Mexico	1-0	Costa Rica
Guyana	0-5	Mexico
Mexico	2-0	El Salvador
Mexico	0-0	Jamaica
Honduras	2-2	Mexico
Mexico	0-0	USA
Jamaica	0-1	Mexico
Panama	0-0	Mexico
Mexico	0-0	Costa Rica
Mexico	1-2	Honduras
USA	2-0	Mexico
Mexico	2-1	Panama
Costa Rica	2-1	Mexico
Mexico	5-1	New Zealand
New Zealand	2-4	Mexico

KEY PLAYERS

Javier Hernandez
Andres Guardado
Giovani Dos Santos

RIGHT Mexico have a host of quality, but after an underwhelming qualifying campaign, they need to improve in Brazil

On the final match day of the Central and North American section, Mexico were bound for failure as they trailed Costa Rica, while USA, already comfortably through, trailed Panama who looked set to take the play-off spot.

That was until the US scored twice in injury time to allow the Mexicans back up into fourth spot and a two-legged play-off against New Zealand, which they navigated easily with a 9-3 aggregate win.

They took maximum points from their preliminary group, which coincided with Olympic success in 2012, where the young Mexican side beat Brazil in the final. However just two wins in their 10-game final qualifying group meant that they very nearly missed out.

Coach Jose Manuel de la Torre lost his job with three games to go as Victor Manuel Vucetich took over for the final group games before Miguel Herrera was appointed for the play-offs, controversially selecting only home-based players for the two legs.

High-profile European-based players are expected to return in Brazil, with Javier 'Chicharito' Hernandez among the best poachers around and with World Cup pedigree, having impressed four years ago. Andres Guardado and Giovani Dos Santos have plenty of talent too, but will need to be on top of their games to impress in Brazil, while Espanyol defender Hector Moreno should be involved.

Otherwise, it is hard to predict how Herrera will go in Brazil. *El Tri* have plenty of quality and their success in 2012 shows that there is talent emerging at home, but they need to find form fast.

At their five previous World Cups, Mexico have reached the knockout rounds, while making the quarter-finals twice on home soil, in 1970 and 1986. This time around they should be aiming for similar, but it is far from guaranteed.

NIGERIA

The reigning African champions, Nigeria's path to Brazil was efficient rather than excellent, but they should have plenty left in the tank for the World Cup.

It is only a year since they lifted their continental championship in a tournament where they gradually grew into champions, rather than sparking from the outset, and their qualifying campaign can be regarded in similar fashion.

Their initial group stage, featuring Namibia, Malawi and Kenya saw Nigeria score just seven goals in their six games, only hitting more than one in their final game against Malawi, when Emmanuel Emenike struck in first-half injury-time and Victor Moses added a second-half penalty. Still, 12 points from six games and an unbeaten record was comfortable, if not convincing.

The play-off draw made Stephen Keshi's side overwhelming favourites to qualify for the finals and, despite falling behind in Addis Ababa, Emenike struck twice, including a 90th minute spot kick, to turn the tie on its head and give the *Super Eagles* the advantage. At home in Calabar, a Moses penalty and a late Victor Obinna goal sealed progression to Nigeria's fifth World Cup.

Their best achievements remain the last 16 in 1994 and 1998 when they had a more dynamic side that featured the magical Jay-Jay Okocha in midfield, but Nigeria are well organised and will be tough to beat.

John Mikel Obi fulfils a slightly different midfield role to that which he is accustomed with club side Chelsea, where he is a pure stopper. On the international stage, Keshi expects Mikel to attack too, and he demonstrated his capabilities with a fine goal in the 2013 Confederations Cup, where Nigeria lost to both Spain and Uruguay.

Victor Moses has burst onto the international scene and is arguably Nigeria's most potent attacker. His pace and trickery have already caused problems for defences and don't be surprised to see him winning, and converting, penalties.

Elsewhere youngsters Kenneth Omeruo and Ahmed Musa will demonstrate their class in Brazil, while experienced goalkeeper Vincent Enyeama is fast approaching his 100th international cap.

If Nigeria were to make the final, Enyeama might just reach that milestone in Brazil, but realistically, the quarter-finals would be a major achievement.

LEFT Victor Moses will be one of Nigeria's biggest threats in Brazil

ROAD TO WORLD CUP 2014

Nigeria	1-0	Namibia
Malawi	1-1	Nigeria
Nigeria	1-1	Kenya
Kenya	0-1	Nigeria
Namibia	1-1	Nigeria
Nigeria	2-0	Malawi
Ethiopia	1-2	Nigeria
Nigeria	2-0	Ethiopia

KEY PLAYERS

John Mikel Obi
Victor Moses
Emmanuel Emenike

RUSSIA

Russia reached their first World Cup since 2002 by sneaking past the well-fancied Portugal in their qualifying campaign.

ROAD TO WORLD CUP 2014

Russia	2-0	Northern Ireland
Israel	0-4	Russia
Russia	1-0	Portugal
Russia	1-0	Azerbaijan
Portugal	1-0	Russia
Northern Ireland	1-0	Russia
Russia	4-1	Luxembourg
Russia	3-1	Israel
Luxembourg	0-4	Russia
Azerbaijan	1-1	Russia

KEY PLAYERS

Igor Akinfeev
Alan Dzagoev
Roman Shirokov

RIGHT Goalkeeper Igor Ikinfeev is back to his best after injury, and a key man for Russia

Upon taking over in the autumn of 2012, Italian coach Fabio Capello instilled a defensive rigidity that proved the foundation of Russian success, with ever-present goalkeeper Igor Akinfeev conceding just five times in 10 games.

The process started excellently with four straight wins, a 4-0 win in Israel followed by an important 1-0 victory over the Portuguese in Moscow, when Alexander Kerzakhov's early goal proved decisive.

It was more than six months until the Russians played another qualifier, however, and momentum had halted. First Portugal and then Northern Ireland, who were on a nine-game winless streak, inflicted 1-0 defeats to put qualification in the balance.

Russia needed to respond and did so perfectly by beating Luxembourg home and away and beating Israel in between to leave them in command at the top of Group F, watching as Portugal slipped up at home to the Israelis.

Eventually it all came down to the final game, where they needed to avoid defeat in Azerbaijan. Midfielder Roman Shirokov had given Capello's side the lead in Azerbaijan, only for a last-minute equaliser from the home side to give them a scare, but they held on to secure their 10th appearance at the finals.

Their previous best was a fourth-place finish in 1966, when legendary goalkeeper Lev Yashin was their leading light. Almost half a century on, it is current stopper Akinfeev who is of most importance to Capello, behind an experienced but ageing backline marshalled by Sergey Ignashevich.

Captain Shirokov, now 32, and Vladimir Bystrov will try to pull the strings from midfield while the powerfully-built Kerzhakov is the most dangerous of Russia's attackers, expected to become their leading goal scorer of all time.

By making them hard to beat, Capello has ensured that Russia have a decent chance of progressing beyond the group stage, a feat they have not achieved since 1986, but they will need the talented Alan Dzagoev to be on his finest form if they are to find a way through the world's finest defences.

SOUTH KOREA

South Korea qualified for their eighth successive World Cup by reaching Brazil, but made hard work of a campaign they were expected to stroll.

Such was the disappointment regarding their efforts that coach Choi Kanghee quit at the end of the process, to be replaced by legendary Hong Myung-Bo, who captained the side during its run to the semi-finals of the World Cup in 2002, his fourth finals appearance at the heart of the Korean defence, where he won 136 caps.

That achievement, on home soil, has become a burden rather than a celebration for Korea's footballing community. Fans have come to expect success rather than appreciate its unlikeliness when viewing their country's resources on a global scale.

Long regarded as an effective unit rather than a side of stars, South Korea lost its golden boy Park Ji-Sung to international retirement after the last World Cup campaign, and now has a side struggling for confidence after a disappointing qualifying campaign. What Hong brings as coach, however, is hope. He led their Under-23 team

to an Olympic bronze medal at London 2012, suggesting there is talent coming through.

Qualification began emphatically with a 6-0 win over Lebanon in the preliminary groups, Korea topping a group that also included Kuwait and the UAE. Into the final stages, they struggled, finishing level on points with Uzbekistan and behind Iran, by whom they were beaten home and away.

Still, they were among the first teams to reach Brazil and now they are there, the new coach will hope to make the most of the attacking talents of Bayer Leverkusen forward Son Heung-Min, Park Chu-Young, the top scorer in qualifying, and Lee Keun-Ho. Young defender Hong Jeong-Ho is seen as a long-term fixture at the back, and will want to impress after missing the Olympics through injury. Midfielder Koo Ja-Cheol will be the team's driving force, and his experience in Europe with Bundesliga side Wolfsburg will prove invaluable as Korea pursue a knockout round appearance.

ROAD TO WORLD CUP 2014

South Korea	6-0	Lebanon
Kuwait	1-1	South Korea
South Korea	2-1	United Arab Emirates
United Arab Emirates	0-2	South Korea
Lebanon	2-1	South Korea
South Korea	2-0	Kuwait
Qatar	1-4	South Korea
South Korea	3-0	Lebanon
Uzbekistan	2-2	South Korea
Iran	1-0	South Korea
South Korea	2-1	Qatar
Lebanon	1-1	South Korea
South Korea	1-0	Uzbekistan
South Korea	0-1	Iran

KEY PLAYERS

Koo Ja-Cheol
Son Heung-Min
Park Chu-Young

LEFT Son Heung-Min will be a goal threat in Brazil

SWITZERLAND

Switzerland will be at their third consecutive World Cup after quietly going about their business and topping their European qualifying group.

ROAD TO WORLD CUP 2014

Slovenia	0-2	Switzerland
Switzerland	2-0	Albania
Switzerland	1-1	Norway
Iceland	0-2	Switzerland
Cyprus	0-0	Switzerland
Switzerland	1-0	Cyprus
Switzerland	4-4	Switzerland
Norway	0-2	Switzerland
Albania	1-2	Switzerland
Switzerland	1-0	Slovenia

KEY PLAYERS

Gokhan Inler
Xerdan Shaqiri
Fabian Schar

Top-seeded for their group after appearances at the finals in 2006 and 2010, they were tipped to succeed and were unbeaten in their 10 games, securing their place in Brazil with the typical minimum of fuss.

Added to that, the Swiss are seeded at the finals, a boost that should help them reach the knockout stages as they did in 2006, when they topped a group that included eventual champions France before bowing out on penalties against Ukraine, having not conceded a single goal in four games.

That run continued four years later in 2010, beating Spain 1-0 in their opening game before losing to Chile, whose first goal ended a run of 559 minutes without the Swiss conceding, a World Cup record. In spite of that, they went no further than the group stages.

Four years down the line and the Swiss are still built on a solid backline, conceding in only three of their 10 qualifying games. Basel centre-back Fabian Schar will be important if this miserliness

is to continue, while goalkeeper Diego Benaglio is the established number one under seasoned coach Ottmar Hitzfeld.

A 4-4 draw against Iceland was the one major blip in qualifying as the Swiss surrendered a three-goal lead against the side that would eventually finish second behind them, but it at least showed an ability to score goals too.

Wingers Xherdan Shaqiri and Valentin Stocker will provide a lively threat to opponents, but nobody scored more than Schar's three goals in the qualifying process and a prolific striker is lacking. Eren Derdiyok is the most experienced of the Swiss attackers, but there is hope for youngsters Haris Seferovic, who packs a powerful shot, and Mario Gavranovic, who netted in each of the last two qualifying games.

Napoli midfielder Gokhan Inler will make things tick from the middle of the pitch, and his physicality and energy will characterise the Swiss effort, though they may lack the killer instinct to spend too long in Brazil.

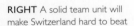

RIGHT A solid team unit will make Switzerland hard to beat

USA

USA secured their seventh consecutive World Cup qualification when they topped a group including Costa Rica, Honduras and Mexico last autumn and they will be eager to match their run to the quarter-finals in 2002.

Four years ago, Bob Bradley's side were eliminated at the last 16. He was replaced a year later by German legend Jurgen Klinsmann and the former World Cup winner led his adopted nation to Brazil with relative ease.

In preliminary qualifying, the *Stars and Stripes* finished comfortably above Jamaica, Guatemala and Antigua and Barbuda. They struggled, however, on the road. Pegged back despite a Clint Dempsey opener in Guatemala City, they were beaten 2-1 in Kingston, only beating the Antiguans thanks to a last-minute strike from forward Eddie Johnson.

At home, however, they had a 100 per cent record that took them through to the final qualifying stage.

Leading once more through top-scorer Dempsey, they were beaten in Honduras before the Texan forward's goal gave them an important win at home to Costa Rica.

A goalless draw away to Mexico was followed by a stunning injury-time victory as they returned to Jamaica, Brad Evans netting the winner just moments after Jermaine Beckford had equalised Jozy Altidore's opening goal.

Two important home wins against Panama and Honduras would follow before being well beaten in Costa Rica, despite another Dempsey strike.

Full points at home in their final two home games, securing eight straight wins on home soil, ensured the USA would top the group, the struggling Mexicans and Jamaicans both brushed aside before incredible late drama in the final group game. Trailing 2-1 in Panama, Graham Zusi and Aron Johannsson both struck in added time to secure another victory and let the Mexicans into the final play-off spot.

Now, Klinsmann's job is to find a way of reproducing that excellent home form in South America. Being there is one thing, but the United States will want to stay rather longer than the group stage.

BELOW Coach Jurgen Klinsmann will hope he can inspire the US like he did his Germany side in 2006

ROAD TO WORLD CUP 2014

USA	3-1	Antigua & Barbuda
Guatemala	1-1	USA
Jamaica	2-1	USA
USA	1-0	Jamaica
Antigua & Barbuda	1-2	USA
USA	3-1	Guatemala
Honduras	2-1	USA
USA	1-0	Costa Rica
Mexico	0-0	USA
Jamaica	1-2	USA
USA	2-0	Panama
USA	1-0	Honduras
Costa Rica	3-1	USA
USA	2-0	Mexico
USA	2-0	Jamaica
Panama	2-3	USA

KEY PLAYERS

Clint Dempsey
Michael Bradley
Jermaine Jones

WORLD CUP MOMENTS 2014

ABOVE Wayne Rooney is mobbed by England team-mates after securing their World Cup spot

RIGHT Uruguay players celebrate after beating Jordan 5-0 in the first leg of their intercontinental play-off

LEFT Radamel Falcao's penalty earned Colombia a 3-3 draw against Chile, and booked their place in Brazil

ABOVE The excellent Dutch put eight past Hungary in their group game on October 11, 2013

RIGHT Bosnia-Herzegovina fans celebrate their first World Cup qualification

ABOVE Germany were top scorers in European qualifying, scoring 36 times in 10 games

ABOVE USA's late winner on the final day of qualifying eliminated Panama, allowing Mexico into the play-offs

ABOVE Goalscorer Josh Kennedy is mobbed after his goal against Iraq secure's Australia's place in Brazil

ABOVE Madjid Bougherra headed the all-important goal for Algeria against Burkina Faso in the African play-offs

RIGHT Carlos Queiroz has delighted the Iranian public by leading them to qualification

ANDRES INIESTA

Andres Iniesta joined the exclusive club of players to have scored a World-Cup-winning goal when he struck in extra time in 2010. Four years on, hopes are high that he can inspire Spain to defend their title.

FACT FILE

Full Name: Andres Iniesta Lujan

Date of Birth: May 11, 1984

Place of Birth: Fuentealbilla, Spain

Height: 5 ft 7 in (1.70 m)

Playing Position: Attacking midfielder

National Team: Spain

1st Appearance: 2006

A goalless encounter in the final match of the 2010 World Cup, memorable more for Dutch defensive tactics than Spanish silk, sprang to life with four minutes remaining. Iniesta played a neat back-heel in midfield as Spain counter-attacked, Fernando Torres crossed, Cesc Fabregas picked up the loose ball and squared it to Iniesta, now unmarked at the far post, and he drove it low into the far bottom corner to bring a first world title to his country.

Two years either side of that night in Johannesburg, there were huge celebrations as Spain won and then became the first side to retain the European Championships. Iniesta, the classy all-rounder, was present throughout.

The Barcelona man, who will be 30 by the time Brazil 2014 kicks off, was also ever-present in qualifying for this tournament, which will be his third World Cup, having been a bit-part player in Spain's 2006 squad.

This time around they qualified in comfort, unbeaten in a group also containing France. Iniesta played a part in all eight games as Spain took 20 points from a possible 24, with 1-1 draws at home to France and Finland the only blemishes in an otherwise commanding run of results.

Anyone who has seen him play will understand why Iniesta is nicknamed 'the illusionist' in his homeland, as he possesses an ability to play anywhere on the park and impress while he does it. He has figured as a winger and as a defensive or attacking midfielder, but is at his best when combining them all and utilising the vision and ball-playing ability that have led to him being labelled among the best Barça players ever.

Having been beaten by Brazil in last summer's Confederations Cup final, Spain's star may have faded slightly, but there is no doubt they remain among the prime candidates to lift the World Cup in Rio on July 13. Should that happen, you can guarantee Iniesta will be at the centre of proceedings.

BELOW He's already won one World Cup but there is every chance Iniesta could lift a second in Brazil

CLINT DEMPSEY

As captain and USA's main goal threat, Clint Dempsey will be hoping to be the all-American hero when he leads his country in Brazil.

2014 will be the Texan's third World Cup and, having scored in each of his previous two, he will be hoping to make a similar mark in South America. His international form suggests Dempsey will do just that, having hit eight goals in a qualifying campaign which ended with the US top of their continental qualifying section.

Goals against their Central American opponents are rather easier to come by however than against the world's top sides, though six years in England's Premier League showed that Dempsey is more than capable of mixing it with the big boys.

He will be 31 when the tournament kicks off, but the former Fulham and Tottenham Hotspur man has lost none of his battling spirit, which makes him a handful for any opposing defender. Good in the air and capable of shooting with both feet, Dempsey scored 57 times in more than 200 Premier League appearances before returning to his homeland with Seattle Sounders in 2013. He is also an accomplished dead-ball specialist.

Alongside Landon Donovan, few players have done as much for football in America as Dempsey. Now, though, with Major League Soccer continuing to grow and domestic youth products improving, there is a chance Dempsey may be appearing at his final World Cup after 10 years as an international that have seen him win more than 100 caps for his country, and two continental Gold Cups.

On the world stage though, there is work to do. As a youngster, Dempsey will have watched the 2002 World Cup, when USA reached the last eight for the first time. It was supposed to be a watershed moment, but the *Stars and Stripes* have stalled in the past two tournaments, exiting at the group stage in 2006 and at the last 16 in 2010. Dempsey will be hoping he can help take the next step. It would be a fitting legacy for one of America's best.

LEFT One of the toughest players around, Dempsey will be USA's main source of goals in Brazil

FACT FILE

Full Name: Clinton Drew Dempsey

Date of Birth: March 9, 1983

Place of Birth: Nacogdoches, Texas, USA

Height: 6 ft 1 in (1.85 m)

Playing Position: Attacking midfielder/ forward

National Team: USA

1st Appearance: 2004

EDEN HAZARD

Having made his international debut as a 17-year-old, Eden Hazard now prepares for his first World Cup after developing into one of the best attacking talents in the world.

FACT FILE

Full Name: Eden Hazard

Date of Birth: January 7, 1991

Place of Birth: La Louviere, Belgium

Height: 5 ft 7 in (1.72 m)

Playing Position: Attacking midfielder

National Team: Belgium

1st Appearance: 2008

Hazard, the son of a former professional, debuted for the Lille first team at just 16 and a year later he was selected in his first Belgian squad, despite interest from France, where he had been resident for seven years.

Slowly integrated into the squad, he featured regularly as a substitute in the early days,

BELOW Belgium's master creator, Hazard can cause any defence problems with his pace and trickery

appearing in five World Cup qualifiers during Belgium's ill-fated 2010 campaign, while at club level he was twice voted the best young player in the French league, his dazzling ball skills making him near impossible to stop. After being encouraged to work harder in training and show greater attention in his defending, Hazard became a regular starter for the Belgians, who were beginning to bring through a number of young talent who will make up the bulk of the team in 2014 .

Two more excellent years in Lille were accompanied by two years of further adaptation to international football. Failure to qualify for Euro 2012 was tempered by more individual awards for his club, but Hazard had outgrown the French league and he transferred to Chelsea ahead of the 2012/13 season.

He took to England like a duck to water and for the first time his form began to transfer to the international stage as Belgium suddenly became a force, dominating their qualifying group for Brazil 2014.

Hazard calmly struck a penalty in the 2-0 win in Macedonia, scoring the only goal of the game against the same opposition four days later, his fourth and fifth goals for his country.

Now in Brazil, Hazard has a further chance to take his slow-burning Belgium career on to the next level.

Far from one of the biggest players, he can be almost impossible to dispossess thanks to a low centre of gravity, quick feet and impressive strength in his lower body. If he can get on the ball in and around opposition penalty areas, there will be no greater danger for defences in the tournament.

FRANCK RIBERY

Long regarded as one of the best wingers in the game, 2013 was the year it all came together for Franck Ribery.

As part of the Bayern Munich side that dominated German football, he lifted an unprecedented treble with his club, including the Champions League after victory over Borussia Dortmund in the Wembley final.

Much-documented injury problems are now long behind him, and a Ballon D'Or nomination was thoroughly deserved for the winger, who has also regularly appeared in the number 10 role behind a main striker for the national team.

Blessed with incredible acceleration, a faultless touch and a fine eye for a pass or a goal, Ribery is a regular on the scoresheet but is even more adept at creating chances for others.

When he first broke into the French side, just in time for the 2006 World Cup, he was seen as a long-term successor to the great Zinedine Zidane in the national side, and he has not disappointed, even though the national team has not fared well.

Ribery started on a high, however, starting six of France's seven games at the 2006 World Cup in Germany, helping them to the final and scoring in the 3-1 win over Spain in the first knockout round. He was substituted before the final reached its penalty shootout conclusion, and watched on from the sidelines as Italy claimed a fourth trophy.

Having helped them qualify for South Africa four years later, albeit only appearing in six qualifiers due to injury, Ribery would have had high hopes, but the tournament was an unmitigated disaster. A goalless draw with Uruguay was followed by defeats to Mexico and South Africa. Off the pitch the team held a strike from training in protest against coach Raymond Domenech, who was dismissed at the end of the tournament.

In 2014, Ribery is part of a more united French squad, but is still the standout performer. He played in all 10 qualifying games, and top-scored with five goals. Even with a talented and fairly settled group around him, the pressure will be on Ribery to produce the goods in Brazil.

LEFT France's inspiration, Ribery had a near-perfect 2013. Can he repeat it in 2014?

FACT FILE

Full Name: Franck Ribery

Date of Birth: April 7, 1983

Place of Birth: Boulougne-sur-Mer, France

Height: 5 ft 7 in (1.70 m)

Playing Position: Winger

National Team: France

1st Appearance: 2006

LIONEL MESSI

When Lionel Messi was awarded the 2012 Ballon d'Or, he became the first player in history to win it a fourth time, taking him beyond Johan Cruyff, Michel Platini and Marco van Basten.

FACT FILE

Full Name: Lionel Andres Messi

Date of Birth: June 24, 1987

Place of Birth: Santa Fe, Argentina

Height: 5 ft 7 in (1.69 m)

Playing Position: Forward

National Team: Argentina

1st Appearance: 2005

The diminutive Argentine has done it all in the club game, twice lifting the Champions League with Barcelona while becoming their top goalscorer of all time despite being just 26 years old. In 2012, Messi scored a world record 91 goals for club and country. Quite simply, he was unstoppable.

BELOW The brightest light in Argentina's galaxy of attacking stars, Messi has done it all for his club but will crave success at international level

For Argentina, there were 10 goals from 14 games during World Cup qualifying. By Messi's standards, that represents a rather modest return, but nobody else scored more for Alejandro Sabella's team and only goalkeeper Sergio Romero played more than Messi's 1,143 minutes during the campaign.

Despite a side possessing a plethora of world-class talent, Argentina will lean on Messi for the magic required to take them all the way in Brazil, just as the side of 1986 required Diego Maradona to produce some of his very best form in Mexico.

Globally, Messi is seen as every bit the equal of his predecessor and is blessed with a rather more clean-cut image. Just like Maradona, he is predominantly left-footed, small but with unparalleled balance and an ability to beat an opponent at will. He can play anywhere across the forward line, but for Argentina will most likely start from the right, cutting inside to look for goal or tee up fellow forwards Gonzalo Higuain and Sergio Aguero.

Unlike Maradona, Messi is not garnered with international honours. Argentina have not lifted a major title since the 1993 Copa America and they are long overdue silverware. Quarter-final exits in each of his previous World Cups have not brought out the best of Messi, who has scored just one goal in eight finals appearances and did not score in five appearances in South Africa four years ago.

This time, Argentina are well placed for success with a squad as strong as they have ever had, but they face stiff competition. At his best, Messi could set them apart from the crowd.

WORLD CUP 2014, STAR PLAYERS
MARIO BALOTELLI

As unpredictable as he is excellent, Italians will be hoping Mario Balotelli
will be making headlines for the right reasons at his first World Cup.

The enigmatic forward's story is like no other at the top level. The son of Ghanaian immigrants, Balotelli was taken into foster care as a toddler before making a professional league debut at 15.

Signed by Inter Milan, he helped them to the 2008 and 2009 Serie A titles as he became a first-team regular under Roberto Mancini and then Jose Mourinho. Disciplinary problems were already an issue, however, as Mourinho accused him of a lack of effort in training and he suffered racism from the terraces.

Balotelli finally gained Italian citizenship to allow him to play for his country of birth, having turned down advances from Ghana. The forward was called into the Under-21 setup and quickly made his mark, but during the 2009 Under-21 European Championships his temper got the better of him and he was red-carded against Sweden.

Progress continued, however, and he earned a full international call after transferring to Manchester City and the Premier League. His club form provided six goals in 17 league outings, but another red card early on typified the fiery forward.

Balotelli scored his first international goal in a friendly against Poland, before adding three more at Euro 2012, his brace against Germany securing Italy's place in the final, though he could not prevent a heavy 4-0 defeat to Spain.

His fifth international goal came in a World Cup qualifier against Denmark, before he moved back to Italy by transferring to AC Milan in January 2013. Since then, he has scored prolifically for club and country, netting both goals in a 2-0 win over Malta and key strikes against both Czech Republic and Armenia as Italy qualified

unbeaten for Brazil 2014. He also scored twice at the Confederations Cup, despite being injured before the semi-final.

Fast, strong and agile, Balotelli could easily be the star of the next World Cup, yet he must keep a lid on his infamous temperament to avoid being Italy's fall guy. Either way, the Mohawk-sporting striker is sure to be in the South American spotlight.

BELOW Fantastic or frustrating? Balotelli has all the talent but his temperament has been questioned

FACT FILE

Full Name: Mario Barwuah Balotelli

Date of Birth: August 12, 1990

Place of Birth: Palermo, Italy

Height: 6 ft 2 in (1.89 m)

Playing Position: Striker

National Team: Italy

1st Appearance: 2010

WORLD CUP 2014, STAR PLAYERS

MESUT OZIL

Mesut Ozil prepares for his second World Cup knowing his creativity could be the key ingredient for Germany as they seek to end a 24-year wait for football's biggest prize.

FACT FILE

Full Name: Mesut Ozil

Date of Birth: October 15, 1988

Place of Birth: Gelsenkirchen, Germany

Height: 5 ft 11 in (1.81 m)

Playing Position: Attacking midfielder

National Team: Germany

1st Appearance: 2009

Ozil was already a renowned talent throughout youth football, but really hit the headlines with his performances at the European Under-21 championship in 2009, leading an outstanding German side to the title. He had already made a full international debut earlier that year, having impressed after transferring to Werder Bremen, and scored his first goal for his country later that year in a friendly against South Africa, the venue of the 2010 World Cup.

His second international goal came in the final group stage game, an important volley to secure a 1-0 victory against Ghana. That win set up a date with England, where Ozil pulled the strings in a devastating 4-1 win, creating two goals as Germany demonstrated a near-perfect counter-attacking display.

They reached perfection in the quarter-final, a 4-0 win over Diego Maradona's lauded Argentina, but came unstuck against eventual champions Spain, losing 1-0 in the semis. Ozil featured again in the third-place play-off, and it was his cross that set up Sami Khedira's winner to earn a bronze medal.

This time, Ozil and co. will want gold. Although he is Germany's main man, with eight goals in their qualifying campaign alone, the playmaker does not carry the burden of his country's expectations single-handedly and can lean on the support of world-class team-mates if he is not on top of his game.

Ozil's off days are rare though, and he has developed further after three years in Spain with Real Madrid, playing under the great Jose Mourinho. His ability to beat a man or pick a pass in an instant is almost unrivalled around the world. His form for Arsenal, after swapping Spain for England last summer, showed he can mix it in tougher conditions too.

At 25, Ozil is still not at his footballing peak, yet the feeling is that this could be Germany's best chance. He was a toddler last time they won the World Cup in 1990, but now the stage is set for this generation to make its mark.

RIGHT The key man in Germany's attack, if Ozil is on form then "Der Mannschaft" could be celebrating come July

JOHN MIKEL OBI

One of the most experienced midfielders of his generation at club level, Mikel now looks forward to his first World Cup after missing out on 2010 through injury.

A defensive lieutenant at Chelsea, where he has been a regular since understudying the great Claude Makelele, Mikel is often asked to play in a more advanced role for his national team, not just breaking up opposition attacks but starting and partaking in those of his own side too.

Adorning the number 10 shirt, there is an expectation on Mikel to play with flair, and he can do it too. His goal at the Confederations Cup last June saw him collect the ball on the edge of the area and swivel to beat his Uruguayan marker before calmly side-footing home into the top corner with his weaker left foot. It was a far cry from the man who went 185 Premier League games without scoring a goal, and more associated with the precocious creative talent that finished runner-up to Lionel Messi as the best player at the 2005 Under-20 World Cup.

Since then, Mikel has experienced a mixed international career, bursting onto the senior scene in the 2006 African Cup of Nations, and stealing the show as a playmaker in parts of the 2008 tournament, but being suspended for not turning up in between and seeing his commitment questioned in the run-up to the 2010 World Cup, which he then missed due to a knee injury. He did not return to the setup until late 2012, but then helped Nigeria become African champions for the first time since 1994 with a string of stellar performances in early 2013.

It was an unexpected success, but one which leaves Nigeria with confidence, and without the weight of previous generations on their shoulders. Mikel now has the opportunity to show he is one of Africa's finest talents, and could yet inspire an organised Nigerian side into new territory at the World Cup finals.

With a calm head and relaxed demeanour, there is little that will faze a player who lifted the Champions League in 2012, and Mikel will be desperate to show the world there is more to him than English audiences see.

FACT FILE

Full Name: John Michael Obinna

Date of Birth: April 22, 1987

Place of Birth: Jos, Nigeria

Height: 6 ft 2 in (1.88 m)

Playing Position: Midfield

National Team: Nigeria

1st Appearance: 2005

RIGHT A steadying presence on Nigeria, will Mikel be able to lead them into the later stages?

NEYMAR

Although the mercurial forward is just 21, it seems as though Neymar's name has been on everybody's lips for an eternity.

FACT FILE

Full Name: Neymar da Silva Santos Júnior

Date of Birth: February 5, 1992

Place of Birth: Mogi das Cruzes, Sao Paulo, Brazil

Height: 5 ft 9 in (1.75 m)

Playing Position: Striker

National Team: Brazil

1st Appearance: 2010

A typical Brazilian protégé, the fleet-footed youngster with a box of tricks emerged in 2009 as a teenager at Santos, the club that had previously produced Pele and Robinho. Being billed as a potential successor to the title of 'Best Player in the World' has proved overwhelming for many before him, yet Neymar appears to love the limelight.

Scoring freely for Santos ensured an international debut at 18, having narrowly missed out on a place in the squad for South Africa in 2010. New coach Mano Menezes picked the youngster in a friendly against USA and it took just 28 minutes for him to convert his first goal, an uncharacteristic header.

Three goals at the 2011 Copa America in Argentina were matched at the 2012 London Olympics, though Brazil were beaten by Mexico in the Wembley final, leaving him waiting for a first international title.

Goals continued to flow for Santos and a move to Europe seemed imminent for the 2012

South American Footballer of the Year. It was finally announced in late May 2013 that Neymar would be joining Barcelona and he was unveiled to more than 50,000 fans at the Nou Camp in early June.

Before he could make his debut for the Catalonian side, however, he returned to Brazil for the 2013 Confederations Cup, wearing the iconic number 10 shirt for his country. If there were doubts about Neymar's ability to produce on the world stage, they would not last long. He thundered home a half-volley against Japan, netted against Mexico and then bent a free-kick against Italy, adding another unstoppable drive against a well-beaten Spain in the final as Brazil lifted the trophy on home soil.

After a bright start in Barcelona, in which he scored in his first meeting with arch rivals Real Madrid, the stage is set for Neymar to light up Brazil 2014.

RIGHT After a lively start to his international career, can Neymar live up to the hype on the biggest stage of all?

WORLD CUP 2014, STAR PLAYERS

OSCAR

It is testament to the young playmaker that he was able to keep
Brazilian legends Kaka and Ronaldinho at bay in order to secure
a place as an automatic starter under two Seleção coaches.

Mano Menezes gave the Sao-Paulo-born youngster his debut as a half-time substitute against rivals Argentina in September 2011, scoring a first goal a year later in a 4-3 friendly win against the same opposition.

By this point, Oscar had already left his native South America for European champions Chelsea, lifted the Under-20s World Cup and been a key figure in Brazil's run to the final of the London Olympics, whetting the appetite of his new fans with a string of eye-catching performances.

His club form, which included a run of five goals in six continental matches, was excellent and replicated on the international stage as Oscar added further strikes in friendlies with China and Iraq.

As hosts of this summer's tournament, Brazil have not had to qualify and so spent two years between 2011 and 2013 playing non-competitive fixtures. Despite his decision to blood young talent like Oscar, Neymar and Paulinho, Menezes was not producing the football demanded of a Brazil coach. The Brazilian Football Confederation opted for change and brought back the 2002 World Cup winner Luiz Felipe Scolari. Would the veteran stick with his young guns or revert to the past?

The answer, with hindsight, was easy. Oscar, playing in the coveted no. 10 role behind the striker, continued to impress with his incisive passing, eye for goal and a surprisingly dogged nature for one with such a slight frame.

Although he did not score in last summer's Confederations Cup, he was a constant in Brazil's midfield as they sampled success at home, seeing off the well-fancied Spain with a commanding performance in the final. They will want to repeat it on the greatest stage this summer.

For 22-year-old Oscar, a World Cup in front of Brazilian support will bring incredible pressure, yet there are few players around with the composure to deal with it as well as the Chelsea midfielder. It is his time to shine.

LEFT Oscar is the latest in a long line of excellent Brazilian playmakers

FACT FILE

Full Name: Oscar dos Santos Emboaba Junior

Date of Birth: September 9, 1991

Place of Birth: Americana, Sao Paulo, Brazil

Height: 5 ft 11 in (1.80 m)

Playing Position: Attacking midfield

National Team: Brazil

Debut: 2011

RADAMEL FALCAO

It is often said that to be a truly great player, you need to have impressed on the greatest stage of them all – the World Cup.

FACT FILE

Full Name: Radamel Falcao Garcia Zarate

Date of Birth: February 10, 1986

Place of Birth: Santa Marta, Colombia

Height: 5 ft 10 in (1.78 m)

Playing Position: Striker

National Team: Colombia

1st Appearance: 2007

For Radamel Falcao, that adage seems especially true. A prolific goalscorer at club level in a career that has taken him from Argentina to Portugal, Spain and France, the Colombian goal machine is yet to take that form truly to the highest level. While he was with Atletico Madrid, he set records in the Europa League but moved on to Monaco before he could add to his

eight Champions League appearances accrued with Porto.

Falcao's career began with River Plate, where his goals earned him a 2007 Colombia debut. This debut may well have come earlier had it not been for a succession of injuries, including a ruptured cruciate ligament. In his first four years as an international, he struck just six goals in 26 appearances and only one in a competitive fixture.

But after swapping South America for Europe, Falcao took his game up a notch and was a major driving force in his country's first World Cup qualification for 16 years, scoring eight times in a campaign that saw Colombia finish second behind Argentina and ahead of 2010's third-placed side and 2011 Copa America winners Uruguay.

Key goals were scored in wins over Bolivia, Chile and Paraguay, while his late brace against Chile to earn a 3-3 draw sealed Colombia's place in Brazil.

Two-footed and stronger in the air than his 5ft 10ins frame suggests, Falcao has the requisite qualities to trouble any defence in the world. He was probably the most hotly pursued forward in the world last summer and can operate as a lone striker or with a partner, who is likely to be Teofilo Gutierrez should coach Jose Pekerman opt for two up-front at the finals.

Whether Falcao can make his mark on the World Cup will depend as much on his team-mates as it will on his own explosive excellence, but if Colombia are to succeed, they will need him at his very best.

BELOW Falcao has been one of the most dangerous strikers in Europe for the past few seasons. Can he fire Colombia to glory?

ROBIN VAN PERSIE

Robin van Persie is among Europe's most feared strikers and scored an incredible 11 goals in nine World Cup qualifying matches on the way to Brazil.

That figure included a hat-trick in his country's 8-1 thrashing of Hungary in October 2013 and braces against Andorra and Romania as Holland stormed their way to the top of their group and confirmed themselves as contenders for the world crown.

Four years ago, Van Persie led the Dutch line as they progressed all the way to the final in South Africa. He was a peripheral figure then however, as his side, under the instructions of coach Bert van Marwijk, attempted to contain rather than outplay Spain and were undone by an extra-time winner. His only goal in the tournament came in the group stage victory over Cameroon.

Back in Germany 2006, the then Arsenal striker also scored once, a free-kick against Ivory Coast as the Dutch went home early in the round of 16.

Since then, Van Persie has shaken the 'fragile' label that marked his early career, finally achieving a regular run of games that has paid dividends. In his final club season with Arsenal, he struck 30 goals in 38 games and hit 26 after a controversial switch to Manchester United a year later.

It has coincided with a fruitful run at international level too and, having suffered frustration so far at the World Cup, he will be desperate to add to his tally of two goals in 11 finals appearances. If Holland are to succeed, they will need Van Persie's goals and there should be no shortage of supply with a talented midfield and wide men lining up the chances.

The Hungarian treble made Van Persie his country's top goalscorer of all time, surpassing Patrick Kluivert's 40 strikes, yet Marco van Basten would probably be the answer if Dutch fans were asked to name their greatest forward of all time. An impressive World Cup, and a winners' medal, would change all that.

FACT FILE

Full Name: Robin van Persie

Date of Birth: August 6, 1983

Place of Birth: Rotterdam, Holland

Height: 6 ft 2 in (1.88 m)

Playing Position: Striker

National Team: Holland

1st Appearance: 2005

LEFT Van Persie is the top Dutch scorer of all time, and looks set to add to his tally in Brazil

CRISTIANO RONALDO

FACT FILE

Full Name: Cristiano Ronaldo dos Santos Aveiro

Date of Birth: February 5, 1985

Place of Birth: Madeira, Portugal

Height: 6 ft 1 in (1.86 m)

Playing Position: Winger/Forward

National Team: Portugal

1st Appearance: 2003

Cristiano Ronaldo is probably more central to his own team's plans than any other player at the forthcoming World Cup.

In 2013, Ronaldo was the best player on the planet, outshining Lionel Messi, his long-running rival, for the first time since winning the 2008 Ballon D'Or. His form was simply stunning as he racked up goals and records like never before.

BELOW Cristiano Ronaldo will be Portugal's most dangerous asset in Brazil

His importance to Portugal cannot be overstated. Captain for the past five years, his four goals in the European play-offs against Sweden showed what Ronaldo is all about. There is nothing he cannot do. In Lisbon, his diving header separated the sides and then in Solna his pace and ability to finish off a counter-attack came to the fore, netting with both feet and delivering an incredible hat-trick.

Ronaldo is not just a finisher though. He can create something from nothing with a dribble, a flick, a dummy or an incisive pass and although his goalscoring game has gone from strength to strength, he remains a wonderful creator of chances and does so with regularity. He is also a dead-ball specialist, his dipping, bending, free-kicks a trademark of a player with huge amount of self-belief.

He will be 29 when the World Cup kicks off, probably at the peak of his powers, yet Ronaldo is still accused of lacking the team ethic of Messi and on the international stage, where Portugal are a less dominant force than his Real Madrid club side, he can cut a frustrated figure. Where in 2006 he was part of a fantastic unit that reached the semi-finals, he is now, as in 2010, the standout talent of a side trying to keep up with the elite.

The thought of missing out this time around must have occurred to Ronaldo, who is among the most marketed footballers in the world, but thanks largely to his own brilliance he will be at the party and is sure to take centre stage.

If he maintains his form of 2013, he has the ability to take Portugal all the way. International honours are missing from one of football's finest CVs, but Ronaldo will be eager to set that right in 2014.

SHINJI KAGAWA

Shinji Kagawa prepares for his first World Cup carrying the hopes of his nation on his shoulders.

A prodigy in Japan, Kagawa signed professional terms before leaving high school, showing an eye for goal with Cerezo Osaka before arriving in Europe with Borussia Dortmund in 2010. There, he impressed with an excellent goalscoring record, frequently timing his arrival in the penalty box to score goals. Close control and tremendous vision make him a potent attacking weapon.

Two excellent seasons with one of the continent's emerging forces were then followed by a switch to England with Manchester United and Kagawa has enjoyed a promising start to life in the Premier League.

Japan's main man, he is most at home playing behind a striker but also comfortable as a wide player supplying opportunities for those ahead of him. He has been used regularly at club level on the left and may yet feature similarly for Alberto Zaccheroni's side.

Still only 25 when Brazil 2014 gets underway, Kagawa's best years should still be ahead of him, but he now has the perfect stage to demonstrate his talents and if he can link with Japan's other star talent, Keisuke Honda, then he may be able to participate in the later stages. Japan has never gone beyond the last 16 and if it is to happen this year, Kagawa will almost certainly be central to any success.

The player himself will be desperate to do well as he missed Japan's Asian Cup final win against Australia through injury, having broken a metatarsal in the semi-final of what had been a strong tournament.

Unlike some of his international team-mates and those Japan have pinned their hopes on in the past, Kagawa is a genuine top class talent and, even if his country still trails the world's elite sides, he would not look out of place in some of the more illustrious squads.

Kagawa scored in Japan's 4-3 defeat to Italy in last summer's Confederations Cup and will relish the opportunity to return to Brazil in 2014.

LEFT Kagawa will be among the most exciting attacking players on display at the World Cup

FACT FILE

Full Name: Shinji Kagawa

Date of Birth: March 17, 1989

Place of Birth: Kobe, Japan

Height: 5 ft 7 in (1.72 m)

Playing Position: Attacking midfielder

National Team: Japan

1st Appearance: 2008

LUIS SUAREZ

Nobody scored more goals in South American qualifying than Luis Suarez, who has emerged as Uruguay's talisman.

FACT FILE

Full Name: Luis Alberto Suarez Diaz

Date of Birth: January 24, 1987

Place of Birth: Salto, Uruguay

Height: 5 ft 11 in (1.81 m)

Playing Position: Forward

National Team: Uruguay

1st Appearance: 2007

RIGHT Suarez is Uruguay's inspiration, but needs to remain focused on his football in Brazil

The Liverpool forward's 11 goals for his country outlined his importance to the cause and Suarez is known to thrive under the pressure of the spotlight.

Unpredictable, and at times in his career unmanageable, Suarez regularly achieves what appears to be impossible. Few players possess the forward's pace, touch or cunning, mixed with an ability to find the net from anywhere around the box. Capable of playing up on his own or alongside a strike partner, Suarez is also capable of providing chances for team-mates and there is an unselfish streak that sets him apart from others.

He will be expected to complement Edinson Cavani for Uruguay at the World Cup and he has formed a deadly partnership with the forward over the past few years, having partnered Diego Forlan at the last tournament in South Africa.

Suarez's tournament ended in disgrace four years ago, when his handball denied Ghana a place in the semi-finals before Uruguay edged out the Africans in the penalty shootout, but before then he had been part of a side that caught the eye with their excellent football.

Since then, a move to England and a starring role in his nation's success at the 2011 Copa America has taken Suarez's profile up a notch and he has remained close to controversy at all times. Yet through it all, his form has been superb.

Uruguay's top goalscorer of all time, Suarez now has a chance to correct his questionable reputation and make people focus on his football. By remaining focused and avoiding a tendency to dive or wind up opponents, he could inspire Uruguay to the later stages once again.

Despite his goals, *La Celeste* were underwhelming in qualifying, however, and others will probably need to raise their game if Suarez is to see the semi-finals. Neutrals will hope that is the case, as on his day, he can be a joy to behold.

TIM CAHILL

The poster boy of football's growth in Australia, Tim Cahill will be appearing in his third World Cup when he leads his country in Brazil.

Sydney-born, Cahill actually represented Samoa at youth level, and it wasn't until eligibility rules changed in 2004 that he could make his debut for the *Socceroos*, having impressed as a combative midfielder with an eye for a goal for Millwall in England's second tier.

Making up for lost time, Cahill quickly became a prolific goal-scorer at international level, helping his side to only their second World Cup and scoring key goals in the Oceanic Nations Cup and the Athens Olympics.

His transfer into the Premier League with Everton saw him take his form onto a higher stage and he raised his profile even higher on his World Cup debut in Germany in 2006.

Australia had not qualified since 1974, and they had failed to score a single goal. In 2006 things started badly against Japan as they fell a goal behind. However, Cahill struck twice in the last 10 minutes to turn the game on its head and earn his country its first World Cup win. This, followed by a draw with Croatia, was enough to see them through to the knockout rounds, where they were narrowly beaten by eventual champions Italy. His efforts were enough to receive a nomination for the 2006 World Player of the Year award.

Fast forward four years and Australia qualified for South Africa, their switch to the Asian Confederation offering a more straightforward route to the finals than they had previously encountered. Frustration was to follow though as, in the opening game, Cahill was harshly sent off for a challenge on Bastian Schweinsteiger as Germany hammered his side 4-0. Cahill subsequently missed the 1-1 draw with Ghana before returning to score in the 2-1 win

over Serbia. Four years earlier, Australia had progressed with four points, but this time they were eliminated.

Cahill, who will be 34 in Brazil, remains the focal point of Australia's side, despite leaving the Premier League for the New York Red Bulls. He contributed important goals in qualifying and will hope he can add more in his third, and probably final World Cup.

BELOW Cahill is Australia's finest footballing export, and has one more chance to make a major impact at the World Cup

FACT FILE

Full Name: Timothy Filiga Cahill

Date of Birth: December 6, 1979

Place of Birth: Sydney, Australia

Height: 5 ft 10 in (1.78 m)

Playing Position: Attacking midfielder

National Team: Australia

1st Appearance: 2004

WAYNE ROONEY

It is now more than a decade since Wayne Rooney, then a prodigious teenager, burst onto the international scene as England's next great hope.

FACT FILE

Full Name: Wayne Mark Rooney

Date of Birth: October 24 1985

Place of Birth: Croxteth, Liverpool, England

Height: 5 ft 10 in (1.78 m)

Playing Position: Striker

National Team: England

Debut: 2003

Rooney became his country's youngest ever player in February 2003, just months after making his Everton debut as a 16-year-old and quickly became the main attacking focus of a team who were long overdue glory.

After cementing a place in Sven-Goran Eriksson's starting line-up, he impressed at Euro 2004, scoring twice against both Switzerland and Croatia before limping off through injury during the quarter-final against Portugal.

A big money move to Manchester United followed for Rooney, where he struck a hat-trick on his European debut, but while England made the World Cup in Germany, the forward failed to score during the qualifying campaign and was again injured, this time in the run-up to the tournament. A nation waited and Eriksson was able to name Rooney in his squad, though he had to sit out the opening group game against Paraguay. A substitute in the next game and substituted in the one after, Rooney was clearly unfit and missed the first knockout round clash with Ecuador, returning to face Portugal. Once again Rooney left the action early, but this time in disgrace after being shown a red card for a stamp on Ricardo Carvalho.

The combustible forward returned to competitive action after suspension, scoring twice in a disappointing Euro 2008 qualifying campaign, where England failed to qualify. However, under the tutelage of Fabio Capello, he led England to the 2010 South Africa World Cup with nine straight victories and nine goals in the qualification process.

Fully fit with a fine club campaign behind him, hopes were high for Rooney, but once again England stuttered, drawing with USA and Algeria and beating Slovenia by a solitary goal to book a knockout meeting with Germany. England were despatched 4-1, with Rooney anonymous.

A low-key European Championship followed, but with Brazil approaching there is optimism once more. Approaching his 100th England cap and with another seven goals in qualifying, Rooney is now England's top World Cup scorer of all time. The problem is none have come in a finals tournament. He will be hoping 2014 is the year all that changes.

BELOW He is England's main man, and Rooney will be desperate to show it in his third World Cup

YAYA TOURE

Yaya Toure has the raw materials to be unstoppable on his day, and his Ivory Coast team-mates will look to him to drive them on in Brazil.

The midfielder, younger brother of international team-mate Kolo, has grown into a dominant force for both club and country. His ability to defend and attack with equal quality is probably unmatched in world football, and his coaches have regularly seen fit to switch him between attacking and defensive roles.

At a huge 6ft 4ins, Toure would be a commanding presence anywhere on the field, but in midfield he can be relied upon to win possession back for his side. When allowed the freedom to do so, he can release the ball and follow his pass, with a growing tendency later in his career to finish off moves he has started. Yet Toure can also provide an effective shield in front of a defensive line, bypassing him is almost impossible for opposition sides, who can find his strength and stamina simply unplayable.

In addition there is a deft touch that defies the Ivorian's size, and he prefers to curl a free-kick into the top corner than rifle it home with power alone. Whether he can prise the ball from Didier Drogba for any such opportunities at the World Cup remains to be seen.

Brazil will be his third finals appearance, yet Toure is still waiting to reach the knockout phase. The Netherlands and Argentina, and then Brazil and Portugal, twice condemned the Ivorians to the traditional group of death.

The midfielder would not have looked out of place in any of those sides, and fans should hope the west African country have a slightly easier time of it in 2014. If that proves to be the case, there is no doubt Toure has the class to lead his nation's charge. However, if Ivory Coast struggle again, there will be nobody better to help contain the opposition's threat.

Whatever his role in South America, the versatile man mountain will perform to the highest standard.

BELOW Nobody will relish facing the irresistible Yaya Toure in Brazil

FACT FILE

Full Name: Gnegneri Yaya Toure

Date of Birth: May 13, 1983

Place of Birth: Bouake, Ivory Coast

Height: 6 ft 4 in (1.92 m)

Playing Position: Midfielder

National Team: Ivory Coast

1st Appearance: 2004

GREAT NATIONS

International power in football is defined by a mixture
of achievement and history. Success or failure at the
World Cup finals is what counts to today's modern critic,
followed by titles in the various regional championships.
Brazil boast five World Cup victories, one more than
mighty Italy. Germany have scored a hat-trick of successes
on the world stage, with Argentina and Uruguay twice
crowned as world champions, while England and
France have each triumphed once. The role of the four
British Home Nations is acknowledged worldwide,
especially as England are major crowd pullers.

GREAT NATIONS

BRAZIL

England may have invented the modern game, but Brazil —and Pelé in particular—have perfected it to such an extent that they can now boast a record-breaking five World Cup wins.

RIGHT A 17-year-old Pelé holds the Jules Rimet trophy

PAGE 102 Brazil star Garrincha skips past Wales defender Terry Hennessey in 1962

PAGE 103 The 1986 France team before their match against Canada

Few dare argue with the Brazilian pre-eminence in post-war football—especially after watching the timeless re-runs of Garrincha and Pelé swaggering their way to Brazil's first World Cup win in 1958 or, 12 years later, witnessing in colour Brazil's third World Cup triumph in the Mexican sunshine. Since then, successive new generations of Brazilians have consistently lived up to Pelé's romantic notion of "the beautiful game".

But the original link was an English one. In 1894, Brazilian Charles Miller, whose father was originally from England, brought over the first footballs to be seen in Brazil, after a study trip in Southampton where he learned the game. Miller envisaged a game for expatriates and their families, but its popularity swiftly spread and Brazil now boasts the proud achievement of being the only nation to have competed in every World Cup.

The country's first footballing hero was Arthur Friedenreich, who, in the early part of the 20th century, was also popularly supposed to have been the first senior player to have scored over 1,000 goals. Emulating him was Leonidas, who spearheaded Brazil's attack at the 1938 World Cup finals in France. Unwisely, the team's selectors decided to rest Leonidas from the semi-final against World Cup title holders Italy in order to be fresh for the final—which, of course, they never reached.

Brazil were awarded hosting rights to the next World Cup, but had to wait until after World War II. It was originally due to be played in 1949, but a mixture of European uncertainty and slow preparation work put the staging back to 1950.

Brazil reached the final only to suffer a shock 2-1 defeat to Uruguay in front of almost 200,000 disbelieving fans. As Brazil had lost the final while dressed in all-white, they superstitiously decided to make the switch to their current strip of yellow shirts and blue shorts—arguably today's most iconic football kit.

Brazil reached the quarter-final stage at the 1954 World Cup finals in Switzerland, returning to Europe to take the world title in Sweden four years later with almost an entirely new team.

Coach Vicente Feola had brought in the mercurial outside-right Garrincha and a 17-year-old inside-left called Pelé. As a teenage sensation, Pelé shared top billing for Brazil with wizard dribbler Garrincha, nicknamed "the Little Bird" and the midfield duo of Didi and Zito.

Four years later they retained the title in Chile despite an early injury to Pelé, who was now the subject of physical marking wherever he played. Brazil struggled in England in 1966 as the star of the side was again roughhoused out of the tournament, but in 1970 he was better than ever, and complemented by the likes of Gerson, Rivelino, Tostao and the explosive Jairzinho, making arguably the greatest side in World Cup history. When Pelé retired in 1977, he boasted over 1,000 goals in a career with Brazil, Santos and New York Cosmos.

Brazil had to wait for 24 years to claim their fourth World Cup, edging past Italy on penalty kicks at the 1994 finals in the United States. Brazil's Bebeto and Romario were the deadliest strike pairing at the tournament going into the match against Italy, yet the match finished goalless. A young Ronaldo was a member of the 1994 squad without playing and, in 1998, he was hampered by injury and illness as Brazil limply surrendered their crown to France. Four years later, Ronaldo was the two-goal hero in the 2002 final victory over Germany and in 2006 became the World Cup's all-time leading scorer when he scored his 15th goal at the finals.

Brazil's immense size long hindered the development of a national league until 1971, and the traditional old regional championships still generate fierce rivalry. Flamengo and Fluminense insist that they are the best-supported clubs, although São Paulo have a record five league titles. The wealth of Brazilian football has always rested on the Rio-São Paulo axis, with the South American country now the world's greatest exporter of players.

Most members of Brazil's recent World Cup squads have been European-based, a stark contrast to 1958 and 1962, when their entire squads played for Brazilian clubs. Santos have been the most internationally acclaimed club in Brazilian football history. This is largely due to their perpetual global touring in the 1960s, when they cashed in on the fame and drawing power of Pelé. Despite the touring, Santos—even at their peak—were an extremely fine team that in 1962 and 1963 won both the Copa Libertadores and the World Club Cup.

Outstanding Brazilian coaches over the years have included World Cup-winning managers Feola, Aimoré Moreira, Mario Zagallo, Carlos Alberto Parreira, and Luiz Felipe Scolari, who leads the team again in 2014, looking for a success on home soil that would make up for the not forgotten pain of 1950.

BELOW Bebeto and Romario celebrate in 1994

GREAT NATIONS

ARGENTINA

Argentina took until 1978 to lift the World Cup despite producing legendary players, coaches and teams. Their greatest player remains the controversial Diego Maradona, who inspired them to a second world title in 1986.

Argentina had come close to the title before, but it was not until they were on home soil in front of their own fans that the famous *Albiceleste*, in their distinctive blue and white stripes, were celebrating becoming world champions. Six goals from forward Mario Kempes, the midfield promptings of Ossie Ardiles, defensive rigidity from captain Daniel Passarella and shrewd managerial guidance by César Luis Menotti fired them to victory.

The country's football federation deserved enormous credit for appointing the attack-minded Menotti as coach, because at the time other coaches such as Juan Carlos Lorenzo (Boca), Manuel Giudice (Independiente) and Osvaldo Zubeldía (Estudiantes de La Plata), were ruthlessly putting the achievement of results above the quality of play and entertainment. Menotti was able to deliver both.

Under Menotti, Argentina's triumph and style of play at the 1978 World Cup finals inspired a significant shift in opinion, and eight years later they added a second crown at the 1986 World Cup finals in Mexico. This time they were inspired by Diego Maradona, the best attacking player in the world, who as a 17-year-old had just failed to make the 1978 squad due to a lack of experience.

Argentina then finished as the runner-up to West Germany in 1990, as they had

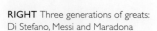
RIGHT Three generations of greats: Di Stefano, Messi and Maradona

done against Uruguay 60 years earlier at the inaugural tournament.

Maradona took the headlines again in 1994, when he failed a dope test and was immediately sent home in disgrace. In his absence, Argentina underperformed and bowed out to Romania in the second round. They reached the quarter-final stage four years later, crashed out in the first round in 2002 and made it to the quarter-finals in 2006 and 2010, when Maradona had been appointed coach. Despite a controversial career, he remains an idol for his outrageous talent and the sheer nerve with which he scored two remarkable goals against England in the 1986 World Cup finals. These goals are legendary. One was helped in with his hand, the other one a solo effort that began on the halfway line.

Argentina have won the South American title 14 times, but just twice in the Copa America era since 1975. Their greatest side prior to their 1978 World Cup win was the class of 1957, when the inspirational performances of Humberto Maschio, Antonio Valentín Angelillo, and Omar Sivori established them as early favourites to win the following year's World Cup, but by 1958, the trio had moved abroad to Italy, and Argentina's hopes went with them. From then on there was a steady stream of Argentinian players heading for the riches on offer in Europe.

By the mid-1990s, as most European countries eased their restrictions on foreign players, a minor industry developed in "finding" European forebears—and European Union passports—for many Argentinian players, with the bulk of the national team now playing club football away from South America.

At club level, Argentina has played a major role in the history of the Copa Libertadores, the South American equivalent of Europe's Champions League, which has been dominated by six clubs —Argentinos Juniors, Boca Juniors, Estudiantes, Independiente, Racing Club, and River Plate, but the domestic game lacks the financial muscle of Europe.

Boca and River remain among the world's most renowned clubs, with the majority of the country's finest players having used them as a springboard to lucrative careers elsewhere. Boca Juniors' colours are navy blue and yellow, while

River Plate play in white shirts with a red sash. In the late 1940s, River carried all before them with a forward line nicknamed "The Machine" for its goalscoring efficiency. They fielded two inside forwards, Juan Manuel Moreno and Angel Labruna, while in reserve was a young Alfredo Di Stefano. The side broke up in the early 1950s, when Argentinian league players went on strike in a demand for improved contracts and wages. Many players, including Di Stefano, were lured away to a "pirate" league in Colombia and never returned. Di Stefano played more games for Spain than he did his native Argentina.

After Di Stefano and Maradona came Lionel Messi, who like many before him moved to Europe as a teenager, coming through the ranks at Barcelona. Messi is now the club's top goalscorer of all time, but at international level has underachieved. He, along with other European-based players in the current generation, know they must succeed on the world stage if they are to live up to Argentina's rich past.

ABOVE Daniel Passarella holds the World Cup trophy aloft in 1978

ITALY

Only Brazil can boast a better World Cup record than Italy, who have recorded four wins to date, most recently in 2006 when they emerged victorious after penalties against France.

FOOTBALL FACTS

LAST 10 CHAMPIONS

2004 AC Milan

2005 No winner – Juventus stripped of their title

2006 Internazionale

2007 Internazionale

2008 Internazionale

2009 Internazionale

2010 Internazionale

2011 AC Milan

2012 Juventus

2013 Juventus

It was Italy's first shootout victory, having suffered heartache in three of the four previous tournaments, at home against Argentina, in Los Angeles against the Brazilians, and against the French in Paris.

Fabio Grosso's winning spot kick in Berlin took them to four World Cup wins, and was their first in 24 years, helping restore faith in the Italian game after a match-fixing scandal had dogged their preparations.

At its origin, Italy had refused to travel to the 1930 World Cup in Uruguay, but won the next two tournaments, in Europe, thanks to the managerial wisdom of Vittorio Pozzo and the genius of inside-forward Giuseppe Meazza. Pozzo fielded three Argentines in the team that beat Czechoslovakia in the 1934 final, responding to criticism by pointing out their eligibility to national service, saying: "If they can die for Italy, then I'm sure they can play football for Italy!"

In 1958, Italy failed for the first time to progress through the qualifying system and into the World Cup finals, not helped by a number of foreign imports to the domestic game. Participation in the 1966 finals remains notorious for their 1-0 defeat at the hands of North Korea, one of the tournament's biggest upsets. Adversity turned to glory when Italy captured the 1968 European Championships after a replay, and two years later, inspired by the legendary figures of Giacinto Faccheti, Sandro Mazzola, Gigi Riva, and Gianni Rivera, Italy took part in one of the greatest games ever played, edging past West Germany 4-3 in extra time to secure a place in the World Cup final. So exhausted were they after the victory, however, that they surrendered 4-1 to a brilliant Brazil.

Italy arrived at the 1982 World Cup finals in the wake of another match-fixing scandal. Coach Enzo Bearzot and veteran captain Dino Zoff

RIGHT Fabio Grosso hits the winning penalty at the 2006 World Cup

imposed a press blackout. Paolo Rossi had just returned from a two-year ban for his alleged role in the scandal and would prove to be their unlikely inspiration, with six goals— including a hat-trick against Brazil—guiding his nation to a stunning victory in Spain.

For the next 24 years, Italy would regularly go close, but the leading league clubs kept the flag flying with a string of European successes, Juventus and AC Milan enjoying periods of dominance, while Parma and Internazionale also lifted trophies.

The Italian league had been founded in the late 1920s, under the Fascist regime of Benito Mussolini. Turin-based Juventus, funded by rich industrialists, proved to be the outstanding pre-war team, winning the league title five years in a row and providing the backbone of the national team that lifted the World Cup in 1934.

Torino also won five consecutive titles in the 1940s with an outstanding squad that was so strong the national team used 10 of their players in one match. However, the Torino squad was tragically killed by a 1949 plane crash returning from playing a testimonial match in Lisbon. The disaster, at Superga, wrecked the national team's prospects ahead of their World Cup defence in Brazil in 1950.

In the following years, clubs invested financial strength in foreign players, which did nothing to help rebuild the national team, but ensured strength in Europe, where during the early 1960s, clubs such as AC Milan and their bitter rivals Inter ruled the scene, as they would again during the late '80s and '90s, when Arrigo Sacchi's Milan dominated thanks to their Dutch trio of Ruud Gullit, Frank Rijkaard and Marco van Basten.

Doping and match-fixing would mar the Juventus successes of the mid-1990s and into the 2000s, when they were relegated to Serie B as punishment. They had been under investigation for the illegal administration of unspecified stimulants to their players when telephone-tap investigators uncovered a match manipulation system created by club director Luciano Moggi. Evidence produced at a variety of hearings suggested that Moggi had used his influence with referees to generate yellow and red cards and suspensions for opposing players before they

were due to play against Juventus and that he had also put pressure on players and coaches over transfers and even national team selection. He went to prison and Juve went down, but have been reborn in the past few years and under Antonio Conte, and with inspirational midfielder Andrea Pirlo steering the ship, they rule once more.

ABOVE The great Roberto Baggio stands dejected after missing his penalty in the 1994 final

GREAT NATIONS

HOLLAND

Dutch football is synonymous with "total football"— the all-action strategy pioneered by Ajax Amsterdam under the inspiration of the great Johan Cruyff in the early 1970s.

Yet while Cruyff provided the brains and leadership out on the pitch, it was Ajax's visionary coach Rinus Michels who masterminded the strategy. With two fabulous feet and mesmeric ball skills, Cruyff was at the heart of the Holland team—all of their goals at the 1974 World Cup finals either started or ended with a contribution from their captain. Cruyff was supported by Johan Neeskens out of midfield, Ruud Krol from full-back, and the duo of Johnny Rep and Rob Rensenbrink in attack. At the peak of their success, the team were nicknamed "Clockwork

RIGHT Rinus Michels, the figurehead behind Total Football

Orange," after the coour of their famous shirts as well as their precision passing.

The Dutch again finished as runner-up at the World Cup finals, even without Cruyff at the helm, in 1978, yet in terms of international status, Holland had been late developers.

A crucial reason was the fact that it was not until the the mid-1950s that domestic clubs such as Feyenoord, Sparta and Excelsior—notably all from Rotterdam—forced the recognition of professionalism, even initially part-time. The amateur status that ruled the Dutch game previously meant star players, such as Faas Wilkes, had been forced abroad to the likes of Italy and Spain to earn a living from their talent. Feyenoord became the first Dutch club to reach the semi-final stage of the European Cup in 1963, losing narrowly to Benfica. This was the start of a remarkable era, during which the Rotterdam club won the domestic double—league and cup—in both 1965 and 1969. They then became the first Dutch club to win a European crown in 1970, edging past Celtic in extra time with a team that included outside left Coen Moulijn—one of the finest of Dutch players before the Ajax era.

Holland's national team had not qualified for the World Cup finals since the inter-war period but this, and the entire international status of Dutch football, changed with the explosive eruption of Ajax, who had reached the 1969 European Cup final and then won it in 1971, 1972, and 1973, before Cruyff was sold to Barcelona. Cruyff stepped out of national team football at the end of 1977 but Dutch football continued to produce an apparently endless stream of talented players and coaches. PSV Eindhoven won the 1988 European Cup under the wily management of Guus Hiddink, while Holland finally lifted their first international trophy, the European Championship, in West Germany six weeks later. The Dutch national hero at that time was AC Milan—and former Ajax—striker Marco van Basten, who scored a group stage hat-trick against England, a semi-final winner against West Germany and a magnificent volleyed winning goal against the Soviet Union in the final at Munich's Olympic Stadium.

Controversy was never far away whenever the Dutch faced their German arch rivals. A spitting incident involving Holland midfielder Frank Rijkaard and German striker Rudi Völler marred a dramatic clash in the second round of the 1990 World Cup finals in Italy, which Holland lost 2-1. Too often at major tournaments, Holland's potential has been undermined by squabbling between players and coaching staff over tactics and team selection. Inspirational forward Ruud Gullit, a former World and European Player of the Year, refused to put on the shirt and play for Holland at the 1990 World Cup finals. Hiddink sent midfielder Edgar Davids home during the 1996 European Championship after internal squabbling among the squad.

The unpredictability of the Dutch game's biggest names was evident up to the spring of 2008. Van Basten, by now manager of Holland, agreed to return to Ajax as coach after the European Championships in Austria and Switzerland, with Cruyff as a senior consultant. However, Cruyff had barely been confirmed in the role before he withdrew in an apparent disagreement with Van Basten—his one-time protégé—over youth strategy. This is a sector that has become more crucial than ever to the Dutch game. The Ajax youth set-up is famed worldwide, with its players coached in a style and tactical system imposed on all the teams right through to the senior professionals. The club raises significant income selling players to the big leagues in England, Italy, and Spain to supplement its income from regular annual participation in European competitions, and it was from this foundation it lifted the country's only Champions League crown, in 1995.

The domestic game has struggled to keep up with the riches elsewhere, but on the international stage, the Dutch remain strong and creative candidates for silverware, and lost their third World Cup final against Spain four years ago.

ABOVE Marco van Basten fires home spectacularly in the 1988 European Championship final

GREAT NATIONS MOMENTS

RIGHT Pelé celebrates Brazil's first in the 1970 World Cup final victory

BELOW Fabio Capello (front, left) lines up for Italy against England in 1973

ABOVE North Korea and Portugal emerge for their sensational 1966 World Cup tie

BELOW The Soviet Union greet their English host fans in 1966

RIGHT Franz Beckenbauer betters rival captain Johan Cruyff in the 1974 World Cup final

1970s   1980s   1990s   2000s

ABOVE Argentina poised to win their first World Cup, in 1978

RIGHT England line up, optimistically, ahead of their 1982 World Cup assault

BELOW Holland in 1978 — about to finish World Cup runners-up once more

ABOVE Didier Six opens up for France against Czechoslovakia in 1982

ABOVE Mexico head for a 2-1 defeat by Portugal in Germany in 2006

LEFT Gary Lineker's penalty goal against West Germany in 1990 is not enough for England

GREAT NATIONS

ENGLAND

England lays justifiable claim to be the home and birthplace of football—the game itself is thought to originate in the Middle Ages, but its rules weren't formalised until the mid-19th century.

The formation of the Football Association in 1863, the first FA Cup competition in 1872 and the introduction of a revolutionary league system in 1888 were major events in the game's development, and they all happened in England. Despite this, the country has only one World Cup triumph to date; the 1966 tournament, played at home. That victory was founded upon Alf Ramsey's coaching, Bobby Moore's captaincy, Bobby Charlton's long-range shooting, and Geoff Hurst's famous hat-trick in the final against West Germany.

Yet historically, England have underachieved. Bobby Robson's team, inspired by Paul Gascoigne and Gary Lineker, came closest to tasting success by reaching the 1990 World Cup semi-final in Italy, but since then, the *Three Lions* failed to qualify in 1994 and have never gone beyond the last eight.

The FA had initially turned their noses up at the concept of a World Cup, and it was not until 1950 that England even entered. At club level, there was a similar story, with Chelsea, the champions, ordered not to enter the inaugural European Cup in 1955. Once the door was opened, Manchester United claimed England's first European Cup by beating Benfica in 1968, some five years after Bill Nicholson's Tottenham had become the first English winners of a European trophy in the Cup Winners' Cup. Under the management of Sir Alex Ferguson, United would win a unique hat-trick for an English club in 1999, with victory in the Premier League, FA Cup, and the Champions League. A third Champions League triumph followed in 2008, when United defeated Chelsea in a penalty

shoot-out in Moscow in the first all-English final in the competition's history.

It was in the 1970s and early '80s, however, that English clubs really dominated, with the European Cup won by an English side for five successive years, yet the national team continued to struggle despite the successes of Liverpool, Nottingham Forest and Aston Villa.

The dark side of the English passion for football has been a long history of hooliganism, which began in the 1960s and developed over the next 20 years. Leeds United were barred from

RIGHT Paul Gascoigne is inconsolable after defeat to West Germany in 1990

European football due to their fans' behaviour, and after the Heysel disaster of 1985, when 39 Juventus fans died in Brussels after being charged by Liverpool followers, the ban was extended to all English clubs for five years.

The Hillsborough tragedy, in which 96 supporters were killed, in 1989, brought calls for safety to be improved, and all-seater demands were imposed on all major sports venues, leading to the building of new grounds and total redevelopment of others. The pace of the stadia and security revolution persuaded UEFA to grant England hosting rights to the European Championship finals in 1996, which proved to be a huge success on and off the pitch. Suddenly football was in fashion once more, thanks in no small part to the performance of Terry Venables's side in that tournament, losing to Germany in the semi-finals on penalties.

English football has led the world game in many ways. In the late 1920s and early 1930s it was Arsenal, thanks to manager Herbert Chapman and forward Charles Buchan, that conceived the "WM" system, a formation, that dominated the sport for four decades until Ramsey's "Wingless Wonders" of '66, while off the pitch the lucrative FA Premier League's 1992 launch have helped tempt over some of the world's top talents.

Manchester United, among the world's best supported clubs, have dominated since 1992, with big-spending Chelsea and Manchester City now wanting a slice of glory as ownership shifts from British families to international businessmen, oligarchs and dynasties. English football is now more popular than ever, though with foreign players and foreign ownership, it is the least English it has ever been.

ABOVE Bobby Moore receives the Jules Rimet trophy from the Queen in 1966

FRANCE

France's contribution to football goes far beyond its national team's significant achievements on the pitch. French administrator Jules Rimet was the brains behind the creation of the World Cup finals.

FOOTBALL FACTS

LAST 10 CHAMPIONS

2004 Lyon

2005 Lyon

2006 Lyon

2007 Lyon

2008 Lyon

2009 Bordeaux

2010 Marseille

2011 Lille

2012 Montpellier

2013 Paris St-Germain

Another French administrator, Henri Delaunay, paved the way for the European Championship. Gabriel Hanot, editor of the daily sports newspaper *L'Equipe*, was the creative force behind the European Cup.

On the field, France's greatest achievement remains their World Cup victory, on home soil, in 1998. Inspired by midfielder Zinedine Zidane, they saw off Paraguay, Italy and Croatia in the knockout stages before crushing Brazil 3-0 in the final.

Two years later, David Trezeguet scored the golden goal that beat Italy 2-1 in the 2000 European Championship final. Zidane, who retired from international football after the 2004 European Championship, made an impressive comeback as France reached the final of the 2006 World Cup, but was sent off for headbutting an opponent during a 1-1 draw with Italy in which he scored, only to watch from the sidelines as the Italians won on penalties.

One of the dominant personalities in the modern French game has been Michel Platini. In 1984, he towered over the Euro finals—in France—scoring nine goals as the home team went on to beat Spain 2-0 in the final. Later, Platini progressed to become the country's national manager and president of the organising committee for the 1998 World Cup before being elected UEFA president in 2007.

French club football has often been overshadowed by the national team, as so many home-grown players have moved abroad. One of the persisting problems for the league has been the lack of an established, successful club in the French capital, Paris. The power of the French game has resided largely in the provinces—the comparatively new team Paris Saint-Germain once reached the final of the now-defunct European Cup Winners' Cup, but sank back into the second tier before recently being taken over

RIGHT The French team before the 1998 final

by rich owners from the Middle East, who by signing stars such as Zlatan Ibraimovic, Ezequiel Lavezzi and Edinson Cavani, look set to turn the Parisians into major European contenders.

The first French club to make an international impression was Reims. Prompted by forward Raymond Kopa, they reached the first European Cup final in 1956 and were losing finalists again three years later. Kopa was the playmaker for the France side that finished third in the 1958 World Cup and helped set up most of Just Fontaine's record tally of 13 goals. Fontaine had been brought into the team only at the last minute because of injury to Reims team-mate René Bliard.

No French club managed to reach the European Cup final again until the eruption of Marseille in the late 1980s and early 1990s. The team were bankrolled by the flamboyant businessman-turned-politician Bernard Tapie. A team starring top-scoring French player Jean-Pierre Papin and England winger Chris Waddle finished as runner-up in the 1991 European Cup, losing on penalties to Red Star Belgrade. Two years later, Marseille defeated AC Milan 1-0, but that triumph was tarnished almost immediately as Marseille were thrown out of European competition over a domestic match-fixing scandal that saw Tapie imprisoned. Other French football clubs and their directors were punished, with sentences ranging from suspensions to fines for financial irregularities.

Lyon president Jean-Michel Aulas said: "What we need in the French game is greater financial freedom to run our own affairs. Then maybe we wouldn't have these other problems. Fans demand success and directors want to give that to them, for their own reasons." Software millionaire Aulas knew his subject well. He had taken over Lyon when the club were in the second division, and supplied both financial and administrative resources to secure promotion and then a record run of seven successive league titles from 2002 to 2008. Aulas even pressed successfully for a relaxation of laws barring sports clubs from obtaining outside, foreign investment. He claimed that, without new revenue streams, French clubs could not afford to buy the best players nor could they develop stadia to such an extent that the country could ever hope to host the finals of the World Cup or European Championship.

The factor that continued to elude Aulas was success in European competitions. Lyon regularly reached the knock-out stages of the Champions League without ever reaching even the semi-finals. Saint-Etienne (1976) and AS Monaco (2004) remain the only other French clubs aside from Reims and Marseille to have reached a European Cup final. Saint-Etienne lost narrowly to Bayern Munich while AS Monaco crashed 3-0 to Porto, but with PSG making progress, there is hope for a breakthrough.

BELOW Raymond Kopa trains in 1958

GREAT NATIONS

GERMANY

Germany have long been one of the most powerful countries in international football, boasting appearances in seven World Cup finals since 1954.

They have never failed to qualify for a World Cup since entering for the first time in 1934, though they did not participate in the 1950 edition following World War II. Since then, they have never gone more than 12 years without playing in the final.

Football had difficulty establishing itself initially in Germany because of the social strength of the gymnastic movement. Attitudes changed gradually, partly because toward the end of World War I, the Kaiser ascribed British strength of character on the battlefield to the morale and physical qualities developed through the team sports played at schools and universities.

Football clubs thrived in the inter-war years even though the domestic game was riven with tension over the issue of professionalism. Even under Hitler's National Socialist government in the 1930s, football was considered a recreation, with payments to players prohibited. This did not prevent many clubs from bending the rules. The leading club in the 1930s were Schalke, from the mining town of Gelsenkirchen in the Ruhr. All their players were paid as miners. The German game was organised in a regional championship, topped off by a play-off series to decide the national champions. The play-off final regularly drew crowds of 70,000–80,000. Schalke were crowned champions six times and won the domestic cup once in the 1930s. Their forward, Fritz Szepan, led Germany to third place in the 1934 World Cup.

After the war, political reality saw Germany divided into west and east. Soviet-supported East Germany developed its own football federation and league, but although it became a force in international swimming and athletics, it did not replicate this success in football. East Germany only ever qualified for the World Cup finals in 1974, and in the same year, Magdeburg won the nation's only European club trophy by taking the Cup Winners' Cup.

RIGHT Jurgen Klinsmann and Bastian Schweinsteiger in 2006

In contrast, football in West Germany went from strength to strength. Wily coach Sepp Herberger and captain Fritz Walter guided the West German team to a shock victory over hot favourites Hungary in the final of the 1954 World Cup in Switzerland. The victory was known as the "miracle of Berne", because Hungary—as Olympic champions—had not been beaten for four years, and quickly took a two-goal lead.

Further World Cup triumphs followed in 1974 and in 1990, when the Germans managed to overcome first Johan Cruyff and then Diego Maradona, having lost their previous final to England in 1966.

In 1990, the collapse of the Berlin Wall led to the reunification of Germany and the integration of East German football into the German football federation. Germany, whether West or unified, have also finished as World Cup runner-up four times (1966, 1982, 1986, and 2002) and third four times (1976, 1992, 2006 and 2010). They have also won the European Championship three times (1972, 1980, and 1996) and three times finished as runner-up (1976, 1992, and 2008).

A significant factor in the national team's success was the creation of the unified, fully professional Bundesliga in 1963. Bayern Munich have been the dominant force over the past 50 years, and in the past few years have used their financial muscle to become a European superpower.

The greatest personality to emerge from within Bayern was Franz Beckenbauer, known as "Der Kaiser," who netted 68 goals in 62 games for his country, including the winning goal in the 1974 final against Holland. As captain and sweeper, Beckenbauer led Bayern to a European Cup hat-trick (1974, 1975, and 1976). He was ably supported by a host of stars that included goalkeeper Sepp Maier, full-back Paul Breitner, midfielder Uli Hoeness, and the greatest goalscorer of the time, Gerd Müller.

Beckenbauer later coached West Germany to 1990 World Cup victory over Argentina in Italy, having guided them to the final four years earlier, and later oversaw the successful bid to host the 2006 tournament, in which Jurgen Klinsmann's entertaining side finished third.

Despite problems with hooliganism, German football continues to thrive, and the Bundesliga recently overtook England's Premier League as the world's most profitable. That, added to the success of Bayern and Borussia Dortmund, who in 2013 competed in the first all-German Champions League final, offers a bright future.

ABOVE Franz Beckenbauer challenges Johan Neeskens in the 1974 World Cup final

GREAT NATIONS

PORTUGAL

The Portuguese team are often known as the "Brazilians of Europe," thanks to the flamboyance of Eusébio in the 1960s, the "golden generation" of Luis Figo, João Pinto, and Rui Costa in the 1990s, and the country's latest idol, Cristiano Ronaldo.

Traditionally the power of the Portuguese game has been dominated by the three leading clubs of Benfica, Porto, and Sporting Lisbon. Only Belenenses in 1948 and Boavista in 2001 have broken their monopoly of the league since its formation in 1934. Benfica lead the way with 32 championships, with Porto, recently gaining ground, on 27.

Football was introduced to Portugal through the ports in the 19th century, but the relatively small size of the country meant the national team had little or no impact internationally. However, Portugal had a source of playing talent in their African territories, such as Angola and Mozambique.

An increasing number of African players were imported by the clubs and, from the late 1950s, also selected for the national team. Such players included Benfica's goalkeeper Jose Alberto Costa Pereira, striker Jose Aguas, and the two forwards

RIGHT Luis Figo at the 2006 World Cup

Joaquin Santana and Mario Coluna. All four were members of Benfica's European Cup-winning side that, in 1961, defeated favourites Barcelona 3-2 in Switzerland. Simultaneously, Benfica had also acquired the greatest African discovery of all in young striker Eusébio. A year later he scored two thundering goals as Benfica defeated Real Madrid 5-3 to retain the trophy. Eusébio would also lead Benfica to three more finals, albeit finishing on the losing side against AC Milan (1963), Internazionale (1965), and Manchester United (1968).

A mixture of Sporting Lisbon's defense, along with Benfica's midfield and attack, provided the backbone for the Portuguese national side that finished third in their first ever World Cup finals, Eusébio a nine-goal top scorer in England in 1966. Like the country itself, Portuguese football suffered from economic decline in the following decades but a new era dawned with triumphs in the 1989 and 1991 World Youth Cups. Ever since the emergence of that so-called "golden generation" on the senior stage, Portugal have been a threat at major tournaments. Portugal reached the semi-final stage of the 2000 European Championship in Belgium and Holland.

At the same time, Porto emerged as the dominant club in the country under coach Jose Mourinho, who delivered victory in the 2003 UEFA Cup and then, more impressively, in the Champions League a year later —before being lured away to Chelsea. The inability to compete in wages with the giants of England, Italy, and Spain meant the departure from Portugal of home-grown stars such as Luis Figo, Deco and Cristiano Ronaldo in the past 20 years, but the national team has been strong.

In 2003, the Portuguese Football Federation hired Luiz Felipe Scolari, Brazil's 2002 World Cup-winning coach, to bring the competitive best out of the country's depth of talent. Scolari succeeded to a qualified degree. Portugal finished as runner-up on home territory in the 2004 European Championship—losing to outsiders Greece in the final—and were fourth at the 2006 World Cup finals in Germany. Under Carlos Queiroz in 2010, they were eliminated by neighbours and eventual champions Spain, ensuring their wait for a major title goes on.

ABOVE Eusebio is consoled after England beat Portugal in the 1966 semi-final

GREAT NATIONS

SPAIN

Three major consecutive honours have finally ended Spain's years of underachievement, with real hopes that they could become the first team in 50 years to retain the World Cup.

No country had been quite as underwhelming as Spain, who until 2008 had only the 1964 European Championship in their trophy cabinet. Since then, first under Luis Aragones and then Vicente Del Bosque, they have produced some of the finest football the world has ever seen, their "tiki-taka" short, passing game, based on the style exploited by the great Barcelona side of the last decade, blowing opponents away.

Spain have a history rich in great players and their recent successes ensured their best players can claim equal billing in the hall of fame with previous heroes. These include legends of the 1920s and 1930s, when goalkeeper Ricardo Zamora, defender Jacinto Quincoces, and inside forward Luis Regueiro helped Spain become the first foreign nation to beat England, 4-3 in Madrid in 1929.

RIGHT Emilio Butragueno in action in Mexico in 1986

At the end of the 1950s, a team packed with stars such as Alfredo Di Stefano, Ladislav Kubala, and Luis Suarez saw Spain ranked as favourites to win the inaugural European Championship. However, when the 1960 quarter-final draw matched Spain against the Soviet Union, dictator Francisco Franco ordered the team to withdraw on political grounds. Even so long after the Spanish Civil War, Spain still had no diplomatic relations with countries from the Communist Bloc.

In 1964, on home soil, Spain won its first title. Relations with the East had thawed significantly enough for the USSR squad to be allowed entry into Spain for the European Championship, and strikers Jesus Pereda and Marcelino each scored in Spain's 2-1 victory over the Soviets.

Spain's failure to achieve national team success in the following four decades remains one of football's mysteries, yet the best they could point to was a runner-up spot at the 1984 European Championship finals and a stunning 5-1 win over Denmark in the second round of the 1986 World Cup finals, when Emilio Butragueno, nicknamed "the Vulture", scored four goals.

It was all put to rest when first, Fernando Torres struck to give a 1-0 win over Germany in the final of Euro 2008, and then two years later Andres Iniesta netted in injury time to deliver the world title at the expense of the Dutch. At Euro 2012, they became the first side to successfully defend the Henri Delaunay trophy, beating Italy 4-0 in the final.

At club level, success has been varied and wide-ranging. Real Madrid were Europe's first club champions in 1956 and retained the trophy for the next four years, during a period of total domination in which the team enthralled with their victories in an entertaining manner. With nine European Cups, two UEFA Cups, and 32 domestic league titles, Real Madrid have their own special place in the history books. They also led the way in European stadium development, which they owed to the vision of Santiago Bernabeu—a former player and coach, who became president in 1943. Bernabeu issued bonds to finance the building of a new stadium that was opened in 1947, and named the Bernabeu Stadium. Its capacity was increased in the late 1950s to 125,000, as fans flocked to watch their heroes and superstars at work. In

terms of power and ambition, however, Barcelona can rival Real, claiming a unique loyalty on and off the field. Although the club has never dominated the European Cup or Champions League in the manner of their bitter rivals, Barcelona are currently enjoying their richest period, claiming their fourth European title, and third in six years, in 2011. Between them, the two great rivals remain the most popular destinations for the world's best players. In the summer of 2013, Brazilian sensation Neymar joined Barça, while Real broke the world transfer record to land Gareth Bale from Tottenham.

ABOVE Captain Iker Casillas after winning the 2010 World Cup

GREAT NATIONS

RUSSIA

Europe's most populous nation has rarely punched its weight in international football. So far, its greatest days came in the early 1960s, while it was a part of the Soviet Union.

Moscow, the capital of the USSR, has been the central force in its national football, boasting all the major clubs—Dynamo, Spartak, Torpedo, Lokomotiv and CSKA—and had all the finest players. The size of the country made it difficult for any other clubs to compete effectively until air travel was possible. Even that was a risk, with the entire first team squad of Pakhtakor Tashkent killed when their plane crashed in 1979.

In the mid-1960s, however, major powers were emerging in the club game in Georgia and Ukraine especially, and also in Armenia and Belarus. Dynamo Tbilisi, Dynamo Kiev, Dynamo Minsk, and Ararat Yerevan may have owed their creation to the Soviet model but all developed a style of football very different to the physical Moscow style. Tbilisi and Kiev played football with a Latin-style touch of flair. Kiev twice won in the European Cup Winners' Cup and Tbilisi won it once.

The Soviet Communist attitude to sport brought other complications. The USSR ignored FIFA and would not compete internationally until after World War II. A tour of Britain by Dynamo Moscow in the winter of 1945 marked a slight thaw. More than 100,000 curious Londoners

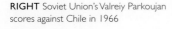

RIGHT Soviet Union's Valreiy Parkoujan scores against Chile in 1966

turned out to see the tourists at Chelsea's Stamford Bridge. Two years later the Soviet Union joined FIFA on condition that it could have a permanent vice-president.

By definition, Soviet footballers were amateurs, not paid for playing football though they were paid for their nominal roles in the armed services or other professions. The Soviet Union felt free to send its strongest possible team to the Olympics, while Western European rivals were weakened by the transparency of their own players' professional status. The Soviet national team competed internationally for the first time at the 1952 Olympic Games, and they duly won it four years later in Melbourne, Australia. Their heroes were world-class footballers, goalkeeper Lev Yashin, and left-half skipper Igor Netto. Yashin was the hero again when the Soviets won the inaugural 1960 European Championship. The Soviet Union lost the 1964 final 2-1 to Spain and finished fourth in the 1966 World Cup finals.

Since then, Russia have underachieved, qualifying for only six World Cups prior to 2014 (though Oleg Salenko became the first player to score five goals in one World Cup game in 1994), when Italian veteran coach Fabio Capello will try to improve upon the good work of Guus Hiddink at Euro 2008, the Dutchman leading the Russians to the semi-finals.

The change in Russia's balance of power is reflected in the league honours list when the Soviet Union was finally wiped off the map after the experiment with perestroika undermined the entire system. Dynamo Kiev had won 13 league titles in the Soviet era, Spartak Moscow 12, Dynamo Moscow 11, CSKA Moscow seven, and Lokomotiv Moscow three. Yet not once in the Soviet era did a club from the Russian Republic win a European trophy. That feat had to wait until 2005 when CSKA Moscow beat Sporting Lisbon 3-1 in the UEFA Cup final. Zenit St. Petersburg followed their example in 2008, when they also won the UEFA Cup, beating Rangers. Those achievements demonstrated how far Russian clubs have come since the breakup of the Soviet Union and the formation of a Russian league—then virtually bankrupt—in 1992.

The collapse of central funding for football clubs from the various state organisations threw

the Russian game into turmoil. Within a decade, only Lokomotiv were still in the controlling, supporting hands of the railway unions. All the other clubs had long since been cast adrift by the secret police (Dynamo), army (CSKA), and farms (Spartak).

The domestic game was rescued by the oligarchs who had taken massive financial advantage of the collapse of Communism and the bargain-basement sell-offs of the major utilities. Roman Abramovich's oil company Sibneft originally supported CSKA and the Russian energy giant Gazprom funded the 2007 champions Zenit. The outcome has been that Russian clubs now import star players from all over the world, and can compete with the financial muscle of their western rivals. Now, they must challenge on the field too.

ABOVE Oleg Salenko scored five in the 6-1 win over Cameroon at USA 1994

GREAT NATIONS

REST OF THE WORLD

From small nations such as Luxembourg and San Marino to the array of African sides and former Soviet states, the status and power of world football is forever changing.

ALBANIA (Europe): Despite being among UEFA's founder members in 1954, Albanian football has been hampered by the country's poverty and isolation. They beat newly-crowned European champions Greece in the 2006 World Cup qualifiers, but are still waiting to reach their first tournament.

ALGERIA (Africa): Having broken away from France in 1958, Algeria's footballers beat eventual finalists West Germany at the 1982 World Cup thanks to Lakhdar Belloumi's goal but were eliminated in a convenient draw between the West Germans and Austria. Their finest moment came when Moussa Saïb captained the hosts to success at the 1990 African Cup of Nations. JS Kabylie have dominated at home, having won 14 league titles, but ES Setif are the current team to beat.

ANDORRA (Europe): Not too much can be expected of a country with a population of 72,000, squeezed between Spain and France. Andorra's team, largely made up of part-timers, only began playing international football in 1997.

ANGOLA (Africa): On the rise after years of being constrained by civil war and having their finest players poached by Portugal, Angola made an encouraging World Cup finals debut in 2006. Petro Atlético have been crowned as Angolan champions 15 times.

AUSTRALIA (Asia): After achieving nothing at the 1974 World Cup, the "Socceroos" did not return until 2006, when Dutch manager Guus Hiddink made effective use of such talents as Tim Cahill, Harry Kewell, and Mark Viduka. Australia left the uncompetitive Oceania Football Federation for Asia later that year, and have since qualified for the 2010 and 2014 World Cups. The national A-League kicked off in 2005–06, and has attracted big name Europeans like Alessandro Del Piero to the region.

AUSTRIA (Europe): The so-called "Wunderteam" of the 1930s, inspired by playmaker Matthias Sindelar and coach Hugo Meisl, finished fourth at the 1934 World Cup. Austrian coach Ernst Happel took Holland to the 1978 World Cup final; the Ernst Happel Stadium in Vienna is named after him. The stadium was also the venue for the Euro 2008 final. Rapid Vienna lead the way in home games, with an astonishing 32 league titles, yet in recent years Red Bull Salzburg have won four of the past seven.

AZERBAIJAN (Europe): This former Soviet state has struggled since independence despite a spell in charge by World Cup-winning Brazil captain Carlos Alberto. The main stadium in Baku is named after linesman Tofik Bakhmarov, who decided England's third goal in the 1966 World Cup final really did cross the line.

BELARUS (Europe): Midfielder Alexander Hleb put Belarus on the map with his club displays in Germany, England and Spain, but the former Soviet state narrowly missed out on a place at the 2002 World Cup finals after a last-gasp defeat to Wales. BATE Borisov have

BELOW Bulgaria's Hristo Stoichkov (left) celebrates another goal for Barcelona

won the past seven titles, and became the first Belorussian club to qualify for the Champions League group stages.

BELGIUM (Europe): Despite its small size, Belgium reached the 1980 European Championship final, beat holders Argentina in the opening game of the 1982 World Cup, and finished fourth in 1986 under Guy Thys. Goalkeeper Jean-Marie Pfaff, defender Eric Gerets, midfielder Jan Ceulemans, and forward Enzo Scifo formed the side's spine. Anderlecht have won not only a record 32 league titles but one UEFA Cup, a pair of European Super Cups, twice been crowned European Champions, and twice won the Cup Winners' Cup.

BOLIVIA (South America): The Hernando Siles Stadium in La Paz is one of the world's highest playing surfaces, at 3,637 metres above sea level. The national side have struggled, although they did win the 1963 Copa America courtesy of a 5-4 win over Brazil, and famously beat Argentina 6-1 in a 2009 World Cup qualifying game. Bolívar FC have won the domestic league 18 times.

BOSNIA-HERZEGOVINA (Europe): This former Yugoslav republic was accepted by UEFA in 1991, but despite a wealth of talent had been able to reach a major tournament until they qualified for the 2014 World Cup. Željezničar have won five Premier League titles.

BULGARIA (Europe): This is one of Eastern Europe's most consistent producers of quality players. The national team's finest achievement was in reaching the World Cup semi-finals in 1994 with a team starring the legendary Hristo Stoichkov and Emil Kostadinov, while Dimitar Berbatov and Stiliyan Petrov have been the outstanding performers of the last decade. The record domestic champions are CSKA Sofia with 31 league titles to their credit, while city rivals Levski have 26.

BURKINA FASO (Africa): Burkina Faso lost to Algeria in qualifying play-offs ahead of the 2014 World Cup, which meant 2013 will be remembered with disappointment despite

reaching the final of the African Cup of Nations for the first time. They have never appeared at a World Cup finals.

CAMEROON (Africa): Known as the "Indomitable Lions", Cameroon were the surprise package at the 1990 World Cup. They upset holders Argentina and pushed England hard in the quarter-finals, spearheaded by veteran striker Roger Milla. Barcelona's Samuel Eto'o holds the scoring record for the African Cup of Nations, a competition that Cameroon have won four times. Canon Yaoundé have won the African Championship three times to match their 10 domestic league titles.

CANADA (Central and North America): Often over-shadowed by CONCACAF rivals such as Mexico and the US, Canada still await their second World Cup qualification, having lost all three group games in 1986.

CHILE (South America): Strike duo Marcelo Salas and Iván Zamorano helped guide Chile to the 1998 World Cup quarter-finals. But Chile's best run came when hosting the 1962 tournament, eventually losing to Brazil in a fiery semi-final. Colo-Colo have won 31 Chilean league titles, more than double the tally of their main rivals.

ABOVE Samuel Eto'o acknowledges the cheers greeting another of his goals for Cameroon

REST OF THE WORLD

CHINA (Asia): The national team faced Manila in Asia's first international match in 1913, but made their World Cup finals debut only in 2002 when they lost all three matches under Serb Bora Milutinovic. Versatile midfielder Zheng Zhi captained the side that hosted but lost the 2004 Asian Cup final to Japan.

COLOMBIA (South America): Carlos Valderrama, Faustino Asprilla and goalkeeper Rene Higuita (famous for his "scorpion kick") made Colombia one of the world's most entertaining yet underachieving sides in the 1990s. Iván Córdoba's goal beat Mexico in the 2001 Copa America final. Club Deportivo Los Millonarios, whose riches lured stars such as Alfredo Di Stefano to a breakaway league in the 1940s and 1950s, have picked up 14 league titles.

CONGO DR (Africa): Under their former name of Zaire, they became the first black African side to reach the World Cup finals. But at the 1974 competition they were humiliated by eventual champions West Germany. They were crowned African champions in 1968 and 1974, and have produced several excellent players for other countries, such as France's Claude Makelele. Lomana Tresor Lua Lua was a Premier League regular at Newcastle United and Portsmouth. Étoile du Congo, of Brazzaville, have won 12 league titles.

COSTA RICA (Central and North America): Consistent performers who reached their first World Cup in 1990 under charismatic coach Bora Milutinovic. They also appeared at the 2002 and 2006 tournaments. with striker Paolo Wanchope as the figurehead. They have won nine CONCACAF championships, though surprisingly none since 1989. Former CONCACAF club champions Deportivo Saprissa have a record 29 domestic league titles.

CROATIA (Europe): This Balkan country taught England a footballing lesson in qualifiers for the 2008 European Championship—just as they did to Germany on their way to third place at the 1998 World Cup. Back then they were inspired by the likes of Robert Prosinecki, Golden Boot winner Davor Šuker, and future national coach Slaven Bilic. More recently, Brazilian-born striker Eduardo and nimble midfielders Luka Modric and Ivan Rakitic have caught the eye. Dinamo Zagreb have won the league 15 times since Croatia achieved independence from the former Yugoslavia in 1992.

CYPRUS (Europe): Cyprus have pulled off some unlikely results down the years, but have never appeared in a major finals, missing out on a European Championship play-off spot in 2000 by a single point. APOEL Nicosia, who have featured in the Champions League, have won the Cypriot league 22 times and are its pre-eminent club.

CZECH REPUBLIC (Europe): The Czechs formed the larger part of the old Czechoslovakia, which reached the World Cup Final in 1934 and 1962—when Czech wing-half Josef Masopust was voted European Footballer of the Year. Czechoslovakia won the European Championship in 1976 thanks to a penalty shootout victory against West Germany. The "new" Czech Republic side lost the Euro 1996 final to the Germans on a golden goal. Sparta Prague have dominated domestic football, winning 11 championships since the Czechs and Slovaks split in 1993. The best Czech players inevitably move to the big clubs in the West. Pavel Nedved of Juventus was voted European Footballer of the Year in 2003, while Petr Cech was a Champions League winner with Chelsea in 2012.

DENMARK (Europe): The Danes' greatest triumph came in 1992, when they beat Germany 2-0 to win the European Championships. The Danes also reached the semi-finals of Euro 1984 and the last 16 of the 1986 World Cup. Denmark has produced many stars for rich Western clubs, such as the

ABOVE Colombia's Carlos Valderrama has earned more than 100 caps playing for his country

Laudrup brothers (Michael and Brian), Morten Olsen, and Manchester United great Peter Schmeichel. FC Copenhagen have won nine titles since 2001.

ECUADOR (South America): Qualified for the last two World Cup finals tournaments and reached the last 16 in 2006, losing to England. They will be in Brazil in 2014. Domestically, Sporting Club Barcelona have won 14 titles, one more than El Nacional.

EGYPT (Africa): Won the African Cup of Nations for a record seventh time in 2010, but have struggled on the world stage with only two World Cup appearances, the last in 1990, and the troubled Egyptians missed out on 2014 with defeat to Ghana. At home, Al-Ahly have dominated.

EL SALVADOR (Central and North America): Reached the 1970 World Cup finals by beating local rivals Honduras. This stoked up an already tense situation between the two countries, culminating in a six-day conflict that became known as "the football war". They also qualified in 1982, but have lost all six games they've played.

ESTONIA (Europe): Estonia are yet to make their mark internationally, though goalkeeper Mart Poom was a Premier League regular at several sides. Flora Tallinn have dominated the domestic championship since Estonia became a republic in 1992, taking nine titles.

FAROE ISLANDS (Europe): Minnows of European football, the Faroes beat Lithuania in 2009 to record their first competitive win in seven years, the same year beating neighbours Iceland in a friendly.

FINLAND (Europe): Noted for producing players for Europe's big clubs, such as Jari Litmanen (Ajax) and Sami Hyypia (Liverpool), Finland have nonetheless struggled on the international stage and still await a major tournament appearance. The domestic championship has been dominated by HJK Helsinki, United Tampere, and Haka Valkeakoski.

GEORGIA (Europe): Their greatest moment came in 1981, when Dinamo Tbilisi, inspired by midfielder David Kipiani, beat Carl Zeiss Jena

2-1 in the European Cup Winners' Cup final. The national side is currently coached by one of Georgia's greatest players, Temuri Ketsbaia.

GHANA (Africa): Ghana reached the quarter-finals of the 2010 World Cup, and were within a penalty kick of becoming the first Africans ever to make the last four, only for Asamoah Gyan to miss his spot kick before the South Americans won a shootout. Featuring stars such as Michael Essien and Kevin-Prince Boateng, they will hope to impress in Brazil. Ghana have won the African Cup of Nations four times. Asante Kotoko have won 22 domestic titles.

GREECE (Europe): Shock winners of the 2004 European Championship when Otto Rehhagel's side beat hosts Portugal 1-0 in the final with a goal from Angelos Charisteas. They then failed to qualify for the 2006 World Cup finals. Panathinaikos reached the 1971 European Cup final, losing to Ajax at Wembley. Olympiakos have dominated the domestic game, winning 15 of the last 17 championships. In 2008, they became the first Greek side to play in the last 16 of the Champions League.

ABOVE Theo Zagorakis, a European title-winning hero for Greece

GREAT NATIONS

REST OF THE WORLD

HAITI (Central and North America): Haiti reached the World Cup finals in 1974 when Emmanuel Sanon scored a historic goal against Italy but have not been back since. They were CONCACAF champions in 1957 and 1973.

HONDURAS (Central and North America): Reaching the World Cup finals for the first time in 1982, they had been CONCACAF champions the previous year. Their team now, driven by Wilson Palacios, is probably as good as it ever has been.

HUNGARY (Europe): The "Magnificent Magyars" were the finest team in the world in the early 1950s. Led by Ferenc Puskas, they included greats such as striker Sandor Kocsis, playmaker Nandor Hidegkuti, flying winger Zoltan Czibor, goalkeeper Gyula Grocis, and wing half Jozsef Boszik. But they were shocked by West Germany in the 1954 World Cup final and the team broke up two years later after the Budapest uprising against Soviet control. A new side finished third in the 1964 European Championship and reached the 1966 World Cup quarter-finals after beating Brazil 3-1. Hungary have struggled at international level ever since. Ferencvaros have 27 titles, but Debrecen have won six of the last 10.

ICELAND (Europe): Yet to make an impact in major competitions, they are, however, well known for exporting star players, such as former Chelsea and Barcelona forward Eidur Gudjohnsen. They were beaten in a play-off for the 2014 World Cup by Croatia.

INDIA (Asia): The team reached the World Cup finals once, in 1950, but withdrew after FIFA barred them from playing in bare feet.

IRAN (Asia): Although they have reached the World Cup finals three times, they have yet to reach the last 16. They have won the Asian Cup

BELOW Haiti's Sanon runs with the ball in a 1974 World Cup match against Italy

three times. Iran's greatest player Ali Daei won 149 caps, and scored a record 35 World Cup qualifying goals.

IRAQ (Asia): Iraq won the 2007 Asian Cup, after a 1-0 win over Saudi Arabia in the final, appearing in the Confederations Cup final two years later. They have had one World Cup appearance, in 1986.

ISRAEL (Europe): Israeli clubs dominated the early years of the Asian Club Championship, before political problems forced the country out into the cold and then into UEFA. The national team were World Cup finalists in 1970.

IVORY COAST (Africa): Winners of the African Cup of Nations in 1992, the national team reached the World Cup finals for the first time in 2006 with a golden generation of players expected to perform in 2010, where they were unfortunate to be drawn alongside Brazil and Portugal. The country is most famous for exporting star players such as Didier Drogba, Salomon Kalou and the Toure brothers, Kolo and Yaya.

JAMAICA (Central and North America): Their best performance was reaching the 1998 World Cup finals with a team that included many England-based players, beating Japan in their final group game.

JAPAN (Asia): Reaching the World Cup finals in 1998, Japan advanced to a best-yet place in the last 16 on home soil in 2002, which they matched in 2010. They have won the Asian Cup four times, and are the current holders after a 1-0 win over Australia in the 2011 final. The J-League continues to develop since its formation in 1992, though most of Japan's top talents move to Europe.

KAZAKHSTAN (Europe): After gaining independence from the Soviet Union, the country

switched from the Asian Confederation to UEFA in 2002. Arguably their greatest player was Oleg Litvinenko, who died tragically in November 2007, just four days short of his 34th birthday.

KUWAIT (Asia): The national team had one appearance in the World Cup finals in 1982. They managed a draw with Czechoslovakia but lost to both England and France. During the last of these, France famously "scored" while some of the Kuwaiti players had stopped playing, having heard a whistle. They walked off the pitch in protest and resumed only after the goal was disallowed. They have previously been coached by both Carlos Alberto Parreira and Luiz Felipe Scolari.

LATVIA (Europe): Having regained their independence in 1991, they are the only Baltic team to have qualified for the European Championship finals when they upset Turkey in the qualifiers for the 2004 tournament in Portugal. At home, Skonto Riga were the dominant side during the 1990s, but have won the league just once in the last nine years, with FK Ventspils winning five of those.

LIECHTENSTEIN (Europe): One of the whipping boys of European football, comprising mainly part-timers, the tiny principality improved in the Euro 2008 qualifiers when they upset Latvia 1-0 and followed that up with a 3-0 win over Iceland. Tournament qualification remains a distant dream.

LITHUANIA (Europe): They came third in their group in both the Euro 96 and 1998 World Cup qualifying campaigns. Since then they have managed away draws with both Germany and Italy but, like many former Soviet states, they lack depth of quality as yet.

LUXEMBOURG (Europe): Historically one of Europe's minor teams, they once went 12 years without winning a competitive fixture, but beat Switzerland in 2008. They are almost exclusively part-timers, though record appearance maker Jeff Strasser had a solid Bundesliga career in Germany.

MACEDONIA (Europe): Only since the breakup of Yugoslavia have they had their own officially recognised team. The inaugural Macedonian side featured Darko Pancev, who won the European Cup with Red Star Belgrade in 1991. Away draws with England and Holland represent two of the country's modest high spots.

MALTA (Europe): With one of the oldest national associations in Europe, Malta owes much of its football fanaticism to the island's former British occupation. With a population of under 400,000, however, the national team draws from one of the smallest on the European continent. Sliema Wanderers, Floriana and Valletta have dominated the domestic league.

MEXICO (Central and North America): World Cup regulars, Mexico relied on a play-off win over New Zealand to seal a place at 2014. They reached the quarter-finals in 1970 and 1986, both times on home soil. Their 2-1 defeat by Argentina in the 2006 World Cup was regarded as one of the finest technical matches of recent tournaments. Chivas Guadalajara and Club America have 11 titles each, with many top players remaining on home soil.

MOLDOVA (Europe): Their two best-ever results came within a month of each other in the mid-1990s during the qualifiers for Euro 96, beating Georgia and Wales. Sheriff Tiraspol have won 12 of the last 13 league titles, overtaking Zimbru Chisinau as Moldova's top club.

ABOVE The Ivory Coast team before their game against Ghana in the 2008 African Cup of Nations

REST OF THE WORLD

MONTENEGRO (Europe): Came into existence only after the 2006 World Cup after being politically tied to Serbia. The 2010 tournament was their first competitive opportunity, and although they did not qualify they impressed with some excellent attacking play, and pushed England and Ukraine all the way in qualifying for 2014. It is felt the future is bright.

MOROCCO (Africa): The first African team to win a group at the World Cup (1986), finishing ahead of Portugal, Poland, and England, and also appeared in the 1994 and 1998 tournaments. Nourredine Naybet, the former Deportivo La Coruna and Tottenham defender, is their record appearance maker of all time.

NEW ZEALAND (Oceania): In a country where rugby union is king, the New Zealand football league is semi-professional. They reached the World Cup in South Africa in 2010, and drew all three games, including against Italy, making them the only unbeaten side at the tournament. They had previously qualified only once, in 1982, but lost all three games. They are now the powerful Oceanic nation after Australia's switch to the Asian confederation.

NIGERIA (Africa): With a rich footballing pedigree, Nigeria has exported a string of exceptional players to Europe, such as Jay-Jay Okocha, Nwankwo Kanu and John Mikel Obi. The current African champions, Nigeria have been at every World Cup, bar 2006, since 1994. Enyimba have been the most successful domestic club in recent years.

NORTHERN IRELAND (Europe): Fans still talk nostalgically about their heyday when they qualified for the 1982 World Cup, reaching the quarter-finals, having beaten hosts Spain. Norman

Whiteside became the youngest-ever player in the finals, at 17 years 41 days. Billy Bingham, a player in the team who had also reached the quarter-finals in 1958, was the manager and led his country to the finals again in 1986, the smallest European nation to qualify twice. Still capable of a shock, they beat England in 2005 and Spain in 2006.

NORTH KOREA (Asia): The North Koreans' shining moment came in the 1966 World Cup when they upset Italy 1-0 to gain a spot in the quarter-finals. There, they went 3-0 up against Portugal, but the brilliance of Eusébio and his four goals stopped the fairytale and the match ended with the Koreans down 5-3. Political isolation has cost their football dear, but they did qualify for the 2010 finals, where they were beaten by Brazil, Portugal and Ivory Coast.

NORWAY (Europe): The greatest moment in Norwegian football, a 2-1 win over Brazil in the 1998 World Cup, sparked wild scenes back home, four years after they had been a well-respected side at USA '94, where they were harshly eliminated at the group stage on goals scored. Rosenborg, the country's leading club, have perennially competed in the Champions League and famously beat AC Milan in 1996, but almost all of Norway's top players move abroad.

PARAGUAY (South America): Although they reached the second round of the World Cup in 1986, 1998, and 2002, they have never advanced beyond that stage. They appeared in four consecutive World Cups between 1998 and 2010, and won the Copa América 1953 and 1979, finishing runner-up to Uruguay in 2011.

PERU (South America): Peru's "golden generation" in the 1970s and early 1980s was highlighted by the skills of Teofilo Cubillas, who scored five goals in two different World Cup

ABOVE Mexico's Rafael Marquez and keeper Oswaldo Sanchez clear their lines at the 2006 World Cup

finals. Defender Hector Chumputaz was one of the first South American players to have 100 international appearances. Universitario and Alianza Lima are the top two clubs at home.

POLAND (Europe): They have twice finished third in the World Cup in 1974 and 1982, thanks to talents of outstanding players such as Zbigniew Boniek and Grzegorz Lato. Goalkeeper Jan Tomaszewski, whose performance at Wembley in 1973 prevented England reaching the World Cup finals in West Germany, remains an icon. More recently, they appeared in the 2002 and 2006 World Cups, but were eliminated at the group stage, where they also exited Euro 2012, which they joint-hosted with Ukraine.

QATAR (Asia): Opening up the domestic league to foreign players turned Qatar into an attractive and lucrative new destination for veteran stars over the last decade. Qatar's wealth has also been invested in a sports academy to help develop home-grown talent, and the country was awarded the 2022 World Cup, though there are concerns about playing football in the heat of the Qatari summer.

REPUBLIC OF IRELAND (Europe): The Irish enjoyed their most euphoric era under the guidance of Jack Charlton and his successor Mick McCarthy. They qualified for Euro 88, reached the quarter-finals of the 1990 World Cup and made the last 16 at both the 1994 and 2002 World Cups. The side gets its strength from the fact that most of the squad feature regularly in the English Premier League. They recently qualified for Euro 2012, while record goalscorer Robbie Keane is now one of the standout performers in the American MLS.

ROMANIA (Europe): The national side contested the first World Cup in 1930, and their golden generation, led by Gheorghe Hagi, reached the 1994 World Cup quarter-finals and the 1998 round of 16. They were beaten by Greece in 2014 qualification play-offs. Steaua Bucharest became the first Eastern European side to win the European Champions Cup in 1985. The domestic scene is dominated by the clubs

from Bucharest, with Steaua and Dinamo holding 42 titles between them, though CFR Cluj were champions three times between 2008 and 2012.

SAUDI ARABIA (Asia): Three-time Asian Cup champions, their former goalkeeper Mohamed Al-Deayea is the most capped international male footballer, with 181 appearances. Al-Hilal have won the league title 13 times since it began in 1972.

SCOTLAND (Europe): The first-ever international game took place between Scotland and England in 1872. The fixture remains one of football's fiercest rivalries. Scotland have never reached the second stage of an international tournament, despite a famous victory over Holland in 1978. The "Old Firm", Celtic and Rangers, have long enjoyed a near-monopoly on the Scottish Premier League, though Rangers were relegated due to financial irregularities in 2012. In 1967, Celtic became the first British team to win the European Cup. Scottish players and managers have contributed enormously to the English League, including Kenny Daglish and Graeme Sounness at Liverpool and Sir Alex Ferguson at Manchester United.

SENEGAL (Africa): Senegal stunned the world by beating defending title-holders France in the 2002 World Cup on their way to becoming only the second African team to reach the tournament's quarter-finals, but have not qualified before or since. Most members of the Senegalese squad play in Europe's top leagues.

SERBIA (Europe): They became a single footballing nation in 2006 after Montenegro gained independence, and reached the World Cup in 2010. Serbia's most powerful clubs remain the ones that dominated within the original Yugoslavia— Partizan and Red Star, both from Belgrade.

SLOVAKIA (Europe): Originally a member of FIFA in 1907, Slovakia rejoined in 1994 after the break-up of Czechoslovakia. They qualified for their first World Cup in 2010, and a memorable 3-2 victory over Italy put them into the knockout rounds.

BELOW Kenny Dalglish, hero of Scotland and Celtic

GREAT NATIONS

REST OF THE WORLD

SLOVENIA (Europe): A decade after gaining independence from Yugoslavia, Slovenia reached its first finals in the 2000 European Championship and the 2002 World Cup. NK Maribor, which beat Villarreal to win the 2006 Intertoto Cup, hold the most Slovenian league titles, with 11.

SOUTH AFRICA (Africa): They became the first African nation to host the World Cup finals in 2010, and also the first home side to be eliminated in the group stage, despite a win over France. Re-admitted to world footballing bodies in 1990 after the end of apartheid, the national team won the African Cup of Nations in 1996 after stepping in at the last minute as hosts. South African players Benni McCarthy, Mark Fish, Lucas Radebe, and Quinton Fortune were all successful at European club level.

SOUTH KOREA (Asia): With their semi-final appearance in 2002, South Korea recorded the best-ever performance by an Asian team in the World Cup. Traditionally strong in Asia, they won the first two Asian Cups. Manchester United's Park Ji-Sung is the most famous South Korean player in the world, but has now retired from international football. Seongnam Ilhwa Chunma are the K-League's most successful team with seven championship trophies.

SWEDEN (Europe): World Cup runners-up as hosts in 1958, Sweden have also reached three other semi-finals, the most recent being third place in 1994. Swedish players have been successful across Europe, and Swede Sven-Göran Eriksson won the Italian title at Lazio before managing England to three successive tournament quarter-finals. Malmö are the leading domestic title-winners with 20 and once appeared in the European Cup final. IFK are the only Swedish club to have won a European trophy, however, twice landing the UEFA Cup.

SWITZERLAND (Europe): One of Switzerland's major roles in the world game is off the pitch—hosting FIFA headquarters in Zurich and UEFA's headquarters near Geneva. Switzerland holds the dubious honour of being the only team to be eliminated from the World Cup (in 2006) in a penalty shoot-out without netting a single spot-kick. The domestic league is dominated by Grasshoppers (27 titles) and the recently resurgent FC Zurich and Basel.

TOGO (Africa): Togo's first-ever appearance in the World Cup in 2006 was blighted by a dispute over player bonuses. The federation was subsequently fined by FIFA for "behaviour unworthy of a participant in the World Cup." Tragedy struck in 2007, when 20 members of their delegation to the African Cup of Nations qualifier, including the Sports Minister but not any players, were killed in a helicopter crash. Then, in 2010, their team coach was ambushed on the way to the African Cup of Nations tournament, killing three and injuring several others. Star player Emmanuel Adebayor retired from the international game afterwards, but has since returned.

TRINIDAD AND TOBAGO (Central and North America): Ex-Manchester United striker Dwight Yorke is such a hero in Tobago that the national stadium bears his name. Other notable players to have succeeded in England include goalkeeper Shaka Hislop, Stern John, and Kenwyne Jones. Trinidad and Tobago qualified for their first World Cup in 2006 under Leo Beenhakker, where they were eliminated without scoring a goal.

TURKEY (Europe): Turkey's biggest footballing success came in the 2002 World Cup, where they finished third. Turkish teams have proved fearsome opposition in the Champions

BELOW Trinidad's Dwight Yorke strikes for goal against Paraguay

GREAT CLUBS

EUROPE

ABOVE Johan Cruyff, three times a European champion with Ajax

PAGE 136 Liverpool celebrate a goal in 2005

PAGE 137 Zarrago, Real Madrid's captain, holds aloft the European cup

AJAX AMSTERDAM (Holland)

Ajax reached their peak in the early 1970s, when they pioneered the style known as "Total Football" and won the European Cup three times in a row. Coach Rinus Michels painstakingly built the side, led by the legendary Johann Cruyff, for five years before their victories from 1971 to 1973. Cruyff was the coach when Ajax lifted their next European trophy, the Cup Winners' Cup, in 1987. The club's renowned youth system cultured another European Cup-winning side in 1995, which finished as runner-up the following season. But the effects of the "Bosman Rule" have diminished Ajax's power, and now their stars inevitably move to richer clubs abroad.
Titles: European Cup/Champions League 1971, 1972, 1973, 1995; UEFA Cup 1992; Cup Winners' Cup 1987; Dutch champions 32 times; Dutch Cup 18

ARSENAL (England)

Arsenal became the dominant force in England in the 1930s. Manager Herbert Chapman created their first truly great side, which won four league titles in five seasons, including three in a row between 1933 and 1935. After two post-war titles, Arsenal went through a barren spell. Victory over Anderlecht in the 1970 Fairs Cup final brought their first trophy for 17 years. They won the domestic "double" the following season and star player George Graham later delivered two more titles as coach with a host of home-grown players. Long-serving manager Arsène Wenger imported a host of foreign players with a French connection. His rewards include two league and cup "doubles."
Titles: UEFA/Fairs Cup 1970; Cup Winners' Cup: 1994; English champions 13 times; FA Cup 10; League Cup 2

ASTON VILLA (England)

Aston Villa were one of the 12 founding members of the Football League in 1888. They were a major force in its early years, winning five championships between 1894 and 1900 and the "double" in 1897. But after lifting the FA Cup in 1920, they went 37 years before gaining another major crown, beating Manchester United in the FA Cup final. Their most remarkable success was winning the European Cup in 1982. A quarter-final defeat by Juventus in 1983 signalled the start of a decline, and they were relegated in 1987. Aston Villa regained their elite status a season later. They finished league runner-up in both 1989 and 1993.
Titles: European Cup 1982; English champions 7 times; FA Cup 7; League Cup 5

ATLETICO MADRID (Spain)

Atletico Madrid have spent years playing second fiddle to neighbours Real Madrid, although they overshadowed their bitter rivals in the early 1950s, when master coach Helenio Herrera guided them to successive titles. Spanish champions in 1973, they came within a minute of winning the European Cup a year later, but were denied glory by a late equaliser that forced a replay, which Bayern Munich won 4-0. Atletico won the 1974 World Club Cup after Bayern Munich declined to compete. The club became synonymous with instability during the reign of president Jesus Gil, who hired and fired 23 different coaches between 1987 and 2003. They revived, and in 2008 secured entry into the Champions League for the first time in over a decade, lifting the Europa League in 2012.
Titles: Cup Winner's Cup 1962; UEFA Cup/Europa League 2010, 2012, Spanish champions 9 times; Spanish Cup 10

BARCELONA (Spain)

Barcelona's motto is *"mes que un club,"* meaning "more than a club," and they have long been a symbol for Catalonia's regional pride. Their bitter rivalry with Real Madrid is a key feature of Spanish football. Ronald Koeman's European

Cup final winner against Sampdoria in 1992 healed Barcelona's wounded pride after so many disappointments in the competition, including defeats in the final to Benfica and Steaua Bucharest. Coach Johann Cruyff, a playing great, created the winning "Dream Team," featuring Koeman, Pep Guardiola, Hristo Stoichkov, and Michael Laudrup—which many regard as Barcelona's best-ever team. Frank Rijkaard, Cruyff's protege, later crafted the 2005–06 side that beat Arsenal 2-1 in the Champions League final and won La Liga. Ronaldinho and Samuel Eto'o were the stars. Guardiola replaced Rijkaard in 2008, and raised the bar still further thanks to the star quality of Lionel Messi, Andres Iniesta and Xavi.
Titles: European Cup/Champions League 1992, 2006, 2009, 2011; UEFA/Fairs Cup 1958, 1960, 1966; Cup Winner's Cup 1979, 1982, 1989, 1997; Spanish champions 22 times; Spanish Cup 26

BAYERN MUNICH (Germany)

Bayern Munich succeeded Ajax as the dominant team in Europe in the mid-1970s, winning the European Cup three times in a row. The great Franz Beckenbauer was their conductor, supported by prolific striker Gerd Müller and goalkeeper Sepp Maier. Bayern came within a minute of losing the 1974 final to Atletico Madrid, winning the replay 4-0. A year later they beat Leeds United 2-0 in the final and they completed their trio with a 1-0 win over Saint-Etienne. Bayern added a fourth triumph in 2001, when goalkeeper Oliver Kahn defied Valencia in a penalty shoot-out and despite losing the 2012 final to Chelsea on their own ground, Bayern triumphed in London in 2013, beating German rivals Borussia Dortmund thanks to a late winner from Arjen Robben to add to their domestic "double". Bayern have been the dominant team in their domestic Bundesliga for more than 40 years.
Titles: European Cup/Champions League 1974, 1975, 1976, 2001, 2013; UEFA Cup Winners' Cup 1967; UEFA Cup 1996; German champions 23 times; German Cup 16

BENFICA (Portugal)

Benfica fans look back on the 1960s as their club's golden years. They succeeded Real Madrid as European champions by beating Barcelona 3-2 in the 1961 final, then retained the trophy with a 5-3 win over Real Madrid. Benfica also reached the final in 1963, 1965, and 1968 and supplied the bulk of the Portugal side that finished third in the 1966 World Cup finals. Benfica's hero was the great striker Eusébio. The team was packed with internationals, with Mario Coluna pulling the strings in midfield. Benfica lost in recent finals to PSV Eindhoven, on penalties in 1988, and AC Milan in 1990. They have since faded as a European power and been eclipsed at home by great rivals Porto, but made the 2013 Europa

ABOVE Henrik Larsson, Carles Puyol and Ronaldinho take the Champions League Cup by tickertape storm in 2006

BELOW Arsenal celebrate their 1971 FA Cup final victory

GREAT CLUBS

EUROPE

League final where they were beaten by Chelsea.
Titles: European Cup 1961, 1962; Portuguese champions 32 times; Portuguese Cup 27

BORUSSIA DORTMUND (Germany)

Borussia Dortmund became the first West German team to lift a European trophy after they beat Liverpool in the 1966 Cup Winners' Cup final. But their greatest day came in 1997, when Ottmar Hitzfeld's side stunned Juventus 3-1 in the Champions League final. Hitzfeld had brought back Matthias Sammer, Andy Möller, Jürgen Koller and Stefan Reuter from Italy to form the core of the team. Five years later, Borussia Dortmund won the Bundesliga and reached the UEFA Cup final, losing to Feyenoord. They came perilously close to bankruptcy in 2005, but recovered to win the Bundesliga again in 2011 and 2012, reaching the final of the Champions League under charismatic coach Jurgen Klopp in 2013.
Titles: European Cup 1997; UEFA Cup Winners' Cup 1966; German champions 8 times; German Cup 3

CELTIC (Scotland)

Celtic were the first British club to win the European Cup when they beat Internazionale 2-1 in the 1967 final at Lisbon. The team became known as the "Lisbon Lions", and were all born within a 30-mile radius of Glasgow. Celtic also reached the final in 1970. They were managed by Jock Stein, and included outstanding figures such as Tommy Gemmell, Billy McNeill, Bobby Murdoch, and Jimmy Johnstone. That team began to break up after losing the 1974 European Cup semi-final to Atletico Madrid. But they still set a domestic record of nine consecutive championships. Celtic revived memories of those glory days with a run to the 2003 UEFA Cup final, and they surprised Barcelona with a 2-1 win during the 2012-13 Champions league group stages.
Titles: European Cup 1967; Scottish champions 44 times; Scottish Cup 36; League Cup 14

CHELSEA (England)

Chelsea's recent transformation into a European power has been bankrolled by Russian oil billionaire Roman Abramovich, the club's owner since 2003. His appointment of Portugal's Jose Mourinho as manager a year later galvanized the club. Mourinho spent heavily to win the Premier League in his first season, and delivered another league title in 2006. He left Chelsea in September 2007, despite guiding them to FA Cup and League Cup victories, after falling out with Abramovich. Israeli Avram Grant then took Chelsea to their first Champions League final, but was sacked after their shoot-out defeat by Manchester United. Four years later they took their first Champions League, beating Bayern Munich on penalties

BELOW Barcelona's Thierry Henry fails to breach Celtic's defense

under caretaker coach Roberto Di Matteo, with Petr Cech saving three spot kicks. Didier Drogba converted the decisive penalty in his last game for the club. Disappointment a year later was eased when they lifted the Europa League under another temporary coach, Rafael Benitez.

Titles: Champions League 2012, Europa League 2013, Cup Winners' Cup 1971, 1998; English champions 4 times; FA Cup 7; League Cup 4

DYNAMO KIEV (Ukraine)

Dynamo Kiev were the first club from the former Soviet Union to win a European trophy when they beat Hungary's Ferencváros in the 1975 European Cup Winners' Cup final. They saw off Atletico Madrid 3-0 to win the same competition 11 years later. The Ukrainians led non-Russian opposition to the Moscow clubs during the Soviet era, winning 13 championships and nine cup finals. They are seasoned Champions League competitors, despite normally needing to start in the qualifying stages, and reached the semi-final stage in 1999. Andriy Shevchenko was their inspiration with eight goals, earning him a lucrative move to AC Milan.

Titles: Cup Winners' Cup 1975, 1986; Soviet/Ukrainian champions 26 times; Soviet/Ukrainian Cup 18

EVERTON (England)

Everton, formed in 1878, were founder members of the Football League, and one of its most successful clubs for many years. They reached their peak under Howard Kendall in the mid-1980s. They won the FA Cup in 1984, the league title (ahead of their great rivals, Liverpool) and the Cup Winners' Cup a year later, and added another title in 1987. In between, they finished as runner-up to Liverpool in the league and FA Cup. However, the ban on English clubs after the Heysel Stadium disaster denied Everton the chance to build on their European success, and eventually the team broke up. A string of managers struggled to rebuild the club in the years that followed, before David Moyes steered Everton to a Champions League qualifying place in 2005. The 2-0 win over Manchester United in the 1995 FA Cup remains their last major honour.

Titles: Cup Winners' Cup 1985; English champions 9 times; FA Cup 5

FEYENOORD (Holland)

Feyenoord became the first Dutch team to win the European Cup when they beat Celtic 2-1 after extra time in 1970 in Milan. Four years later, they lifted the UEFA Cup after drawing with Tottenham in the first leg in London and winning the return game 2-0. Three of that victorious side, Wim Rijsbergen, Wim Jansen, and Wim Van Hanegem, played for Holland in the 1974 World Cup final. Following almost 20 years without further European success, Feyenoord were surprise UEFA Cup winners in 2002, beating Borussia Dortmund 3-2. They have failed to make any impact in Europe since, and have not won the Dutch title since 1999. Instead, they have become a supplier of stars, including talents such as Robin van Persie, Dirk Kuyt, Salomon Kalou to clubs in richer leagues.

Titles: Intercontinental Cup 1970; European Champion Clubs' Cup 1970; UEFA Cup 1974, 2002; Dutch champions 14 times; Dutch Cup 11

INTERNAZIONALE (Italy)

Internazionale were a dominant world power in the mid-1960s. European champions in 1964 and '65, they were beaten finalists in 1967. However, coach Helenio Herrera's *catenaccio* tactics were criticised for being too defensive, and they were an unpopular side with neutral spectators, despite fielding greats such as full-back Giacinto Facchetti, midfielder Luis Suarez, and attacker Sandro Mazzola. Internazionale reached another European Cup final in 1972, when they were swept aside by Ajax. They won only two domestic championships between 1972 and 2005, but collected three straight under Roberto Mancini and Jose Mourinho, with the latter lifting the Champions League in 2010, ending a 45-year wait and in the process becoming the first coach to lead an Italian side to a "treble".

Titles: Intercontinental Cup 1964, 1965; European Cup 1964, 1965, 2010; UEFA Cup 1991, 1994, 1998; Italian champions 18 times; Italian Cup 7

JUVENTUS (Italy)

Juventus boast an enviable record of appearing in seven European Cup finals. The tragedy of the Heysel Stadium disaster dwarfed their first success, when Michel Platini's goal edged out

ABOVE Alessandro Del Piero of Juventus celebrates a goal against Celtic in 2001

EUROPE

ABOVE Liverpool captain Steven Gerrard lifts the 2005 European Cup in Istanbul

Liverpool in the 1985 final. They won again in 1996, when Marcello Lippi's team beat Ajax on penalties. Juventus have also lost finals to Ajax, Hamburg, Borussia Dortmund, Real Madrid, and AC Milan, most recently in 2003. They have amassed a record number of Italian titles, but recent successes have been dogged by controversy. Their three title wins between 1995 and 1998 were the subject of a doping enquiry. In 2006, Juventus were stripped of their 2005 and 2006 Serie A titles following a match-fixing scandal. The punishment included relegation, sending them to Serie B for the first time. Despite a 30-point deduction, they won promotion and have now returned to the top of Serie A, going unbeaten through the 2012-13 campaign.
Titles: Intercontinental Cup 1985, 1996; European Cup/Champions League 1985, 1996; Cup Winners' Cup 1984; UEFA/Fairs Cup 1977, 1990, 1993; Italian champions 29 times; Italian cup 9

LIVERPOOL (England)
Liverpool remain the most successful English club in European competition. They have lifted the European Cup five times, the UEFA Cup three times, and have a hat-trick of European Super Cup prizes. Manager Bob Paisley, who succeeded the great Bill Shankly, was the architect of their success, steering Liverpool to a hat-trick of triumphs in 1977, 1978, and 1981 before handing over to Joe Fagan for their 1984 triumph. The Steven Gerrard-inspired comeback known as "the Miracle of Istanbul" brought Liverpool their fifth European Cup, and their first of the Champions League era in 2005. Paisley's team dominated in England as well as Europe. Such stars as Kenny Dalglish, Alan Hansen, Ian Rush, Graeme Souness, and Phil Thompson helped Liverpool to win a total of 18 championships. They have not, however, won the league since 1990 and ending that run has become the club's priority.
Titles: European Cup/Champions League 1977, 1978, 1981, 1984, 2005; UEFA Cup 1973, 1976, 2001; English champions 18 times; FA Cup 7; League Cup 7

LYON (France)
Lyon monopolised French football from 2002 for seven straight seasons, a domestic record. In 2008, they completed a league and cup "double." The 2002 title was Lyon's first, and a realisation of the dreams of Jean-Michel Aulas, club president since 1987. Despite that dominance, Lyon failed to dominate in Europe, regularly losing key players to Champions League rivals, such as Michael Essien to Chelsea and Karim Benzema to Real Madrid.
Titles: French champions 7 times; French Cup 5

MANCHESTER CITY (England)
Life has rarely been dull for fans of Man City. Recent history has seen them suffer the indignity of dropping into the third tier of English football before climbing back to the Premier League. They were relegated again, only for Kevin Keegan to lead them up again in 2002. A huge injection of cash by new Arab owners in 2008 elevated City into the big time, and they immediately sought to challenge for England's top honours, bringing in top players like Brazilian Robinho and Belgian Vincent Kompany, the latter leading them to their first league title in 44 years in 2012 under Roberto Mancini, bringing back the glory years of the late 1960s when manager Joe Mercer guided them to the championship in 1968, the FA Cup in 1969 and the European Cup Winners' Cup and League Cup the next season. Their challenge now is to lift the Champions League for a first time.
Titles: Cup Winner's Cup 1970; English champions 3; FA Cup 5; League Cup 2

MANCHESTER UNITED (England)
Scottish managers have crafted Manchester United's record-breaking post-war achievements.

Sir Matt Busby built the team known as "the Busby Babes" who won two championships and reached the European Cup semi-finals twice, before being torn apart by the Munich air disaster in 1958. Busby went on to create another great side—featuring Bobby Charlton, Denis Law and George Best—which won two more championships and became the first English team to lift the European Cup, ten years after Munich. Sir Alex Ferguson then achieved greatness in his own style after delivering Manchester United's first league title for 26 years in 1993. His sides dominated the lucrative Premier League era, claiming 13 of the 21 titles. Ferguson added two Champions League triumphs—in 1999 and 2008, the first bringing the club a unique "treble", adding to the prizes of the Premier League and FA Cup. Nine years later, United keeper Edwin van der Sar held his nerve in the final shoot-out against Chelsea after Cristiano Ronaldo's goals had propelled Manchester United to another domestic league title, but they were beaten in their next two finals in 2009 and 2011, both by Barcelona. Ferguson retired in 2013, to be succeeded by David Moyes.

Titles: European Cup/Champions League 1968, 1999, 2008; Cup Winners' Cup 1991; English champions 20 times; FA Cup 11; League Cup 4

AC MILAN (Italy)

AC Milan come second only to Real Madrid in terms of Champions League successes, having captured the prize seven times and appeared in four other finals. They first lifted it in 1963 by deposing holders Benfica 2-1, and six years later crushed Ajax Amsterdam 4-1. They had to wait 20 years for their next victory, when the Dutch trio of Ruud Gullit, Frank Rijkaard, and Marco van Basten inspired Arrigo Sacchi's cultured side to a 4-0 win over Steaua Bucharest, beating Benfica to retain the trophy a year later. AC Milan triumphed again in 1994, tearing Barcelona apart 4-0 under Fabio Capello. Defeat by Ajax Amsterdam the following year signalled the end of an era. The Dutchmen had already gone, but two defenders remained who would star in the next decade— Alessandro Costacurta and Paolo Maldini. Milan edged past Juventus on penalty kicks in 2003, then lost one of the most dramatic finals in 2005,

having led Liverpool 3-0 they were defeated on penalties. They gained revenge two years later, winning 2-1 as Maldini collected his fifth winner's medal in the competition.

Titles: European Cup/Champions League 1963, 1969, 1989, 1990, 1994, 2003, 2007; European Cup Winners' Cup 1968, 1973; Italian champions 18 times; Italian Cup 5

OLYMPIQUE MARSEILLE (France)

Marseille's greatest achievement also led to their greatest crisis. They became the only French team to have won the Champions League when they saw off AC Milan in the 1993 final. Club president Bernard Tapie was jailed for his involvement in a match-fixing scandal which saw the club relegated. The club, who had won the previous five championships, were also stripped of their domestic crown. UEFA disqualified them from competing for a short period, but they returned to reach the UEFA Cup final in 1999 and 2004.

Titles: Champions League 1993; French champions 9 times; French Cup 10

PORTO (Portugal)

Porto tasted glory under Jose Mourinho as the new century unfolded. He steered them to the

ABOVE Andrea Pirlo of AC Milan takes a free kick against Atalanta in 2008.

WORLD CUP MOMENTS

ABOVE Tottenham's Jimmy Greaves shoots for goal against Burnley

BELOW Celtic keeper Ronnie Simpson defies Internazionale in Lisbon

ABOVE Zico (left) is a legendary figure for Flamengo and Brazil

LEFT Benfica's Portugal hero Eusébio bears down on goal

BELOW Manchester United parade the Champions Cup in 1968

1980s   2000s

ABOVE Hugo Sanchez top-scored for Mexico, Real and Atletico Madrid

RIGHT Carles Pujol and Ronaldinho raise the Champions Cup

BELOW Alex (Santos) tackles Boca's Carlos Tevez

RIGHT David Beckham takes to the wing for LA Galaxy

ABOVE Milan forward Kaka eludes Inter's Nelson Rivas

ABOVE RIGHT Etoile Sahel carry off the African Super Cup

THE WORLD CUP ⚽ **145**

GREAT CLUBS

EUROPE

championship and a 2003 UEFA Cup final victory over Celtic. A year later, they were crowned champions of both Portugal and Europe, destroying AS Monaco 3-0 in the Champions League final, to deliver Porto's second such triumph. Mourinho then left for big-spending Chelsea, taking defensive duo Paulo Ferreira and Ricardo Carvalho with him, while playmaker Deco left for Barcelona. Still a Champions League regular, Porto have supplied many more of Europe's top players in recent seasons, notably Radamel Falcao, who helped them to the 2011 Europa League.

Titles: European Cup/Champions League 1987, 2004; UEFA Cup/Europa League 2003, 2011; Portuguese champions 27 times; Portuguese Cup 16

PSV EINDHOVEN (Holland)
PSV broke the dominance of Ajax and Feyenoord, Holland's "Big Two" in the 1970s, when they won three championships in four seasons, and snatched the UEFA Cup in 1978 with a 3-0 aggregate win over Bastia. PSV's greatest moment came ten years later, when they beat Benfica on penalties in the European Cup final, coached by Guus Hiddink. The side have continued to challenge in the UEFA Champions League despite losing stars to England (Arjen Robben and Park Ji-Sung), Germany (Mark Van Bommel), and Spain (Arouna Kone). They lost on away goals to AC Milan in the 2005 semi-finals and reached the quarter-finals two years later.

Titles: European Champion Clubs' Cup 1988; UEFA Cup 1978; Dutch champions 21 times; Dutch cup 9

RANGERS (Scotland)
Rangers' run to the 2008 UEFA Cup final, which they lost 2-0 to Zenit St. Petersburg, marked the end of a 36-year gap since their last appearance in a European showpiece. In the previous final, they beat Dynamo Moscow 3-2 to lift the European Cup Winners' Cup—their only European prize. In 1961, Rangers had lost the first European Cup Winners' Cup final to Fiorentina. A year earlier, Rangers reached the European Cup semi-finals, but crashed 12-4 on aggregate to Eintracht Frankfurt. They made their biggest

RIGHT Jorge Costa and Vitor Baia lead Porto's European victory parade in 2004

impact on the Champions League in 1993, when they finished a point behind winners Marseille in the last eight group stage. Rangers have won a record 51 Scottish League titles, but were relegated to Scotland's lowest tier amid financial scandal in 2012.

Titles: Cup Winners' Cup 1972; Scottish champions 54 times; Scottish Cup 33; League Cup 27

REAL MADRID (Spain)

Real Madrid are the best known club in the world. They won each of the first five finals of the European Cup—defeating Reims twice, Fiorentina, AC Milan, and Eintracht Frankfurt. Real were guided by visionary president Santiago Bernabeu, with the team ably led by the legendary Argentinian forward Alfredo Di Stefano—who played in all five finals. The most renowned final was the 7-3 victory over Frankfurt in 1960, when Di Stefano hit a hat-trick and Hungary great Ferenc Puskás netted four goals. Winger Paco Gento was the only attacking link with that golden past when Real Madrid's new-look team edged Partizan Belgrade 2-1 to win the trophy again six years later. They had to wait until 1998 for their next success, when Predrag Mijatovic scored the clincher against Juventus. Vicente Del Bosque revived past glories, steering Real Madrid to victories in 2000 and 2002, but was sacked after their 2003 semi-final loss, and club president Florentino Perez put together a star-studded side with the top players known as "*Galacticos*." Their hunt for a tenth European Cup continues however, with even the great Jose Mourinho failing to win the famous trophy under the shadow of Barcelona and Bayern Munich.

Titles: European Cup/Champions League 1956, 1957, 1958, 1959, 1960, 1966, 1998, 2000, 2002; UEFA Cup 1985, 1986; Spanish champions 32 times; Spanish Cup 18

AS ROMA (Italy)

AS Roma have enjoyed their most successful decade recently, winning Serie A in 2001 and finishing runner-up five times since. The fulcrum of the club's success has been the excellence of forward Francesco Totti, who holds club records for games and goals. After a dip in form, Roma

look back to their best under French coach Rudi Garcia during 2013-14.

Titles: Fairs Cup 1961; Italian champions 3 times; Italian Cup 9

TOTTENHAM HOTSPUR (England)

Tottenham Hotspur became the first English club to win a European trophy when they beat Atletico Madrid 5-1 in the 1963 European Cup Winners' Cup final. The team, built by Bill Nicholson and skippered by Danny Blanchflower, are considered Tottenham's best ever. They won the first league and cup "double" of the 20th century in 1961, collecting the FA Cup again the following season, and reached the European Cup semi-final. Tottenham have since added two UEFA Cup victories to their European honours, and qualified for their first Champions League campaign in 2010, reaching the quarter-finals thanks largely to the form of Gareth Bale and Luka Modric who have both since been sold to Real Madrid.

Titles: European Cup Winner's Cup 1963; UEFA Cup 1972, 1984; English champions 2 times; FA Cup 8; League Cup 4

ABOVE Tottenham Hotspurs' double-winning players enjoy their open-top bus parade in 1961

GREAT CLUBS

AMERICAS

ABOVE Juan Román Riquelme, a latter-day hero for Boca Juniors

BOCA JUNIORS (Argentina)

No South American club has won more international titles than the Argentinian club from La Bombonera, the Buenos Aires stadium whose affectionate nickname translates as "The Chocolate Box." Their "*Superclásico*" rivalry with River Plate is one of the fiercest in the world, with Boca Juniors' supporters considering themselves as the city's working-class underdogs. Diego Maradona spent a title-winning season with the club before leaving for Spain in 1982, before returning 13 years later. Juan Román Riquelme was a modern-day heir whose return for a second spell led to Copa Libertadores glory in 2007, and has a statue outside the stadium.
Titles: Copa Libertadores 1977, 1978, 2000, 2001, 2003, 2007; Copa Sudamericana 2004, 2005; Argentine league 30 times

COLO COLO (Chile)

The "Snow Whites" of Santiago became the first, and so far only, Chilean club to win the Copa Libertadores—the South American equivalent of the UEFA Champions League—in 1991 when they beat Paraguay's Olimpia Asuncion 3-0 on aggregate. They are Chile's most successful club, with 41 domestic trophies and the only club to have contested every season without relegation since the league was founded in 1933.
Titles: Copa Libertadores 1991; Chilean league 27 times; Chilean Cup 10

FLAMENGO (Brazil)

Flamengo began life in 1895 as a rowing club but embraced football 16 years later, after a breakaway by aggrieved members of neighboring Fluminense. They have since become Brazil's best-loved club, with an estimated fanbase of 40 million. It was not until the late 1970s and early 1980s that they extended their domestic brilliance to the international arena, inspired by the brilliance of Zico.
Titles: Copa Libertadores 1981; Brazilian league 6 times, Brazilian Cup 2

INDEPENDIENTE (Argentina)

Years of decline and debts forced Independiente to sell wonder-kid Sergio Aguero to Atletico Madrid in 2006, yet the club's history remains as glorious as any in Argentina—including a record seven Copa Libertadores titles. These include four in a row between 1972 and 1975 that were inspired by midfielder Ricardo Bochini, who played for 20 years with the club. They have also been home to the World Cup-winning trio of Daniel Bertoni, Jorge Burruchaga and Oscar Ortiz.
Titles: Copa Libertadores 1964, 1965, 1972, 1973, 1974, 1975, 1984; Argentine league 16 times

PENAROL (Uruguay)

Uruguay's most prestigious club provided the two scorers when Brazil were amazingly beaten in the 1950 World Cup finals, namely Alcides Ghigghia and Juan Schiaffino. At times in the 1960s, Peñarol could even outshine Pelé and Santos, including a 5-0 win in 1963, featuring a hat-trick by Alberto Spencer. He remains the all-time top scorer in the Copa Libertadores, leading the Montevideo club to three of their five triumphs. Peñarol have also been crowned World Club champions three times.
Titles: Copa Libertadores 1960, 1961, 1966, 1982, 1987; Uruguayan league 49 times

RIVER PLATE (Argentina)

Along with Buenos Aires arch rivals Boca Juniors, River Plate remain one of Argentina's biggest, best-supported teams. Their formidable five-man forward line of the early 1940s was dubbed "*La Máquina*" (The Machine) but a sixth striker that decade was perhaps their greatest of all, Alfredo Di Stefano. Argentina's 1978 World Cup-winning captain Daniel Passarella spearheaded a club revival in the 1970s, before boyhood fan Hernan Crespo shot to fame at the Estadio Monumental in the 1990s. 1986 was a perfect year for River hinchas, not only were Argentina crowned World Champions, but River captured the league, the

LEFT Pelé takes aim for Santos in 1973

Copa Libertadores and the World Club Cup, beating Steaua Bucharest. Recent years have brought struggles, however, and they were relegated from the top flight for the first time ever in 2011, though they returned a year later.
Titles: Copa Libertadores 1986, 1996; Supercopa Sudamericana 1997; Argentine league 35 times

SANTOS (Brazil)

For much of the 1960s, Santos were the side the whole world wanted to see—largely thanks to their iconic number 10, Pelé. As well as clinching two world club titles, beating Benfica and AC Milan, and several state championships, the Brazilian entertainers toured the world almost non-stop to play money-making exhibition matches for huge crowds. Pelé's departure in 1972 inevitably signalled an end to the glory days, and they had to wait until 2002 for their next Brazilian league title. In recent years the club has produced such young stars as Robinho, Elano, Diego and Neymar, who looks set to take the 2014 World Cup by storm, and helped the side to its third Copa Libertadores in 2011.
Titles: Copa Libertadores 1962, 1963, 2011; Copa CONMEBOL 1998; Brazilian champions 8 times, Brazilian Cup 1

SÃO PAULO (Brazil)

Brasilia is the country's capital, Rio's clubs have the most fervent support, and neighbours Santos boasted Pelé, but São Paulo can claim to be Brazil's most successful club. Leonidas da Silva in the 1940s, Gerson in the 1970s, Careca in the 1980s and more recently Kaka in the 2000s have contributed to their collection of domestic and world titles. Their Copa Libertadores win in 2005 made them the first Brazilian club to claim a hat-trick of titles, and the first team to beat a side from the same country in the final, Atletico Paranaense.
Titles: Copa Libertadores 1992, 1993, 2005; Copa Sudamericana 2012, 1994; Brazilian champions 6 times

VASCO DA GAMA (Brazil)

Vasco da Gama was founded in 1898 by Portuguese immigrants, taking their name from the revered Portuguese explorer of the 14th and 15th centuries, and call for much of their support on Rio's Portuguese communities. World Cup-winning striker Romario started his career at Vasco in 1985 and retired in 2008 after his fourth term at the club, which included the goal he claimed was the 1,000th of his career. But his 316 goals for Vasco da Gama were less than half the tally of their leading goalscorer, Roberto Dinamite. He scored 698 in 1,110 games between 1971 and 1993. Vasco have not won the league since 2000, but did lift the domestic cup in 2011.
Titles: Copa Libertadores 1998; Brazilian champions 4 times, Brazilian Cup 1

GREAT CLUBS

REST OF THE WORLD

ABOVE Jaime Moreno of DC United looks for an opening against the New York Red Bulls

AL-AHLY (Egypt)

Little wonder the Cairo side were named in 2000 as the Confederation of African Football's club of the century. Egypt's so-called "People's Club" has won a record five African club championships, and a major haul of domestic titles. They even managed to remain unbeaten from 1974 to 1977. The "Red Devils," whose former players include Egypt's record scorer Hossam Hassan, have a ferocious rivalry with city rivals Zamalek, and have recently had the upper hand, lifting the past two Champions League titles.

Titles: African Champions League 1982, 1987, 2001, 2005, 2006, 2008, 2012, 2013; African Cup Winners' Cup 1984, 1985, 1986, 1993; Egyptian league 36 times, Egyptian Cup 35

CLUB AMERICA (Mexico)

Club America have been Mexico's big spenders since a 1959 takeover by television giant Televisa. Until recent years at least, such power guaranteed success, including a record five crowns as CONCACAF Champions (the same number won by rivals Cruz Azul) and 11 league titles (a joint record with Chivas Guadalajara). Big-name foreign imports have included Argentina's Oscar Ruggeri, Chilean Ivan Zamorano, and Romania's Ilie Dumitrescu. But they have also developed home-grown talent such as Mexican playmaker Cuauhtemoc Blanco. Club America play at the huge Azteca Stadium in Mexico City, the only stadium to have hosted two World Cup finals.

Titles: CONCACAF Champions Cup/ Champions League 1978, 1987, 1991, 1993, 2006; CONCACAF Cup Winners' Cup 2001; Mexican league 11 times, Mexican Cup 5

DC UNITED (United States)

Captain John Harkes, returning home from the English Premier League, and coach Bruce Arena led the Washington DC-based club to the first two MLS titles in 1996 and 1997. They also became the first US club to win the CONCACAF Champions' Cup in 1998. But trophies have proved harder to come by since Arena left to become national coach in 1998, despite high-profile signings such as iconic Hristo Stoichkov and Freddy Adu—who made his debut aged 14. Other notable former players include Bolivian pair Jaime Moreno and Marco Etcheverry.

Titles: CONCACAF Champions Cup 1998; US MLS Cup four times; US Open Cup 3

ETOILE DU SAHEL (Tunisia)

Tunisia may have underachieved internationally, with only one African Cup of Nations triumph, but their oldest club has proved the pride of a nation, with impressive performances in all continental competitions. They achieved surprise Champions League glory in 2007, beating Egyptian holders Al-Ahly, making them the first club to have won each of the African Federation's club trophies.

Titles: African Champions League 2007; African Cup Winners' Cup 1997, 2003; Tunisian league 8; President's Cup 8

LOS ANGELES GALAXY (United States)

LA Galaxy pulled off the most high-profile signing in MLS history when world superstar, England's iconic David Beckham, joined from Real Madrid in 2007. Another great, Holland's Ruud Gullit, was then appointed LA Galaxy coach after a disappointing first season for Beckham. The midfielder's arrival helped the club sell 700 times as many replica shirts as before, bringing global attention to the MLS for the first time. Beckham left after lifting the MLS Cup in 2012, by which time he had been joined by Robbie Keane from Tottenham Hotspur.

Titles: CONCACAF Champions Cup 2000; MLS Cup 2002, 2005, 2011, 2012; US Open Cup 2

KAIZER CHIEFS (South Africa)
Kaizer Chiefs, one of South Africa's first professional clubs, take their name from the former international midfielder, Kaizer Motaung. He co-founded the club in 1970 after returning from a spell in the US. He has since served them as a player, in three separate stints as coach, and now as club president. The Chiefs passionately contest the Soweto derby with Orlando Pirates, another of Motaung's old teams. Their home at Johannesburg's FNB Stadium was rebuilt as Soccer City to host the 2010 World Cup final between Spain and Holland.
Titles: African Cup Winners' Cup 2001; South African league 3, South African Cup 8

POHANG STEELERS (South Korea)
Pohang Steelers dominated in Korea during the 1970s and '80s, then suffered a 15-year barren spell in the K League until their 2007 title triumph. In 1997, they became the third South Korean team to win the Asian Champions League by beating compatriots and defending champions Seongham Ilhwa Chunma. They retained the trophy the following year against China's Dalian Wanda. Crucial to their success in the 1990s was reliable defender Hong-Myung Bo, who went on to become his country's most-capped player, and now coaches his country at Brazil 2014.
Titles: Asian Champions League 1997, 1998, 2009; South Korean league 4; South Korean Cup 4

UNAM PUMAS (Mexico)
UNAM Pumas, the club affiliated to Latin America's largest university, has long put a useful emphasis on youth and proudly produced Mexican legends such as Luis Garcia, Jorge Campos and Hugo Sanchez. The inspirational striker scored 96 goals for UNAM Pumas from 1976 to 1981, then returned as coach 19 years later, guiding the club to four trophies in 2004.

Colourful goalkeeper Campos loved to roam upfield but also occasionally played in attack with 35 goals to his credit in 199 games. UNAM Pumas' home in Mexico City was the main venue for the 1968 Olympics Games.
Titles: CONCACAF Champions Cup 1980, 1982, 1989; Copa Interamericana 1981; Mexican league 7, Mexican Cup 1

URAWA RED DIAMONDS (Japan)
Urawa Red Diamonds won four league titles and four Emperor's Cups before the Japanese game turned professional in 1993. They made a bad start in the J League, finishing bottom in the first two seasons. The team nicknamed "The Nearly Men" lived up to their image by just missing out on the 2004 and 2005 titles, but they finally sparkled to become J League champions in 2006 and win the Asian Champions League in 2007. Star players have included Japanese midfielder Shinji Ono and Brazilian striker Edmundo.
Titles: Asian Champions League 2007; Japanese league 5; Emperor's Cup 6; J League Cup 1

ABOVE Urawa Reds Diamonds take the glory after their Asian Champions League triumph in 2007

GREAT PLAYERS AND MANAGERS

Match and trophy-winning performances depend on a combination of teamwork and spirit from both the players and their managers. Even the stars that shine like no other—such as Stanley Matthews, Diego Maradona, Ronaldo, Pelé, and Zinedine Zidane—would have been unable to express their genius without a manager to guide them. Nowadays, players are not only chasing the ball but also the opportunities to earn fame, fortune, and even notoriety for their successes and failures, goals and gaffes.

MANAGERS

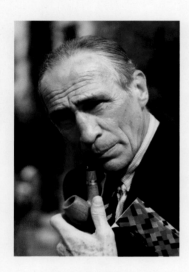

TOP Enzo Bearzot

ABOVE Vicente del Bosque

PAGE 152 Guus Hiddink

PAGE 153 RIGHT Thierry Henry

ENZO BEARZOT (born 26 September 1927, died 21 December 2010)
Greatest success: 1982 World Cup (Italy)
After a decent playing career and a coaching apprenticeship with the national Under-23 side, Bearzot took charge of the senior national team, leading Italy to a fourth-place finish in Argentina in 1978. Four years later, he famously banned the media from the squad's training camp after a poor start, but performances improved and Italy beat Brazil 3-2 in one of the all-time great World Cup games, before eliminating Argentina and Poland and beating West Germany 3-1 in a scintillating final. It was the first time in 44 years that Italy had been world champions. Bearzot stayed in the job until 1986.

VICENTE DEL BOSQUE (born 23 December 1950)
Greatest success: 2010 World Cup (Spain)
Del Bosque replaced Luis Aragones as Spanish coach following their success at Euro 2008 and would go on to raise the bar further by bringing the country its first world crown in 2010. Pre-tournament favourites in 2010, Spain were beaten in their opening game against Switzerland, but recovered to top their group, winning each of their knockout matches 1-0 and beating the Dutch after extra-time. After leading the Spanish to Euro 2012 success too, Del Bosque is looking for his third consecutive major title in 2014 and will be aware that no country has successfully defended the World Cup since Brazil in 1962.

VICENTE FEOLA (born 1 November 1909, died 6 November 1975)
Greatest success: 1958 World Cup (Brazil)
The portly Feola guided Brazil to their first World Cup triumph in Sweden, although he took some persuading from senior players to pick both Garrincha and Pelé in the middle of the tournament when they appeared to be floundering. Because of illness, Feola missed their successful defence of the World Cup in 1962. He returned for the luckless 1966 finals in England, when his side went out in the group stage. Feola finished with an outstanding career record of only losing six matches out of the 74 his team played.

JOSEF "SEPP" HERBERGER (born 28 March 1897, died 20 April 1977)
Greatest success: 1954 World Cup (West Germany)
Herberger became manager of Germany in 1938 and used all his sports and political influence to try to keep his players away from the battle fronts during World War II. He returned as national manager after the war and won West Germany's first World Cup in 1954. The final was aptly labeled the "Miracle of Bern" after his team came from two goals down to defeat the famous Hungarian side 3-2, thanks in no small part to their removable, screw-in studs designed by German manufacturer Adidas.

GUUS HIDDINK (born 8 November 1946)
Greatest success: 2002 semi-finals (South Korea)
Hiddink is a coaching icon around the world, having achieved back-to-back World Cup semi-final appearances in 1998 and 2002. With his native Dutch team in 1998, he reached the last four playing an entertaining and attacking brand of football, eliminating Yugoslavia and Argentina after topping the group, before coming unstuck on penalties against Brazil in the semis. Holland were beaten into fourth place by Croatia. Four years later, Hiddink was in charge of hosts South Korea, who were tipped to struggle. However, group stage wins over Poland and Portugal brought unexpected momentum and Italy were controversially beaten after extra time before Spain were knocked out on penalties. Germany ended the party at the semi-final stage and Turkey took third place in the play-offs, but in

Korea, Hiddink remains a hero and became the first person ever to be given an honorary citizenship. He also led Australia to their first World Cup in 32 years in 2006.

AIMÉ JACQUET (born 27 November 1941)
Greatest success: 1998 World Cup (France)
France had not even qualified for the 1994 World Cup and Jacquet was appointed shortly after this disappointment, initially on a temporary basis. Early results and a good showing at Euro 96 were impressive, though the lead-up to the 1998 World Cup, to be played on home soil, brought complaints from the French public about Jacquet's side's lack of cohesion. They need not have worried, as inspired by Zinedine Zidane, they won all three group games, beat Paraguay after extra time and Italy on penalties. Croatia were beaten 2-1 in the semi-finals thanks to two goals from defender Lilian Thuram. Brazil were then swept away in the final with a stunning performance, as Zidane scored twice in the first half before Emmanuel Petit wrapped up the win in injury time. Jacquet retired afterwards, as a world champion.

MARCELLO LIPPI (born 12 April 1948)
Greatest success: 2006 World Cup (Italy)
A distinguished club coaching career led to Lippi's appointment as Italy's national team coach for

2006. Scandal in the domestic game lowered expectations ahead of the finals, but Lippi created an impressive sense of unity and Italy performed well, topping their group before beating Australia and Ukraine. Italy met hosts Germany, who had impressed with their attacking football, in the semi-finals but two goals in extra time put the Italians into the final. Falling behind to a penalty, they equalised through Marco Materazzi before Fabio Grosso struck the winning penalty to win the shootout 5-3. It was the Italians' first success in a shootout from five attempts. Lippi left his post immediately afterwards but returned in 2008 as he led Italy to the World Cup in South Africa, although this time they underperformed and were eliminated at the group stage.

CÉSAR LUIS MENOTTI (born 5 November 1938)
Greatest success: 1978 World Cup (Argentina)
In 1978, the left-leaning César Luis Menotti made himself immune from action by the ruling military junta because he was busy leading Argentina to their first-ever World Cup success. Menotti believed in positive, attacking football, which set him at odds with other top Argentinian coaches of the era such as Juan Carlos Lorenzo and Osvaldo Zubeldía, and they beat the great Dutch side of the 1970s in the final after thrashing Peru 6-0 in their final group game. Menotti quit after Argentina's shock second round group exit at the 1982 finals in Spain, suffering defeat at the hands of Brazil and Italy.

ABOVE Guus Hiddink

LEFT Sepp Herberger

MANAGERS

ABOVE Bora Milutinović

RIGHT Vittorio Pozzo

BORA MILUTINOVIĆ (born September 7, 1944)

Greatest success: 1986 quarter-finals (Mexico)
Milutinovic is one of only two men to have led five different countries to the World Cup finals and the only manager to have led four into the knockout stages. A Serb, he spent his playing career in Europe but coached Mexico in their home tournament in 1986, leading them to the quarter-final where they were eliminated on penalties by finalists West Germany. Four years later, he took over Costa Rica just before the Italy finals and took them into the second round having beaten Sweden and Scotland, losing narrowly to Brazil. He led USA in 1994 to their first knockout stage since the 1930s and then took Nigeria past well-fancied Spain at France 1998. Milutinović then led China to their first World Cup in 2002, for the first time leaving the tournament without a victory. He has also coached Honduras, Jamaica and Iraq.

AYMORÉ MOREIRA (born 24 April 1912, died 26 July 1998)

Greatest success: 1962 World Cup (Brazil)
One of three coaching brothers, Moreira had been a Brazilian international himself, beginning his career as a winger before becoming a goalkeeper. Appointed to the post in 1961, he successfully defended Brazil's 1958 crown despite the absence of star player Pele through injury for much of the 1962 tournament in Chile. The forward had injured himself in a group game against Czechoslovakia and it was against the same opposition in the final that his replacement, Amarildo, equalized after Brazil had fallen behind, before a sensational display from Garrincha led the holders to a memorable 3-1 victory.

CARLOS ALBERTO PARREIRA (born 27 February 1943)

Greatest success: 1994 World Cup (Brazil)
Parreira is the only man to coach at six World Cups and one of two on this list to lead five different countries at the tournament. He lifted the trophy with his home nation in 1994, their first title since 1970 when he had been in the coaching setup. Parreira led Kuwait and the United Arab Emirates to their first finals tournaments in 1982 and 1990 respectively and was then sacked after two games when in charge of Saudi Arabia at the 1998 tournament in France. Despite links with the Brazil job once more, he sat out in 2002 before returning to the position in 2003 and led his country to the quarter-finals in 2006. He then managed South Africa, the hosts, in 2010, but they became the first hosts to be eliminated at the group stage. He retired after the tournament, his sixth World Cup as a head coach, but remains involved with the Brazilian national team.

VITTORIO POZZO (born 12 March 1886, died 21 December 1968)

Greatest successes: 1934 and 1938 World Cups (Italy)
Pozzo, who was also a journalist, learned to love football during a period of study in England. In

1934 he had no doubts about using former Argentina internationals, such as Luis Monti and Raimundo Orsi, to strengthen his first World Cup-winning side. Ruthlessly, he then scrapped almost the entire team to build a new side for the 1938 competition. In between these triumphs, Pozzo guided Italy to gold medal success at the 1936 Olympic Games. Sadly, Pozzo retired in 1949 after the Superga air disaster wiped out the entire playing staff of Torino, around whom he was planning to build a team for the 1950 World Cup.

SIR ALF RAMSEY (born 22 January 1920, died 28 April 1999)
Greatest success: 1966 World Cup (England)
Ramsey will always hold a special place in the hearts of England fans as the only manager to have brought the country success in a major competition. A tactical pioneer, Ramsey's side was built unusually for the time without wingers, instead having four narrow midfielders. The "Wingless Wonders" began poorly with a 0-0 draw against Uruguay before springing to life with 2-0 wins over Mexico and France. Argentina were beaten 1-0 in a bad-tempered encounter before the great Eusebio's Portugal were knocked out in the semis. The final brought more controversy, with arguments continuing to this day on whether Geoff Hurst's third goal for England had crossed the line, but the forward added another to claim the first World Cup final hat-trick. A year after his achievement, Ramsey was knighted, and went on to lead England to the quarter-finals in Mexico in 1970.

HELMUT SCHÖN (born 15 September 1915, died 23 February 1996)
Greatest success: 1974 World Cup (West Germany)
Under Schön's 14-year-leadership, West Germany won the World Cup on home territory in 1974, after finishing third at Mexico in 1970 and runner-up to England in 1966. West Germany hosted the World Cup finals as worthy winners of the 1972 European Championship under Schön. No coach has overseen more than Schön's 25 World Cup matches, or won more than his 16.

LUIZ FELIPE SCOLARI (born 9 November 1948)
Greatest success: 2002 World Cup (Brazil)
Scolari holds the record for both consecutive wins, 11, and games unbeaten, 12, at the World Cup. Brazil coach in 2002, he utilised a system to bring the best of Ronaldinho, Ronaldo and Rivaldo, with attacking full-backs Roberto Carlos and Cafu becoming important parts of the Brazilian attack. After disappointment four years earlier, they were excellent in Japan and Korea, winning all of their games, including the quarter-final against England with 10 men. After lifting the trophy, Scolari took over Portugal and turned them into contenders in 2006, leading them to the semi-finals where they were beaten by France. He is back in charge of Brazil for 2014.

ALBERTO SUPPICI (born 20 November 1898, died 21 June 1981)
Greatest success: 1930 World Cup (Uruguay)
Suppici was the first coach to win the World Cup, doing so in his own country as Uruguay followed up their 1928 Olympic victory with the inaugural world crown in Montevideo. Nicknamed 'the professor', Suppici was actually technical director and masterminded an excellent comeback against Argentina in the final. Trailing 2-1 at half-time, the Uruguayans scored three second-half goals in front of 93,000 supporters to become champions. Having left the position in 1932, Suppici returned three years later, and coached Uruguay until 1941.

MARIO ZAGALLO (born 9 August 1931)
Greatest success: 1970 World Cup (Brazil)
Mario Zagallo is a Brazilian icon, having enjoyed a magnificent career in football, both as a player and a coach. He played as an industrious left winger in the World Cup-winning sides in 1958 and 1962, then graduated to manage the side in 1970, winning in Mexico. With this victory, he became the first person to win the World Cup as both a player and a coach. His career with Brazil has continued in various roles, including the post of technical director at the 2006 World Cup finals. His Brazilian team won the World Cup in 1994 but finished as runner-up to France in the 1998 World Cup finals.

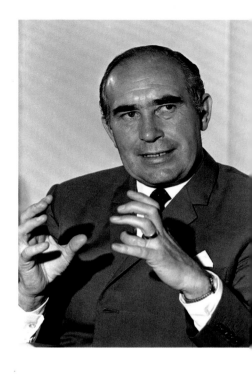

ABOVE Sir Alf Ramsey

EUROPEAN PLAYERS

ABOVE Franz Beckenbauer

RIGHT Sir Bobby Charlton

MARCO VAN BASTEN (born 31 October 1964)

Holland: 58 games, 24 goals

Marco Van Basten scored one of the finest goals in international history when he volleyed home Holland's second in their victory over the Soviet Union in the final of the 1988 European Championship. The goal sealed Van Basten's reputation as one of the finest center forwards to grace European football, not only with Holland but also with top club sides Ajax Amsterdam and Milan. Injury forced his premature retirement.

FRANZ BECKENBAUER (born 11 September 1945)

West Germany: 103 games, 14 goals

Franz Beckenbauer is one of the few defenders guaranteed a place in any football hall of fame. Initially a playmaker, "Der Kaiser" was converted into a creative sweeper by Yugoslavian coach Tschik Čajkovski at Bayern Munich in the 1960s. With more than 100 international appearances, he appeared in two World Cup finals and lifted the trophy as the West German captain in 1974 and again as national coach in 1990. In recent years, he has served as president of Bayern, as a member of the FIFA executive and has chaired the organizing committee for the 2006 World Cup.

DAVID BECKHAM (born 2 May 1975)

England: 102 games, 17 goals

A boyhood Manchester United fan, David Beckham went on to win a historic treble with the club in 1999. He was subsequently sold to Real Madrid in 2003, winning the Spanish league in the last of his four seasons with the club, then joined LA Galaxy. Beckham played in three World Cup finals for England, which included a controversial sending off against Argentina in 1998.

GEORGE BEST (born 22 May 1946, died 25 November 2005)

Northern Ireland: 37 games, 9 goals

Best was arguably the greatest player never to have made an appearance in the World Cup finals. A magical talent, one of the most exciting to grace English football, he made his Manchester United debut as a winger aged 17 in 1963 and went on to win the European Champion Clubs' Cup in 1968 and two league titles, before being driven out of the British game by the pressures of his own fame. His greatest exploit was in United's 5-1 thrashing of Benfica in Lisbon in a European Champion Clubs Cup quarter-final in 1966. He was voted European Footballer of the Year in 1968.

SIR BOBBY CHARLTON (born 11 October 1937)

England: 106 games, 49 goals

Having overcome the tragedy of the Munich air disaster in 1958, Charlton helped lead the reconstruction of the devastated Manchester United side. At international level, his powerful shooting had helped England to their sole

World Cup success, alongside his brother Jack, a defender. With 49 international goals, he remains England's top goalscorer of all time and went on to play in the 1970 tournament in Mexico. He was substituted by manager Alf Ramsey with England leading West Germany, only for the Germans to come from behind to win 3-2.

JOHAN CRUYFF (born 25 April 1947)
Holland: 48 games, 33 goals
Johan Cruyff, son of a cleaner at the Ajax Amsterdam offices, grew up to be the epitome of Holland's "Total Football" revolution, as well as being voted European Footballer of the Year three times in the 1970s. He led his nation to the final of the 1974 World Cup, but they were beaten by hosts West Germany. Cruyff controversially refused to play in the 1978 World Cup finals in Argentina because of the kidnap threats made to him and his family. Holland reached the final, but were once again beaten by the hosts. Critics believe that with his presence they could have returned from South America with the coveted trophy.

KENNY DALGLISH (born 4 March 1951)
Scotland: 102 games, 30 goals
Kenny Dalglish achieved a remarkable feat by winning league titles as both a player and a manager in England with Liverpool and in Scotland with Celtic. A nimble, quick-thinking forward, Dalglish moved from Glasgow to Anfield in 1978 as replacement at Liverpool for the legendary Kevin Keegan. He duly proved that he could fill the boots of the Kop hero—he was the club's leading scorer in his first season. After a glittering playing career for Liverpool, he successfully made the transition to managing the club in 1985, and became the only player-manager in modern times to steer his club to a domestic double in both league and FA Cup. His glittering career saw him equal the scoring record with Denis Law for Scotland, but he stands alone with the record for most appearances.

EUSÉBIO (born 25 January 1942)
Portugal: 64 games, 41 goals
Eusébio da Silva Ferreira, a Mozambican-born Portuguese striker, was nicknamed the "Black Panther" for his valuable goals. A star for club side Benfica, he guided Portugal to third place at the 1966 World Cup and won the Golden Boot as top scorer in the competition with nine goals. His finest performance was in the memorable quarter-final against North Korea. The Koreans raced to a 3-0 lead before Eusébio came on and scored four goals to give his country a 5-3 victory.

JUST FONTAINE (born 18 August 1933)
France: 21 games, 30 goals
Just Fontaine was a fast, brave forward who wrote his name into World Cup history by scoring 13 goals for third-placed France in the 1958 finals—Fontaine scored in all six games. His goalscoring record remains unbeaten. Fontaine, born in Morocco, only got his chance in the 1958 World Cup finals because Reims team-mate Rene Bliard was ruled out with an ankle injury. Fontaine's career was ended prematurely in 1961 due to two serious leg fractures.

ABOVE Eusébio

EUROPEAN PLAYERS

FRANCISCO GENTO (born 21 October 1933)

Spain: 43 games, 5 goals

"Paco" Gento set a record in 1966 when, as captain of Real Madrid, he collected a sixth European Champion Clubs' Cup Winner's medal. Gento, from Santander in northern Spain, was nicknamed "El Supersonico" for his electric pace on the left wing. His distracting effect created valuable extra space to assist the goal-scoring exploits of team-mates such as Alfredo Di Stefano and Ferenc Puskás. Gento was a key figure in Real Madrid's triumphs of the 1950s and 1960s, scoring 126 goals in 428 games over 18 years. He won the domestic league title 12 times, represented Spain in the 1962 and 1966 World Cup finals, and played a key role in the side that dominated the first five European Champion Clubs' Cup finals with successive victories in the late 1950s.

RUUD GULLIT (born 1 September 1962)

Holland: 66 games, 17 goals

Ruud Gullit was hailed as Europe's finest player in the late 1980s, when he moved from Dutch football to help inspire a revival at AC Milan. Gullit, World Player of the Year in 1987 and 1989, was a favorite of AC Milan owner Silvio Berlusconi, winning two European Champion Clubs' Cups and three Italian league titles. He captained Holland in the 1988 European Championship, heading home the opening goal in the 2-0 victory over Russia in the final. He moved to Chelsea as a player and later became their coach—he was the first non-British manager to win the FA Cup. He subsequently had brief spells as manager of Newcastle United and Dutch giants Feyenoord.

GHEORGHE HAGI (born 5 February 1965)

Romania: 125 games, 35 goals

Gheorghe Hagi was nicknamed the "Maradona of the Carpathians" during the late 1980s because of his cultured left foot and silky skills. His huge self-confidence helped him to push forward from midfield to score goals, but his main strength lay in his skill and vision as a playmaker. Such outstanding talent earned special permission, in a restrictive political era, to move abroad to ply his trade. He played for Real Madrid, moved to Brescia in Italy, and then on to Barcelona before ending his career at Turkish side Galatasaray. Hagi was the fulcrum of the Romanian side that reached the quarter-final stage of the 1994 World Cup.

BELOW Thierry Henry

THIERRY HENRY (born 17 August 1977)

France: 100 games, 44 goals

A raw and pacy winger, Thierry Henry had impressed at club level and earned a first international call as a 20-year-old just eight months before the 1998 World Cup. He earned a place in the squad and scored three times in the group stages, appearing both out wide and as a centre-forward, but was an unused substitute in the final as France beat Brazil 3-0. A goalless 2002 campaign meant an early exit for the defending champions, but he returned in 2006 as the lone striker, his three goals helping France to the final where they were beaten on penalties by Italy. France's 2010 campaign was another poor one and, no longer an automatic starter, Henry made just one substitute appearance as they were eliminated in the group stages.

SIR GEOFF HURST (born 8 December 1941)

England: 49 games, 24 goals

Sir Geoff Hurst remains the only player to have scored a hat-trick in a World Cup final, an achievement which ultimately earned him a belated knighthood. Hurst only came into the 1966 England side because first-choice forward Jimmy Greaves was injured. His header had drawn England level against West Germany before he put England ahead controversially in extra time, his shot bouncing down off the crossbar and on to the line, before he raced away to hit a late third, and England's fourth. As well as his match-winning performance in the final, Hurst scored what proved to be the decisive goal in the quarter-final against Argentina.

MIROSLAV KLOSE (born 9 June 1978)

Germany: 130 games, 68 goals

Born in Poland, Klose opted to play for Germany in 2001 and sprang to prominence at the World Cup in 2002, where he became the first player to score five headed goals at one finals, including a hat-trick against Saudi Arabia in an 8-0 win. Germany were eventually beaten in the final by Brazil and Ronaldo is the only man to score more World Cup goals than Klose's total of 14. On home soil in 2006, he added another five as he took the Golden Boot and a second successive appearance in the All-Star XI. In 2010, Germany reached the semi-finals and Klose was among the goals again, scoring against Australia, England and Argentina to help his country to a second successive third-place finish. If selected, Klose could yet add to his tally in 2014.

RAYMOND KOPA (born 13 October 1931)

France: 45 games, 18 goals

Raymond Kopa was the son of a Polish mining family from northern France. His talent was first spotted by Angers, who then sold him on to Reims in 1950. He was sold to Real Madrid after the Spanish club defeated Reims in the European Champion Clubs' Cup final in 1956. At Real Madrid he won the European Champion Clubs Cup three times and was crowned 1958 European Footballer of the Year. Kopa won four French and two Spanish league titles.

HANS KRANKL (born 14 February 1953)

Austria: 69 games, 34 goals

Hans Krankl was one of the great Austrian center forwards. In 1978 he scored 41 goals for Rapid Vienna, winning the Golden Boot as Europe's leading league scorer. He starred for Austria at the World Cup finals in Argentina, where he netted the winning goal against West Germany—Austria's first victory over their neighbors for 37 years. He went on to play for Barcelona, where he won the 1979 European Cup Winners' Cup.

ABOVE Geoff Hurst

BELOW Miroslav Klose

1930s   **1940s**   **1960s**

GREAT PLAYERS & MANAGERS MOMENTS

ABOVE Herbert Chapman,
Arsenal's first great manager

BELOW Jimmy Hogan staging
a coaching lesson for troops

ABOVE Alfredo Di Stefano scores
for Real Madrid against Eintracht

RIGHT England boss Sir Alf Ramsey
(right) with Bobby Charlton

BELOW Bobby Charlton shoots for
goal against France at Wembley

1970s   1990s   2000s

ABOVE Sir Bobby Robson points the way for Newcastle

ABOVE Giovanni Trapattoni brings the winning touch to Ireland

ABOVE Nottingham Forest's Brian Clough in trademark green jumper

ABOVE Mario Zagallo, a World Cup winner as player and manager

ABOVE Arsène Wenger took Arsenal to the double in his first full season

LEFT Sir Alex Ferguson lifted Manchester United to new glory

EUROPEAN PLAYERS

ABOVE Josef Masopust

RIGHT Gary Lineker

MICHAEL LAUDRUP (born 15 June 1964)
Denmark: 104 games, 37 goals
Michael Laudrup stood out in Denmark's outstanding team that reached the semi-finals of the 1984 European Championship and the second round at the 1986 World Cup finals. He achieved club success with Juventus before moving to Lazio, and he was part of Johan Cruyff's "Dream Team" at Barcelona where he won four league titles. He also played for Real Madrid and Ajax.

DENIS LAW (born 24 February 1940)
Scotland: 55 games, 30 goals
Denis Law, whatever the competing talents of Bobby Charlton and George Best, was the king of Old Trafford in the 1960s. His ebullient personality, and his ability to create chances and goals out of nothing, earned him the adulation of Manchester United fans. Law started at Huddersfield Town, and had brief spells at Manchester City and Torino before being brought to Manchester United in 1962. He repaid the club's financial investment with 171 goals in 309 league games. He won the European Footballer of the Year prize in 1964.

GARY LINEKER (born 30 November 1960)
England: 80 games, 48 goals
The only Englishman to win a World Cup Golden Boot, Lineker struck six times in Mexico in 1986, including a hat-trick against Poland, all three goals scored from within the six-yard box, when their campaign was struggling. He added two more against Paraguay in the knockout round, before England were cheated by Diego Maradona's infamous "Hand of God" goal. Lineker did score a consolation to take his tally to six and he added four more in Italy in 1990 as England went one better to the semi-finals. He ended his international career with 48 goals, one less than Sir Bobby Charlton.

JOSEF MASOPUST (born 9 February 1931)
Czechoslovakia: 63 games, 10 goals
Josef Masopust was a midfield heir in the 1950s and early 1960s to the great pre-war traditions of Czechoslovak football. An attacking midfielder, he reached his peak at the 1962 World Cup in Chile, where he helped to inspire his side all the way to the final. Although he opened the scoring against Brazil for an unexpected lead, the holders fought back to triumph 3-1. Masopust won the 1962 Footballer of the Year award following his outstanding displays in Chile, where he was nicknamed "the Czech Knight".

LOTHAR MATTHAUS (born 21 March, 1961)
Germany 150 games, 23 goals
Having led West Germany to the World Cup in Italy in 1990, Matthaus became the first and only outfield player to play in five different tournaments in 1998. Nobody has played as many as his 25 World Cup matches. An energetic

and disciplined midfielder, Matthaus collected a runners-up medal in both 1982 and 1986, playing in the latter, before captaining his country to success four years later. Quarter-final exits in 1994 and 1998 followed for one of his country's most-capped players ever.

SIR STANLEY MATTHEWS (born
1 February 1915, died 23 February 2000)
England: 54 games, 11 goals
Sir Stanley Matthews was the first active player to be knighted as reward for extraordinary service to the game both before and after World War II. He was an outside right whose mesmerizing talent earned him the nickname the "Wizard of Dribble." Matthews achieved his ambition to win the FA Cup with Blackpool in 1953, when, aged 38 he famously rescued his side from a 3-1 deficit by setting up three goals. In 1956, he received the inaugural European Player of the Year. His fitness and enthusiasm saw him play at the 1954 World Cup finals and then lead his original club, Stoke City, to promotion back into the old first division in 1962.

GIUSEPPE MEAZZA (born 23 August
1910, died 21 August 1979)
Italy: 53 game, 33 goals
Giuseppe Meazza is one of only two Italian players—Giovanni Ferrari was the other—to have won the World Cup for the Azzurri both at home and also away from Italy. Meazza was a powerful, goal-scoring inside forward with Internazionale in the 1930s, scoring 287 goals in 408 games for the club. He was a World Cup winner at home in 1934 and was the captain in France when Italy triumphed in 1938, scoring three goals at the finals overall.

BOBBY MOORE (born 12 April 1941, died
24 February 1993)
England: 108 games, 2 goals
Bobby Moore proved to be an ideal captain for England, leading them to glory at the 1966 World Cup and also during their unsuccessful defence of the trophy in 1970. Respected by his team-mates and opponents alike for his tough tackling and silky skills, Moore was regarded as among the best defenders in the world. A bronze statue of Moore stands outside the new Wembley Stadium. Nobody has led England more times than Moore's 90.

GERD MÜLLER (born 3 November 1945)
West Germany: 62 games, 68 goals
Gerd Müller was the most prolific goal scorer in modern German football and the all-time top scorer at the World Cup finals, until Brazilian Ronaldo surpassed his 14 goals in 2006. Müller scored 10 times at the 1970 World Cup finals in Mexico—hitting successive hat-tricks against Bulgaria and Peru—to finish as the highest scorer and win the Golden Boot. He also scored the winning goal for West Germany in the 1974 World Cup final victory over Holland, taking his total tally to 14. Short and stocky, he was nicknamed "Der Bomber" by the adoring German public.

FERENC PUSKÁS (born 2 April 1927, died
17 November 2006)
Hungary: 85 games, 84 goals
Spain: 4 games, no goals
Ferenc Puskás is one of the game's all-time greats, famed for his goals, his leadership and the way

ABOVE Giuseppe Meazza

EUROPEAN PLAYERS

ABOVE Ferenc Puskás

RIGHT Hristo Stoichkov

that he reconstructed his career after the 1956 Hungarian Revolution. Puskás and Hungary were unbeaten for four years going into the 1954 World Cup finals as Olympic champions, but fell 3-2 to West Germany in the final, despite leading 2-0 inside the first 10 minutes. Puskas had opened the scoring in the final, despite not being fully fit.

CRISTIANO RONALDO (born 5 February 1985)
Portugal: 55 games, 20 goals
Cristiano Ronaldo became Britain's most expensive teenager when, aged 18, he cost Manchester United the remarkable sum of $25 million (£12.4 million) in 2003. At first, the self-indulgence of his trickery on the right wing frustrated fans and team-mates alike, but once he adapted to the difficult demands of the English game, he proved to be equally dangerous on the left wing and a real handful to deal with in the air. In the 2007–08 season, he scored 42 goals in all competitions, which helped guide Manchester United to a double of the English league title and the Champions League.

PAOLO ROSSI (born 23 September 1956)
Italy: 48 games, 20 goals
Paolo Rossi looked a great prospect after the 1978 World Cup finals, but he was banned for two years over a match-fixing scandal. The striker only returned to top-class action weeks before the 1982 World Cup finals kicked off, and he started slowly, yet finished as the top scorer with six goals to his credit. These strikes included a hat-trick to deliver the knock-out blow to Brazil in the quarter-final, one of the all-time great World Cup encounters, before both Italian goals against Poland in the semi and the opener against Germany in the final. A stunning return from the wilderness had seen Rossi lead his country to their first World Cup in 44 years.

MATTHIAS SINDELAR (born 10 February 1903, died 23 January 1939)
Austria: 43 games, 27 goals
Matthias Sindelar was the inspirational forward of the Austrian "Wunderteam" that ruled European football in the late 1920s and early 1930s. Sindelar, nicknamed the "Man of Paper" because of his delicate build, was a World Cup semi-finalist in 1934, but suffered at the bruising hands of his marker, Italian Luis Monti. Five years later he died of carbon monoxide poisoning in his Viennese apartment in unexplained circumstances.

HRISTO STOICHKOV (born 8 February 1966)
Bulgaria: 83 games, 37 goals
Stoichkov was the star man of the Bulgaria side, which unexpectedly reached the semi-finals in America in 1994. A 3-0 defeat to Nigeria in their opening group game suggested they would struggle, but wins over Greece and Argentina,

with three goals from the forward, sent them into the knockout stages for the first time. Stoichkov's penalty expertise helped eliminate Mexico in a shootout before they came from behind, with him scoring again, to beat world champions Germany. Eliminated by Italy in the semis and beaten in the play-off by Sweden, Bulgaria finished third, and Stoichkov shared the Golden Boot.

FRITZ WALTER (born 31 October 1920, died 17 June 2002)
West Germany: 61 games, 33 goals
Fritz Walter owed his life to national manager Sepp Herberger and repaid him in glory. Walter, an inside forward from Kaiserslautern who made his international debut just before World War II, was kept away from the front by Herberger's string-pulling before finally being drafted in 1942. He was captured and eventually repatriated by the Soviet army. He relaunched his football career and captained Herberger's West Germany to their unexpected World Cup final victory over the mighty Hungary in 1954.

LEV YASHIN (born 22 October 1929, died 20 March 1990)
Soviet Union: 78 games, no goals.
Lev Yashin, nicknamed the "Black Spider" due to his all-black kit and ability to make the most unlikely of saves, ranks as arguably the game's greatest ever goalkeeper, revolutionising the role and constantly barking instructions at his defenders. A veteran of three World Cups, Yashin appeared in 13 finals matches, reaching the quarter-finals twice and the semis once, where they were beaten by West Germany, in 1966. In 1994, FIFA introduced the Lev Yashin Award for the best goalkeeper at a World Cup.

ZINEDINE ZIDANE (born June 23, 1972)
France: 108 games, 31 goals
Zidane was the outstanding French playmaker of the late 1990s and early 2000s. He was making headlines until the very last moment of his career—he was sent off in extra time in the 2006 World Cup Final, his last game, for headbutting Italy's Marco Materazzi, having already opened the scoring with a brilliant chipped penalty. Zidane also scored twice in France's 1998 World Cup

ABOVE Lev Yashin

final win over Brazil, but was injured for their disastrous 2002 campaign, coming back early to take part in their final group game, although he could not prevent their elimination.

DINO ZOFF (born 28 February 1942)
Italy: 112 games, no goals
Another great goalkeeper, Zoff was Italy's captain when they swept past all opponents at the 1982 World Cup finals. Aged 40, Zoff was the oldest player to win the World Cup after the Azzurri thumped West Germany 3-1 in the final, after which he was voted the best goalkeeper in the tournament. His 112 caps saw him play in three World Cups.

AMERICA'S PLAYERS

ABOVE Gabriel Batistuta

RIGHT Teófilo Cubillas

GABRIEL BATISTUTA (born 1 February, 1969)

Argentina 78 games, 56 goals

Nicknamed "Batigol", Gabriel Batistuta led the Argentine line at three consecutive World Cups and hit a hat-trick on his tournament debut in a 4-0 win over Greece. He became the first player to score triples in two different tournaments four years later when he repeated the trick in a 5-0 thrashing of Jamaica. In total, Batistuta netted 10 goals at the World Cup, but his international career ended in disappointment when Argentina were eliminated at the group stage in 2002.

ANTONIO CARBAJAL (born 7 June 1929)

Mexico: 48 games, no goals

Antonio Carbajal became the first player to appear in the finals of five World Cup competitions, but ended up on the winning side only once. The goalkeeper's debut in the finals was against Brazil in 1950, when he conceded four goals. He played in the 1954, 1958, and 1962 World Cup finals before bowing out after a scoreless draw against Uruguay in the 1966 finals.

ROBERTO CARLOS (born 10 April 1973)

Brazil: 125 games, 11 goals

Roberto Carlos da Silva Rocha proved to be one of Brazil's most loved players due to the power of his shooting and the exuberance of his attacking play from left-back. He played in three World Cups, where with Cafu on the right he became a Brazilian icon and lifted the 2002 trophy in Japan, having scored against China in the group stages with a trademark free-kick. He retired from international football after Brazil were eliminated by France in the 2006 quarter-final.

JOSÉ LUIS CHILAVERT (born 27 July 1965)

Paraguay: 74 games, 8 goals

José Luis Chilavert was renowned for his scoring achievements despite being a goalkeeper. His ultimate ambition was to score a goal in the World Cup finals, but he failed, even though he had scored four in qualifying matches for the 2002 tournament. He was voted the world's top goalkeeper three times and was included in the 1998 team of the tournament.

TEÓFILO CUBILLAS (born 8 March 1949)

Peru: 81 games, 26 goals

Teófilo Cubillas shot to stardom as an inside forward in the outstanding Peru team that reached the 1970 World Cup quarter-finals, scoring in all four of his country's games and five goals in total, including against eventual champions Brazil. Just 21, he was named the best young player in the tournament and returned in 1978 when he scored twice against Scotland and scored a hat-trick against Iran.

DIDI (born 8 October 1929, died 12 May 2001)

Brazil: 68 games, 20 goals

Didi, full name Waldyr Pereira, won the World Cup twice with Brazil in 1958 and 1962, having also played in 1954. Brazil might not have even been at the finals in 1958 at all but for a remarkable free-kick from the midfielder that bent in the air and flew into the net against Peru

in a qualifying tie. The "Falling Leaf" became Didi's trademark and has been copied by players all over the world ever since. He is regarded as among his country's best ever midfield players and was voted the best player of the tournament in Sweden in '58, his performances however overshadowed by the 17-year-old Pele.

LANDON DONOVAN (born 4 March 1982)
United States: 100 games, 35 goals
Landon Donovan is the long-serving, outstanding international that US football has been waiting for. He debuted at the World Cup in 2002, helping his country beat the highly-rated Portugal before scoring in the 2-0 win over Mexico. He was named the tournament's best young player and returned in 2006 for a disappointing campaign, before scoring three further times in South Africa in 2010 as the US again reached the knockout rounds. No player from the American qualifying region has scored as many World Cup goals and Donovan could yet return for his fourth finals in Brazil in 2014.

ENZO FRANCESCOLI (born 12 November 1961)
Uruguay: 72 games, 15 goals
Enzo Francescoli, nicknamed "The Prince", is arguably the last great Uruguayan player. However, he played the majority of his club career in Argentina, France, and Italy. He played the 1989–90 season with Olympique Marseille, where he was the footballing hero and inspiration for the teenage Zinedine Zidane. A tall, graceful inside forward, Francescoli was a three-times winner of the Copa America with Uruguay and played twice at the World Cup finals. He was voted South American Player of the Year in both 1984 and 1995.

GARRINCHA (born 28 October 1933, died 20 January 1983)
Brazil: 50 games, 12 goals
Garrincha, full name Manoel dos Santos Francisco, lived a life that was a tale of triumph and tragedy. Nicknamed "the Little Bird", he won the World Cup in 1958 and 1962, with his goals and creativity proving to be decisive. His dribbling ability was unmatched despite birth defects that left him bow-legged and one limb six centimetres shorter than the other. Yet his love of the good life meant he was also his own worst enemy and a nightmare for coaches. He died tragically of alcohol poisoning.

JAIRZINHO (born 25 December 1944)
Brazil: 81 games, 33 goals
Jairzinho, full name Jair Ventura Filho, was the free-scoring successor to the Brazilian tradition of great outside rights, from Julinho in the mid-1950s to Garrincha in the late 1950s and 1960s. In 1970, he recovered twice from a broken right leg and became the only player to score in every round

LEFT Didi

BELOW LEFT Garrincha

GREAT PLAYERS & MANAGERS
AMERICA'S PLAYERS

ABOVE Mario Kempes

of the World Cup finals in Mexico, scoring seven goals overall. Jairzinho, nicknamed "God", also played in the World Cup finals of 1966 and 1974, and famously discovered an outstanding 12-year-old in Rio de Janeiro, a talent called Ronaldo.

KAKÁ (born 22 April 1982)
Brazil: 59 games, 22 goals
Kaká, full name Ricardo Izecson dos Santos Leite, was generally hailed as having established himself as the world's top player in 2007. During 2007, he set up AC Milan's victory in the European Champions League and was voted both FIFA Player of the Year and European Player of the Year. The supremely gifted Brazilian forward originally made his name with São Paulo, following a remarkable recovery from a swimming pool accident that left him temporarily paralysed. AC Milan paid a comparatively low $10 million (£5 million) for him in 2003.

MARIO KEMPES (born 15 July 1954)
Argentina: 43 games, 20 goals
Forward Mario Kempes emerged at the 1974 World Cup finals, but it is his performances four years later for which he is remembered. As Cesar Luis Menotti's only foreign-based player called up to the squad, he was under pressure to perform, but did so magnificently to take the Golden Boot with six goals, including a brace in the final against Holland. Powerful, direct and clinical, Kempes returned to the squad in 1982, and played 18 World Cup games in total.

DIEGO MARADONA (born 30 October 1960)
Argentina: 91 games, 34 goals
Diego Maradona ranks among the greatest ever players, despite a career shrouded in controversy. Small but strong, Maradona was entirely left-footed and his dribbling ability made him almost impossible to shake off the ball. Captain and

inspiration of the Argentine side which lifted the 1986 World Cup, his second strike against England is considered to be one of the all-time great finals goals, though the infamous "Hand of God" is what most people remember from that quarter-final tie. Such was Maradona's importance to his side, he scored twice more in the semi, and was involved in 10 of their 14 goals in total. A runner-up in the 1990 World Cup, he was suspended from the sport in 1991 after failing a drugs test, and three years later failed a World Cup finals' doping test, having scored in a 4-0 win over Greece. He played 21 World Cup games in total.

PELÉ (born 23 October 1940)
Brazil: 92 games, 77 goals
Pelé, full name Edson Arantes do Nascimento, is synonymous with the World Cup. One of few who could realistically claim to be the best footballer who ever played, he was a World Cup winner at 17—scoring twice in the 5-2 victory over Sweden in the 1958 final, including a brilliant flick over a defender's head and volley into the bottom corner. Injury prevented Pelé playing in the 1962 World Cup final and he endured an unhappy tournament in 1966, when he was the subject of rough marking by Portuguese defenders, but he was back at his best in 1970 and scored in the 4-1 win over Italy. He is the only player to have three World Cup winner's medals.

RONALDINHO (born 21 March 1980)
Brazil: 80 games, 32 goals
Ronaldinho, full name Ronaldo de Assis Moreira, was the third of "the three Rs" in the Brazil team of 2002, joining Rivaldo and Ronaldo in attack. Incredibly talented, he scored in the group game win over China and netted the winner against England in the quarter-final with a long-range free-kick before being sent off, returning for the final and a 2-0 win over Germany. Ronaldinho was voted FIFA World Player of the Year in 2004 and 2005

and was in the squad once more in 2006, when Brazil were beaten by France in the quarter-finals.

RONALDO (born 22 September 1976)
Brazil: 97 games, 62 goals
Ronaldo Luis Nazário de Lima was discovered as a 12-year-old by World Cup-winning hero Jairzinho. Five years later, he was at the 1994 World Cup, albeit as a non-playing member of the winning Brazilian squad. In 1998, he was the best player in the world, his pace, power and clinical finishing making Brazil the favourites, but before the final against France he was taken ill, played anyway and was anonymous as his side lost 3-0. Ronaldo made amends by scoring twice in the 2002 World Cup final win over Germany and nine times in total, adding a record 15th goal at the 2006 World Cup finals.

HUGO SÁNCHEZ (born 11 July 1958)
Mexico: 58 games, 29 goals
Hugo Sánchez numbers among the most prolific scorers in the history of Mexican football and as one of its greatest personalities. He led the attack in three World Cup finals, at 1978, 1986 and as a veteran in 1994.

HECTOR SCARONE (born 1 January 1900, died 4 April 1967)
Uruguay: 51 games, 31 goals
Hector Scarone, nicknamed "the Magician", was the original star of the World Cup after leading Uruguay to victory over Argentina in the inaugural finals in 1930, scoring in a 4-0 win over Romania. His all-time Uruguayan goalscoring record was broken only in 2011.

ALFREDO DI STEFANO (born 4 July 1926)
Argentina: 6 games, 6 goals
Spain: 31 games, 23 goals
Alfredo Di Stefano remains, for many experts, the greatest ever player because of his all-action performances as a pitch-roaming, high-scoring center forward. He starred for Argentina's River Plate and Colombia's Millonarios, before inspiring Real Madrid to victory in the first five European Champion Clubs' Cup competitions. Di Stefano scored in all five finals, and totalled 216 league goals for Real Madrid over 11 years.

CARLOS VALDERRAMA (born 2 September 1961)
Colombia: 111 games, 11 goals
Carlos Valderrama, nicknamed "The Kid", was a colourful character who led Colombia from midfield at the World Cup finals of 1990, 1994, and 1998, all of which ended in disappointment. Valderrama was renowned almost as much for his outrageous, frizzy blonde hair as for his supreme talent, which ensured a 13-year international career.

OBDULIO VARELA (born 20 September 1917, died 2 August 1996)
Uruguay: 49 games, 10 goals
Obdulio Varela was the attacking centre-half who captained Uruguay to World Cup victory in 1950. Varela apparently told the team to ignore their manager's talk and follow his orders—they bounced back with two goals to spring one of the World Cup's greatest shocks: a 2-1 win over hosts Brazil, despite trailing. He returned to the World Cup in 1954 as a 37-year-old, but injury before the semi-final meant he could not help Uruguay avoid defeat against the great Hungarians.

IVAN ZAMORANO (born 18 January 1967)
Chile: 69 games, 34 goals
Ivan Zamorano was Chile's iconic hero in the 1990s, when he led the national team's World Cup attack and starred in European football. Zamorano was brought to Europe by the Swiss club Saint Gallen. After three terms he moved to the Spanish La Liga for six seasons. In 1995 he was the league's top scorer, with 27 goals for Real Madrid. He went on to win the 1998 UEFA Cup with Internazionale before returning to Chile with Colo Colo via a two-year stint in Mexico.

ZICO (born 3 March 1953)
Brazil: 88 games, 66 goals
Zico was arguably the best player in one of the best sides never to win the World Cup, Brazil's 1982 team, which was beaten in the quarter-finals by Italy and Paolo Rossi. A typical number 10, he could create or score prolifically himself and netted four times in the 1982 World Cup, having also been a member of the squad in 1978. In 1986, he was only a substitute for Brazil, who underperformed, and after coming on against France he missed a vital penalty that saw his side eliminated.

ABOVE Zico

BELOW Obdulio Varela

MOMENTS

GREAT PLAYERS & MANAGERS

ABOVE Gerd Müller, triple European champion with Bayern Munich

BELOW Franz Beckenbauer (left) closes in on England's Colin Bell

ABOVE Sepp Maier in training in Munich's Olympic stadium

LEFT Franz Beckenbauer hoists aloft the World Cup in 1974

BELOW Uli Hoeness finds space in the World Cup final

ABOVE David Beckham strikes a winning penalty against Argentina

ABOVE France winger Didier Six (right) takes on the Czech defense

BELOW Ossie Ardiles in English action for Tottenham

ABOVE Eric Cantona making his debut for Manchester United

ABOVE Steve Gerrard celebrates another of his England goals

LEFT Cristiano Ronaldo top-scored with 31 goals in the 2008 Premier League

GREAT PLAYERS & MANAGERS
REST OF THE WORLD

ABOVE Roger Milla

SAMUEL ETO'O (born 10 March 1981)
Cameroon: 76 games, 31 goals
Samuel Eto'o is an explosive Cameroon striker who was brought to Europe by Real Madrid. However, he failed to impress the club and was sold. He has made them regret it with four wonderful seasons each at Mallorca and then Barcelona. In 2006, Eto'o won the Golden Boot as Europe's leading league scorer with 26 goals, helping to fire Barcelona to their Champions League success over Arsenal as well as winning the Spanish Super Cup.

HOSSAM HASSAN (born 10 August 1966)
Egypt: 170 games, 69 goals
Hossam Hassan is the world's second most capped player with 170 appearances for the Pharaohs, just behind Mohammed Al Deayea's 181 games for Saudi Arabia. He has yet to announce retirement and continues to break Egyptian records: winning 41 titles as a player, playing 21 matches over seven African Nations' Cup competitions, and being the oldest scorer in an Egyptian national shirt. Hossam has also played for Paok Saloniki in Greece, Neuchatel Xamax in Switzerland, and El-Ain in the UAE.

DIDIER DROGBA (born 11 March 1978)
Ivory Coast: 52 games, 33 goals
Didier Drogba was a late starter, not making his professional breakthrough until he was 20 with French club Le Mans. He moved on to Guingamp in the French first division at the age of 24 before being bought by Marseille, who he led to the 2004 UEFA Cup final. His next step was a transfer to newly-enriched Chelsea for a then club record $48 million (£24 million). He has scored over 70 goals in four seasons for the club and has won the Premier League, FA Cup, and League Cup. He was named African Player of the Year in 2007.

ROGER MILLA (born 20 May 1952)
Cameroon: 102 games, 28 goals
Roger Milla had long been an African hero before his goal-celebrating dance around the corner flags brought him global fame at the 1990 World Cup. Milla scored four times at those finals, making him the oldest ever World Cup goalscorer at the age of 38. He returned to the World Cup finals four years later, before retiring with an impressive career record: he twice picked up the African Player of the Year award (1976 and 1990) and in 2007 was voted the best African Player of the last 50 years.

HONG MYUNG-BO (born 12 February 1969)

Korea Republic: 135 games, 9 goals

Hong Myung-Bo was the first Asian player to appear in four World Cups. Originally a powerful defensive midfielder, he was soon switched to central defence. He made his international debut in 1990 and was chosen to be part of the Korea Republic World Cup squad in Italy later that year. He earned international admiration for his displays in the 1994 and 1998 World Cup finals, despite the first round exits, and was a national hero long before he captained Korea Republic to the final four on home territory at the 2002 World Cup finals. He will coach his country in Brazil in 2014.

HIDETOSHI NAKATA (born 22 January 1977)

Japan: 77 games, 11 goals

Hidetoshi Nakata was the first Japanese player to make a major impact in Europe. Nakata had been hailed Asian Player of the Year before his 1998 World Cup finals debut. He played in the next two World Cup finals, announcing his shock retirement immediately after the 2006 World Cup match against Brazil in Germany. Nakata played seven seasons for various sides in Italy's Serie A and had a short spell in England's Premier League with Bolton Wanderers.

ABOVE Jay-Jay Okocha

JAY-JAY OKOCHA (born 14 August 1973)

Nigeria: 74 games, 14 goals

Augustine "Jay-Jay" Okocha provided the midfield command that lifted Nigeria's "Super Eagles" out of the also-rans of Africa to regular appearances at the World Cup finals. He played in the 1994, 1998 and 2002 finals, regularly lighting up games with his flair, dribbling and passing. Okocha was the mercurial playmaker around which the side was built and after reaching the knockout rounds at their first finals tournament, he helped Nigeria win the 1996 Olympic gold medal before reaching the last 16 once more in 1998.

SAEED AL-OWAIRAN (born 19 August 1967)

Saudi Arabia: 50 games, 24 goals

Saeed Al-Owairan won the accolade of Asian Player of the Year in 1994, largely thanks to his memorable solo strike against Belgium in that year's World Cup finals. His goal for Saudi Arabia was comparable with Diego Maradona's sensational strike against England in 1986 and has been voted the sixth best World Cup goal of all time.

LEFT Hong Myung-Bo

WORLD CUP 2014 INDEX